ANCESTORS *and* IMMIGRANTS

Ancestors *and*
Immigrants

A Changing New England Tradition
Barbara Miller Solomon

The University of Chicago Press
Chicago and London

THE UNIVERSITY OF CHICAGO PRESS, CHICAGO 60637
The University of Chicago Press, Ltd., London

Phoenix Edition published 1972
Printed in the United States of America

International Standard Book Number: 0-226-76808-2
Library of Congress Catalog Card Number: 73–172102

To Peter

Foreword

In the forming of American civilization New England was as much a state of mind as a geographic entity.* That New England thought which is part of our culture, was bred in a small group whose Puritan ancestors settled in Massachusetts. Predominantly of English stock, their society attained a distinctive character in the half century following the American Revolution; by then, overseas trade and manufacturing had created Yankee families of substance. By then, two hundred years had set patterns of thought and service in the community. Its leading citizens, self-named Brahmins, though they may have lived in neighboring towns, regarded Boston as the Hub of the Universe.

All over the country, writers and reformers respected this New England leadership. Often descendants of New Englanders returned there fully identified with its traditions, or preserved them in the far-removed sections of the United States. Others whose careers led to the Boston community, were converted while they lived there. Thus, Brahmin criteria reached beyond the little group, with important consequences. "The criticism we valued was New England criticism, or more strictly speaking . . . Boston criticism," William Dean Howells later recalled.† Maintaining a unique reputation in the nineteenth century, the New England heart pumped its peculiar ideas through the intellectual veins of the nation.

This study analyzes only the association of ideas which produced

* For this view of New England "as a region of the heart and mind," see George Wilson Pierson, "The Obstinate Conception of New England: A Study of Denudation," *New England Quarterly,* XXVIII (1955), 17.

† William Dean Howells, *Literary Friends and Acquaintance* (New York, 1900), p. 115.

a rationale for immigration restriction. Other Americans were thinking about the immigrants in the second half of the nineteenth century, but Brahmin thought had significant social and intellectual implications for the whole nation. This book does not treat the immigrants themselves, or their actual influence upon the Boston community. Rather it takes the development of the ideology of restriction as a vantage point from which to examine Brahmin attitudes toward themselves in their local society, in the nation at large, and in the world beyond, from the 1850's to the 1920's.

By 1850 Brahmins had a code of values governing their relations with man and God in their democratic society. Their view of immigration fitted naturally into that code. After mid-century this code was subjected to new tests as the feelings of younger generations and the conditions of American life inevitably changed. Then differing affirmations and negations of the old values evolved among conscientious, civic-minded Bostonians; and, revolving about the issue of immigration restriction, an ideology of race absorbed the old values into another intellectual framework which was based upon contemporary historical and scientific hypotheses.

The growth of this ideology of race accompanied the changes in Brahmin society at the turn of the century. The process by which the group lost its unity and gradually divided into opposing channels of thought and action went on for several generations among individuals only partly conscious of the changes within themselves. The introspective writings of New Englanders provided the first insight into the anxieties which beset all but a few hardy souls from the 1850's to the 1890's. Cumulatively, as this loss of faith pervaded a mellow society, its human relations in every phase of experience—family, education, religion, or domestic service—and responses to politics, economics, social crises, foreigners, and their countries, all influenced the Brahmin state of mind. In these later decades, immigrants especially were a focus of altering perspectives, for the newcomers were visible reminders of the strangeness and unpredictability of the United States after the Civil War. From these perspectives came a new chapter in the intellectual history of old New Englanders.

In seeking to understand this interplay of ideas, attitudes, and social change, I benefited immeasurably from the sympathetic guidance of Oscar Handlin. During the course of supervising this book in its various stages, he communicated the stimulus of his creative standard and the vision which, in his own work, has uncovered new meaning in historical fact.

During the long process of research and composition I have been impressed with the number and variety of human relationships aiding the process from start to finish—family, friends, acquaintances, and unknown persons. In gathering the initial material, I enjoyed the facilities and courtesies of the academic community. To its members who permitted the use of private family manuscripts or who graciously granted personal interviews I have made individual acknowledgments on pages 215-218. I wish to thank the various staffs of the libraries mentioned on page 211; and, I am particularly appreciative of the helpful efforts of Kimball C. Elkins of the Harvard University Archives, Isaac Sprague, Jr. of the Boston Athenaeum, and of Stiena E. Benson of the Simmons School of Social Work Library.

Others contributed to the final product in important ways. Mary Flug Handlin's thoughtful and constructive reading of the manuscript was of great value. Evelyn Rexford Bender typed the successive drafts and prepared the manuscript with competence and devoted care. Ann Louise Coffin demonstrated skill and interest in editing the copy.

This book is dedicated to my husband, whose invaluable judgment and generosity sustained me through all the trials. To him and to our children—Peter Jr., Maida, and Daniel—my thanks are inadequate.

Cambridge, Massachusetts   Barbara Miller Solomon

July 19, 1956

Contents

We have unquestionably a great cloud-bank of ancestral blindness weighing down upon us, only transiently riven here and there by fitful revelations of the truth. It is vain to hope for this state of things to alter much. Our inner secrets must remain for the most part impenetrable by others, for beings as essentially practical as we are are necessarily short of sight. But, if we cannot gain much positive insight into one another, cannot we at least use our sense of our own blindness to make us more cautious in going over the dark places? Cannot we escape some of those hideous ancestral intolerances and cruelties, and positive reversals of the truth?

William James, *Talks to Teachers on Psychology; and to Students on Some of Life's Ideals* (New York, 1902), p. 268.

CHAPTER I

New Englanders Between Two Worlds

I wish I could feel, as I did then [July 4, 1826], that we were
a chosen people, with a still valid claim to divine interpositions . . .
Here was a great gain to the sum of human happiness, at least,
however it be with the higher and nobler things that make a
country truly inhabitable. Will they come in time, or is Democracy
doomed by its very nature to a dead level of commonplace?
— James Russell Lowell[1]

In 1850 proper Bostonians were self-conscious members of a
society which had already reached a peak in economic and intellectual attainment. In their own eyes and in those of the outside world
they were heirs to all that New England stood for in religious,
humanitarian, and literary creativity. They believed that their remarkable present had grown purposefully out of the seeds of a
sheltered past. This present, like the past, was not at a standstill;
this sure world was changing in response to new conditions and
human needs. Yet, although an unknown future was slowly moving
nearer, in Boston, "that blessed centre of New England life," never
had destiny seemed brighter.[2]

That sense of destiny was partly rooted in a feeling of continuity
with the great tradition shaped by their New England forbears over
the past two hundred years. What these ancestors had thought of
themselves, of their God, of their country, and of strangers provided
a peculiar binding heritage.

The first settlers of the seventeenth century had been English Puritans, and, like the ancient Jews, had known they were a chosen people. Picked by God to found a just commonwealth on earth, the emigrants entrusted the government of the Massachusetts Bay Colony to a pious minority. These "elect," as stewards of God, fostered a rigid community in which dissenting Puritans as well as adherents of other religions were unwelcome. Like Quakers, Anabaptists, and Catholics, Roger Williams, Anne Hutchinson, and Thomas Hooker discovered that the Bay Colony had no room for those who defied the Boston hierarchy. Its dominance prevailed again when French Huguenots, permitted to establish their own Calvinistic church in 1685, disbanded to merge with the Puritans.[3]

When the Puritan theocracy was ended by the British king in 1692, it was no longer legal to exclude those who differed with the "elect." Still the Anglicans, who were the first to avail themselves of the new religious liberty, "ran the full gamut of social persecution." Many others, including Irish Catholics, were "not approved by the selectmen of Boston to be inhabitants of ye Towne." A few Jews were tolerated because the Puritans longed to convert them. In effect, the clergy were still powerful censors for the established, chosen way of life.[4]

Despite these tenacious guardians, the days of Puritan rule were numbered. Religious fervor dissipated in the eighteenth century, and new sects attenuated the earlier unanimity of thought. The American Revolution hastened the era of positive tolerance and brought "unexpected" freedom of worship to Catholics in Massachusetts. The formation of the Diocese of Boston (encompassing all of New England) in 1818 brought to a close the essential exclusiveness of the whole colonial tradition.[5]

Although no longer religiously orthodox, the descendants of the Puritans kept a "lingering faith" in their destiny as a chosen people. None doubted that New England was morally superior to the rest of the country. Few immigrants had been attracted to New England before the Revolution and the European wars prevented mass emigration from 1789 until 1818.[6]

But this provincial community was not isolated. Foreign travelers found a gracious welcome in Boston homes. And, ever since the Revolution had sent John Adams to France, each generation had dispatched sons across the Atlantic. There they learned from French medicine, English letters, German philosophy and music without disrupting their sense of superiority and difference. From her port trading ships also took young men all over the world and brought them back safely to the "Athens of America." New Englanders were ingrown despite studies, travels, and worldly experience. The scattered foreigners who happened to arrive were absorbed in the homogeneous native society. In this beehive of culture and reform these Bostonians boasted of their town where everyone knew everyone else.[7]

Their town was, however, a growing city which would, by 1850, contain more than 200,000 residents in its environs, of whom only a relatively small group knew each other. While some of them were descended from the old Puritan clergy, many others were enterprising newcomers, sons of simple colonial farmers who had made their way up through the fortunes of trade after the Revolution. In the fluid state of republican society, the intimately associated new merchant families and the increasing number of intellectuals of the old stock formed a select gentry, later called by Oliver Wendell Holmes "the Brahmin caste of New England." By no means a closed caste, the group was nevertheless distinct from the rest of the Yankees who remained farmers, seamen, fishermen, artisans or who became industrial workers. Yet the common tie of rural antecedents, religious affiliations, and Revolutionary experiences cemented a strong feeling of kinship between Brahmins and the larger mass of Yankees from which they had risen. Although the ways of life of the two groups diverged more and more with each decade, the assumption that they shared a common core of values was taken for granted. By this identification of Yankee with Brahmin leadership the New England capital exerted a pervasive influence on Yankees at home, among those who migrated west, and through them upon all other Americans.[8]

In the first half century of the young republic the spokesmen for the New England colonial tradition defined its code of values more plainly, and steadily broadened its applications. The Revolution which had claimed the right of every man to life, liberty, and the pursuit of happiness was dedicated to the rational idea of progress that all men had the natural ability to develop in a democratic environment. This ideal wavered in Boston during the nation's insecure founding years, while Brahmins wrestled with the fuller meanings of these values which were being extended in the new American society. After 1820 Brahmins were self-confident and ready for the religious, intellectual, and social affirmations of the idea of progress which now flowered out of the old New England tradition.

Two representative men—William Ellery Channing and Ralph Waldo Emerson—in their forms of Unitarianism and Transcendentalism, preached the divinity of man, the dignity of man, and the capacity of man. Respect for the individuality of each man plus faith in the universality of all men added up to the code of values upon which specific Brahmin attitudes were based. Religiously, this code impelled respect for the creeds and consciences of all individuals; intellectually, it stimulated new avowals of cultural independence from England; and socially, the inevitable corollary was that the condition of human slavery was intolerable. Moreover, repudiating the Puritan concept that sin and poverty were an inevitable part of God's plan for mankind, Unitarian ministers supplemented the Puritans' duty to the poor with a new impetus to reform. The relation of environment to intemperance, insanity, and criminality assumed major importance as the ministers set out to improve the conditions of living in the fresh slums of their town. By the 1840's a "curious wave of feeling" swept over Boston in which ministers, philosophers and reformers, poets and writers proclaimed their faith that America was creating a new manhood consistent with their democratic ideal.[9]

New industrial conditions in the 1840's and 1850's tested Brahmin faith in the potentialities of mankind. In the very years of fulfillment of this ingrown group, industrialization also stimulated Brahmin expansiveness. The New England élite felt itself part of pioneer America and welcomed the immense challenge of the dawning

machine age. Foreseeing the enlarged scope of activity which ingenious Yankees would gain from the new power, Ralph Waldo
Emerson and Theodore Parker shared the exhilaration of the community. With excitement and pride, Brahmins dreamed new dreams
for the America, the New England, and the Boston they loved.
Indeed, imaginative New Englanders extended their economic horizons and soon led the way in railroading and manufacturing
throughout the country. But while their practical spheres of interest
and influence extended to all sections of the nation, Boston remained
their true Hub of the Universe.[10]

At home, economic expansion attracted strangers in unprecedented numbers. After 1835 Irish immigrants increasingly worked
in the mills and railroads. Small groups of French, German, Jewish,
and other newcomers also found places in the economy. Although
the foreigners were objects of curiosity and distaste in the streets of
Boston, they were valued as useful additions to the laboring population.[11]

Growing immigration, of course, intensified the problems which
urbanism had already begun—crowded tenements, increased pauperism and insanity, inept domestic help—and created new ones. But
Unitarian self-reliance felt equal to these problems. Brahmins, secure
in their own destiny, did not doubt that all mankind was perfectible,
or at least capable of improvement. Immigrants, they assumed, would
learn how to behave in Boston. And just as readily, humanitarians
chastised the behavior of their own merchants and industrialists lest
enthusiasm for money-making lower the ethical standards of the
whole clan. Part and parcel of the same group—dining and wining
and conversing in the same clubs, marrying into each other's families
—the intellectual representatives censured the business practices of
their kin without losing their faith in the growing capitalistic
economy. Self-confident in any case and savoring the positive side
of industrialization, these leaders considered urban hazards annoy-
ing but surmountable blocks on the road to progress.[12]

Since all men could improve in a decent environment, immigration was not only an economic good benefiting New England but
a genuine benevolence for "the poor wretches of the old world."

Parker, a Unitarian minister, urged that America be "the Asylum of Humanity for this century as for the seventeenth." For Emerson, immigration was an integral part of the process of creating a democratic civilization. America would be "a smelting-pot" forged from Irishmen, Germans, Swedes, Poles, Cossacks, and all other European tribes; and from all of them would be born "a new race, a new religion, a new state, a new literature." The feeling of expectancy was as potent as it had been in the Revolutionary years: out of the brawn and brain of the Old World, Young America would grow powerful and unique.[13]

So much was this faith taken for granted that an organized nativist movement in Massachusetts from 1845 to 1855 shocked most Brahmins deeply. Yankee politicians, irked when conservative Irish Americans blocked reform measures, aimed to disenfranchise them. Although Brahmins also objected to the obstruction of reform legislation, they refused to exploit prejudices against Catholic foreigners even to attain desirable political ends. Parker described himself, "as far removed from Catholicism as any man in America," and thought the Irishmen "the worst people in Europe to make colonists of . . ." Yet like his fellow Brahmins he opposed Know-Nothingism: it signified the opposite of democracy, "which allows every man his natural right because he is a *Man*—not a *red* man or a *white* man, or an *American* man." Indeed the Yankee nativists were not immune to this stand and, once in power, the Know-Nothing leaders tried to drop the anti-Catholicism in their program. Nor did it occur to them to propose any kind of restriction of immigration. In Boston's heyday the leaders of the old society limited the effects of the nativist blight on the community.[14]

But although the nativist tension dissipated and the New England tradition seemed intact, a whole Brahmin generation unknowingly stood at the crossroads. Young men in the 1840's and 1850's, nurtured upon the democratic code of values which their society had evolved, dedicated themselves to the continuing challenges of Young America. They shared their fathers' aspirations, yet the metal of the younger generation was not as sure and strong and unbending. The purposes of the sons were just as high but there was a barely discernible difference in their dedication. Their faith was inherited. What their fathers had created independently could never be quite the same for the children who had simply accepted it. The fathers had definitively stated that their democratic ideal applied without limit to outsiders. But, amid the changing course of the children's lives, the faith which idealized the dreams and hopes of their society had to meet unexpected challenges. Inhibited in the face of new adjustments, the ideal became a burden. The changing reactions of two individual leaders of that generation—James Russell Lowell and Charles Eliot Norton—baffled and tormented by their heritage, foreshadowed the ethical conflicts of the group through the rest of the century.

For Lowell and his friends, the essence of mid-century New England, like that of all America, was its dynamic character. Lowell, already a promising poet who graduated from Harvard College in 1838 and from Harvard Law School in 1840, stood out as a younger participant in the flowering culture of his society. Although he would live out his days in a very different world after the Civil War, his values were molded in the 1840's, and he echoed the declarations of Emerson and Parker. In America he watched "the action and reaction of different races . . . and higher or lower civilizations"; and unlike the "dead precipitate" of Europe, in the New World all the human "elements" were "in solution" and would "combine" in time into a new people.[15]

This respect for the unknown American future acted as a gadfly, stimulating Anglophobe sentiment among creative Brahmins. Since the War for Independence, New Englanders had experienced complex feelings toward old England and Englishmen. To Cambridge boys of Lowell's youth, the British lion was "but a dethroned deity, who might again be restored should such boys relax for a moment their defiance to tyrants." But family ties, religious affiliations, habits of thought, and everyday customs often contradicted the dictates of conscience. Forward looking Brahmins appreciated the paradox of their community which, though anti-English in principle, often abased itself before English standards. Again following the leadership of Channing and Emerson, young Lowell battled against English imitativeness and chided his countrymen:

> You steal Englishmen's books and think Englishmen's thoughts,
> With their salt on her tail your wild eagle is caught
> Your literature suits its each whisper and motion
> To what will be thought of it over the ocean.[16]

By contrast, he invented Hosea Biglow, a Yankee in his dialect as well as his antislavery, anti-English views, "to express the American Idea." Not that Lowell intended to forget his English roots. The readers of the *Biglow Papers* were still exposed to the edifying influence of British history, heroes, statesmen, and poets. Ideally, Lowell hoped that between America and England "a balanced life would revolve" in which the American would be himself and not, as in the eyes of English visitors, "a kind of inferior and deported Englishman."[17]

Believing in the "American Idea" of human capacity, Lowell reported the studies of ethnologists in his antislavery journalism of the 1840's to show that the progress of mankind depended upon the influence of environment. Negroes, Irishmen, Jews, Poles, and other oppressed peoples shared alike "the capacity ... for self-government." But "in our moral atmosphere ... so dense and heavy with prejudice," the Negro could not "stand erect or ... breathe freely." Likewise the Irish, kept down by England, were in a "constant state of insecurity" which made them "shiftless and prodigal." The Jews in Europe, "a people remarkable above almost all others for the possession of the highest and clearest intellect," were warped because they were not permitted to exercise their "mental capacity." Similarly, ethnic differences in physical structure and in color of skin were the results of climatic and other factors of environment. Lowell, who had set out to defend the capacity of the Negro to grow in American society, had then pondered the meaning of race as it applied to other oppressed groups, and denied its validity.[18]

Turning upon oppressors, whether Southerners against Negroes or Englishmen against Irishmen, he saw through the tendency of dominant groups to glorify their own origins and to justify their protection of underdogs, as inferiors by race. Centuries ago the Normans had looked down on "their Saxon serfs as mere cattle," and now those very serfs acclaimed "that famous Anglo-Saxon race, concerning whom we have seen so much claptrap in the newspapers for a few years past." Amused by the "vague assertions of our Anglo-Saxon descent," Lowell reduced Anglo-Saxonism to a mere "cause or . . . apology of national oppression."[19]

But although deprecating the use of race as an instrument of the powerful, his statement encompassed more than he really felt. The eighth generation of his family in Massachusetts, Lowell was, like all Brahmins, proud of his heredity. One of the extremists among antislavery Bostonians, he never suggested that all peoples were equal in capacity nor minimized the differences in the qualities of the various ethnic stocks. Brahmin magnanimity toward the oppressed was humanitarian and usually limited. Thus Lowell deplored the status of the Jew, the degraded vender of old clothes and the money-changer of Europe. From this recognizable image, the reformer Lowell wanted to liberate the victim. But when Disraeli's novel *Tancred* wittily embroidered the thesis that all world forces—intellectual, social, and material—originated with the Jews, the Brahmin Lowell lost his sense of humor and descended to the very technique of racial attack which he criticized elsewhere.[20]

With the passing of each year of that decade it became more difficult to retain the anti-racist evaluations which antislavery had inspired. For in the process of combating the nativist politicians, the anti-racist link in Brahmin humanitarianism was weakened. As the differences between old Bostonians and Irish aliens were publicly articulated, those differences were defined by racial categories: Anglo-Saxon was the label for the true American, and Celt for the immigrant. Ten years earlier, James Russell Lowell had placed environment first in the shaping of human character. Now, editor of the new *Atlantic Monthly,* which dedicated itself to "the American Idea," he confessed to a friend how easy it was to become "quite a German in respect to Race . . . inclined to settle all questions by that easy formula." Lowell's self-consciousness, however, demonstrated that for the present "the ideas of the earlier time . . . were still felt, still dominant," and the implications of the racist idiom were ambiguous.[21]

But the society which had been unified was now splitting into sectors which lacked the common ties and the values established through the colonial and the Revolutionary experiences. The weak communication between native and immigrant groups revealed more plainly the proportions of the Brahmins' dilemma in the changing democratic society. The dilemma had created a great divide. In the 1850's most Brahmins ignored the divide in order to quell the nativist crisis, but Charles Eliot Norton broke with his society's values and brought to the foreground its growing concern. While many publicly denounced the Know-Nothing persecutors, a private letter of young Norton registered a discordant note. Disagreeing with his idol Emerson and with his dearest friend Lowell (who was eight years his senior), he approved of the nativist program to exclude the foreign-born from office and to prevent "the growing political influence of the Catholic Church." Better still, Know-Nothingism might initiate "a widespread popular movement" to stem the tide of immigration. A minority view then, Norton's judgment upon immigration emerged from his reappraisal of the pursuits of religion, business, and culture in a democratic society.[22]

Charles Eliot Norton was the son of Andrews Norton, the religious leader once dubbed the Unitarians' pope, whose fifty-acre estate, "Shady Hill," was a center of New England's aristocratic clergy in the early decades of the century. At Harvard in the class of 1846, the son exhibited the scholarly bent of generations of preachers. Upon graduation, he went to work for a few years in a Boston import firm and even started his own East India trade company. Obviously unsuited for a business career, in later life he considered his brief apprenticeship the most arduous discipline he had ever encountered. After this failure to find a place among Boston's merchants, Norton dutifully edited the works of his recently deceased father, only to conclude that for him the inherited religious tradition was outmoded. Despising Calvinism and Catholicism alike,

Norton found the skepticism of his philosopher friend Chauncey Wright a truer norm.[23]

Norton had lost both the tenuous spiritual balance of Unitarian-Transcendentalist Boston and the pride of this community in its expanding capitalistic ventures. Lacking the motivations of merchants and industrialists and the visions of intellectuals, he feared that the incredible prosperity of the country in the 1850's would deprave the national character. Although the United States was the most interesting place to live "were it only for the sake of seeing the mass of people comfortable," materialism threatened to destroy the meaning of the republic. Talk of manifest destiny obsessed the average citizen, and in this crass atmosphere Norton saw no hope for real distinction in literature and art. Despite his admiration for Emerson and the great company of New Englanders, he questioned their assurance of national progress.[24]

The American people lacked "wisdom and intelligence" but there was one chance of saving them. Although Norton criticized John Stuart Mill's theory of upper-class trusteeship for English society, he looked to the leadership of the few "intelligent and prosperous classes" to stabilize his own democracy.[25]

He had no doubt that the growing American people, "misled, troubled and exasperated," needed guidance from his group. For that purpose he had helped organize the first night school for laborers in Boston and had studied the new housing problem caused by the Irish and German immigration. With the interests of the people foremost in his conscientious mind, Norton had no inkling that he looked upon "the lower classes" with contempt and alarm. Yet in 1852 he described immigration as a "sea of ignorance . . . swollen by the waves of misery and vice . . . pouring from revolutionized Europe upon our shores." Uncomfortable at the prospect of increasing popular initiative, whether in Europe or America, he extended his censorious view of his own society to the incoming foreigners.[26]

Under doctor's orders, this dispirited man went abroad in 1855. In Europe Norton found new focus, becoming absorbed, like other Brahmins, in the art and architecture of Dante's world. Earlier in the century, professors George Ticknor and Henry Wadsworth Longfellow had introduced at Harvard the study of the great Catholic poet, and Lowell, now the third Smith Professor of Modern Languages, was conducting his seminar on Dante. From the 1850's, in trips to Italy and France, although still repelled like their "sterner fathers" by Catholic theology, Brahmins increasingly recorded their fascination with the cathedrals. Norton was only one distinguished son of the Unitarians who turned from the dogma grown sterile to the aesthetics of European Catholic civilization. With a scholar's interest, he would later formalize his personal experiences in cultural studies of the medieval world.[27]

But Norton's interest in Catholic art did not increase his tolerance for Irish immigrants of Romanist faith, for they impinged on the core of things troubling to Brahmins in the 1850's. Although he recognized that "the larger share of evils in our cities" was not the fault of the newcomers, Norton stressed the difficulty of absorbing the "sudden influx of a people so long misgoverned . . . of a race foreign to our own." More frankly than some of his friends, he resisted the industrialization which had separated the old New England community into dissident sectors, part native, part foreign. Without the faith in mankind of a Channing or an Emerson, younger men like Norton were losing their heritage of "optimism" and "contentedness." The other side of the Atlantic held a different attraction from that which had drawn their fathers and grandfathers earlier. In time, European monuments and churches would be sanctuaries for New Englanders adrift between two worlds.[28]

Their society was splintering as the old assumptions no longer bound every member of the community, but for a few brief years the old unity returned. In 1861 the Civil War suffused the inherited faith with a new ardor. Relatives, friends, and humbler Americans like immigrants and Negroes demonstrated the North's solidarity. In this righteous crusade, Brahmins were undaunted, fearless. "Can we be too glad to belong to New England, to be her children, and to be living in these days?" asked Charles Eliot Norton. Once again Lowell wielded his pen for the antislavery cause, and Norton too became a molder of public opinion, editing the broadsides of the New England Loyal Publication Society.[29]

War evoked intense rededication to the democratic ideals of their society. In Lowell's view, England's official support of the South reaffirmed the "irrepressible conflict between the Old World and the New." Bitter Anglophobia was again universal in Boston. Even Norton agreed with Lowell that England symbolized "one idea," and America "another . . . innately hostile. . ." England could keep her "valuable institutions—state-church, peerage, pauperage!" For New England, Lincoln (after a period of trial) became the emblem of faith, the embodiment of the manhood which "America made . . . out of the very earth, unancestried, unprivileged, unknown."[30]

War took Norton by surprise: it was "a striking development of the democratic principle" strengthening his lukewarm belief in the present way of life of the American people. For the first and only time Norton was enthusiastic about the economic and cultural state of the nation. The material prosperity, the public education, and the lack of class distinctions had made the population which emigrated from Europe, morally superior to those who had stayed behind. The future strength of the United States lay in the continued migration of "intelligent . . . workingmen" from England and the Continent. Although Norton did not go so far as to praise the Irish newcomers, his approval of immigration was significant. In this moment of faith in both the people and the economy, Norton emphasized the essential role of the European immigrant in American life.[31]

But disillusion followed military victory. The war was "a cataclysm." Destroying relatives and friends, destroying even Southerners whom one had also loved at Harvard or summered with at Newport, it swept away "the old period." With war's end, the breach between past and present deepened; in retrospect, war had been the high water mark for the old ideals.[32]

And, beyond the basic satisfaction of Northern victory, what had been accomplished was not clear. The crucial issue of the 1860's was the fate of the freed men, but few Brahmins supported Negro rights unequivocally. They had made their moral stand against slavery; the fiascos of Reconstruction made them wonder how far their ideals applied. Antislavery views had not necessarily involved a belief in racial equality. The question of universal suffrage for Negroes awakened grave doubts. To Lowell, the ex-abolitionist, the resolution of the Negro's future brought conflict and tension. Just after the war he applauded the forceful measures of the Radical Republicans to "Americanize" the Southerners' treatment of the Negro; but when the Irish help in his kitchen loudly expressed their superiority to the freed slaves, he agreed that "Niggers" were hopeless for "Northern service" in this generation. Unsure, Lowell wavered back and forth between hopes and fears. Finally, after many discussions with Norton who had always been more concerned with the moral taint which slavery placed on the character of the white people and, with E. L. Godkin of the *Nation,* Lowell gave up the humanitarian assumption that all men as human beings were entitled to the ballot as their natural right. Disgusted with the policies of the dominant Republicans, Lowell accused them "of . . . pretending to believe that human nature is as clay in the hands of the potter instead of being . . . the result of a long past . . . to be reshaped by the slow influences of an equally long future." In the end, he accepted the emerging Brahmin view that political expediency rather than the moral antislavery principle was the only justification for Negro suffrage.[33]

And however much the Negro question weighed on Boston consciences, local issues were still paramount. Despairing of the constant problems of pauperism, crime, and other forms of corruption, as well as of "the ignorant white foreigner," Brahmins recalled bygone days with longing. The disappointment with the present enhanced the past. Earlier Lowell had enjoyed recording the charm and security of his childhood home, the Tory mansion "Elmwood," when Cambridge had been "essentially an English village." The only foreigners had been two Scotch gardeners and "almost every dweller in the town had been born in it." Now that vanished time and place was described with painful nostalgia, as Lowell contrasted the idyllic domestic harmony which had prevailed in the kitchen when "servant and master were of one stock."[34]

Even in the midst of the Civil War, Norton had not completely submerged his discontent with contemporary America. In 1864 he found at Ashfield, Massachusetts, a summer retreat and a way of life that was disappearing in Cambridge and Boston. There were no reminders of modern industrialization in this little Berkshire town: railroad, telegraph, and plumbing were unknown. Moreover, Ashfield was a prosperous village, unsullied by the changed population of urban New England. Norton wrote delightedly to Lowell that there was "but one Irish family . . . in the township." Two miles away, however, in "the little village of Tin Pot" there was "a good deal of loafing and drinking," but "the loafers and drunkards" remained where they were; "the line" was "one of positive separation between the two villages."[35]

In practical terms it was inexpensive to live, even on "the salary of a German professor," at Ashfield; here the Cantabrigian did not dread his annual bills. The serenity of this protected world inspired Norton to romanticize: the air was "cool and fresh," the fields were "gardens of wild fruit," the thick, dark woods were as "beautiful as the forest of Broceliande" and "the glades" looked "like the openings in a park." Surely, "in this happy, tranquil region," he reflected, "one could write Massachusetts idylls or a New England 'Arcadia.'"[36]

Ashfield was congenial to Norton's deepest needs and to his inherited standards. He understood its stable society where generations of citizens continued to create an ingrown rural community, oblivious to the urban cleavages of rich and poor, native and foreign-born. Reminiscent of the small college community into which he had been born, the attractions of his Berkshire home betrayed Norton's desire for the vanished Cambridge, Massachusetts of 1827.

But summertime retreats could not solve the problems of postwar Brahmin existence. New Englanders who treasured their leadership in the democratic society would not retire from the contemporary destiny of the United States. As in the 1850's, they again traveled in search of the meaning of their own lives in the changing civilization. The quests abroad in the 1870's gave more occasions to think about their beloved country. To one still proud of the "American Idea," its defects were the more distressing, when in Europe. There

Lowell had to swallow humiliating attacks on the democracy which produced politicians like Ulysses Grant and Boss Tweed. In true Puritan fashion, Lowell railed at his countrymen, only to face the hue and cry of the press denouncing him as an Anglophile and lover of dukes. Disturbed and bewildered, he asked, "If I am not an American, who ever was?"[37]

The presence of rich American tourists was embarrassing to Norton. The very industrialization and commercialism which he had hoped to leave behind encroached in Italy. He did not want to be reminded of "Americanism out of America"; abroad, it was "detestable . . . out of harmony with the nature of the land and with the spirit of the associations." He was relieved that Rome was resisting "the flood of 'American' barbarism and of universal materialism . . . desolating Europe." Norton was happy in Siena, which was pure in its medieval tranquillity. It still had monuments and manners—it had not been vulgarized.[38]

Above all, England seemed to offer all that America could not. Wartime antagonisms ebbed as Bostonians once again enjoyed the society of English writers and intellectuals. Norton reveled in the good company of old friends like Carlyle, Dickens, Mill, Ruskin, and the painter Burne-Jones. The Cambridge, Massachusetts of 1873 provided a terrible contrast. There, alas, only Norton and Lowell and a few others cared for "the ideal side of life." Lowell, too, as Minister to Spain in 1877 and to England in 1880, acutely felt the charm of English life and suffered pangs of conscience for this.[39]

In his later years Lowell became confused by his reactions to England. Surely, he pondered, "the differences between an American of English descent and an Englishman" were "mostly superficial." How had his ancestor had the strength of mind to leave "the most beautiful bit of the Earth's surface?" Interviewed by an English journalist at "Elmwood" in 1891, Lowell welcomed the comment upon the "very English aspect of his little home." He displayed the royal arms in his kitchen and recalled that his grandmother had been a Loyalist, who had mourned, until the day she died, on the Fourth of July. Such boasting of family Anglophilia illustrated the distance Lowell had traveled from his days of resistance to things English.[40]

Lowell was a halfway ambassador in the shifting relations of old and New England. Becoming accustomed to English ways, he attended the Episcopalian services from time to time, and lessened "a certain protest against institutional religion which was characteristic of the community" into which he was born; still, bound by the past, he did not become a church member. He had inherited the New England belief that the "Episcopalian Church was an exotic." Despite the increased attractiveness of English ways, he still rebuked younger men for adopting English accents. Yet he himself had shifted by 1870 from his early nationalistic use of American dialects as a literary medium to an emphasis on the universal English language of tradition. In the total perspective, Henry James was right, Lowell had a "double existence—the American and the English sides of his medal, which had yet so much in common."[41]

While Lowell's ambivalence toward the English was an index to his altering spirit, in a different way his attitude toward Jews revealed confusion with the changing world. English culture and Englishmen had been an intimate part of Brahmin experience, whereas he had known Jews so slightly that his impressions were usually derivative. From his intellectual background the Brahmin inherited two opposing images: one of the noble ancient Hebrew, another of the repugnant modern Jew. Although not religious, Lowell, a minister's son, retained the Puritans' admiration for the chosen people of the Old Testament. And as a learned philologist in his own right, he read Hebrew fluently and liked to recall its hieratic importance in the Harvard College of his ancestors. The Old Testament was still a standard of human wisdom as it had been for his forbears. Truly the Hebrews were the predecessors of the Puritans in quenching "the spiritual thirst of mankind." But, however, since the Middle Ages, the Hebrew had also come out of the ghettos as a wretched street vender. When Lowell had denounced Jewish oppression in the 1840's, his point of departure had been the contrast between these two images.[42]

Significantly, in the last decades of his life these images, bred primarily of literary and historical associations, became a means through which he expressed his loss of inner poise in an unstable world. When he felt out of place in New England, Lowell likened himself to the Hebrew Joseph who had also lived among a younger generation who knew him not. Moreover, when he felt less noble, in a mood of self-ridicule, he would describe himself as the stock Jew who hated pork or pulled a sharp trade. Oddly, Lowell, who had grown up in homogeneous New England, established a personal identity which involved both an attraction toward and a revulsion from Jews.[43]

Finally, he came more and more in contact with Jews who did not fit into either of the inherited images. Not only did he really hear in the early morning the cries of Jewish peddlers selling cast-off clothes on the streets of London and Paris, but now he became aware of other Jews rising in modern European society. To his irritation he found that he mistook for Germans some people who proved to be "rank Jews."[44]

The presence of Jews emerging from ghettos into polite society became a recurring topic of conversation among Lowell, Norton, and others of the Cambridge circle of the 1870's. When George Eliot's novel, *Daniel Deronda,* was in vogue in 1876, they, like Englishmen, were amazed by its dénouement. The hero, discovering his Spanish Jewish origin, gives up his English identity and departs for the East with his bride, an English Jewess, to work for restoration of their people as a political nation. Mrs. Eliot's "mission to restore the lost tribes of old cloe's men," as Norton described it, seemed a romantic attempt to surmount both the ancient past and the immediate past of the Jews with a better future.[45]

Lowell also, during his long stays abroad, probed the meaning of the actual contemporary contacts of the Jewish group with European life. During his diplomatic missions he was more than ever conscious of Jews. In Spain, there was "a very large infusion in the upper and middle classes of the most intense, restless, aspiring, and unscrupulous blood of all, the Jewish." In England, he labeled the poet Browning a Jew and Henry James's heroine in *The Tragic Muse* a Jewess. Suggesting that there was a Jewish nature more passionate and more aggressive than the Anglo-Saxon, Lowell involved Brahmin self-esteem in his interpretations.[46]

The modern Hebrew was still a usurer to him, but in his Anglo-phile sympathies Lowell endorsed the function of those Jews who gave financial support to England's empire. Partially reversing his opinion of Disraeli, Lowell commended the British political policy in the Near East which strengthened the power of the English. Now he considered "a good deal of prejudice against Beaconsfield . . . medieval" for there were "plenty of other modern versions of the story of Joseph." Lowell who was a Joseph in New England felt a personal bond with Disraeli.[47]

But Lowell's fascination with the Jew on three different levels—as the ancient Hebrew of the Bible, as the European scapegoat, and as the emancipated citizen—was mingled with resistance to these outsiders. They seemed to be everywhere in the strange modern world. With his flair for paradox, Lowell made his favorite after-dinner conversation a monologue on "the ubiquity" and "universal ability of the Hebrew." Claiming that "everybody in some way descended from the Jews," Lowell insisted that he himself was a Jew. The Semitic blood strain appeared in European royalty and nobility; in addition, all bankers, most barons, and prime ministers were Jews. The climax of this discourse was a forecast of their "control of finance, the army and navy, the press, diplomacy, society, titles, the government, and the earth's surface." In a stage whisper, the Brahmin ended, "What do you suppose they will do with them—and with us?" The speech of a raconteur, this talk betrayed the deepest fears of the speaker.[48]

To Lowell, as to his English friends, the participation of a few prosperous Jews in affairs of state and their presence in private upper-class homes represented a loss of fixed social distinctions. Could the Christian world of his ancestors survive? But even though he feared modern capitalism and associated the Jews with it, he defended them in his last public address in England. This "race in which ability seems as natural and hereditary as the curve of their noses," had been wronged by the western world, and now ruled "with the ignoble sceptre of finance," declared Lowell, the Puritan descendant who had fought human oppression in his youth. Bewildered and insecure, he was yet incapable of anti-Semitism.[49]

Nevertheless the mobility of Jews had added another dimension to an already unrecognizable world. While Lowell echoed the democratic values of his past, he could not quite reconcile them with his new reactions of fear and hostility toward Jews who no longer corresponded to his inherited stereotype. Indeed, the future of the Jews he met in Europe seemed as unpredictable as the future of his native land.

Although the United States seemed far away, the idea of expatriation was unthinkable to Brahmins of that generation. After Lowell had completed his diplomatic services, for all his pleasure in English life, he came home to die at "Elmwood." At mid-century, he had urged the sculptor William Wetmore Story to return from Italy to Cambridge. Although he was more tolerant with Henry James's removal abroad in the 1870's, Lowell even in 1888 rebuked the "commonplace of our newspapers, that an American who stays long enough in Europe is sure to find his own country unendurable when he comes back." At heart, Lowell was ashamed of the idea of expatriation.[50]

And Norton, despite the changes in New England, wanted his children to be rooted in the community of their ancestors, even though the beloved streets would lose their familiar character to make room for the new and straight sidewalks. Before the city of Cambridge taxed him out of his inherited "Norton Woods," he wanted his children to grow "familiar with the trees and fields" he "used to belong to." Though life would never again seem as promising as in the old days, Norton never renounced his part in American society.[51]

As a professor of the history of fine arts at Harvard and as the first citizen of Ashfield, Norton surely enriched New England culture. Still he knew Harvard and Ashfield were but fragile shields against the impact of industrialization. Speaking for his generation, Norton felt himself being "swept along with irresistible force," while watching "old landmarks disappear." The whole "civilized world" was entering "a transformation, the precise character of which" no one could foresee. Eventually Norton suffered from the knowledge that his neighbors did not always know who he was, nor care how long the Norton family had lived in New England.[52]

Ultimately, he concluded, emigration, first from Europe to America and then from east to west, had intensified the social rupture. There were no hereditary homes in the United States to give continuity to the past; and home-changing did not do justice to the moral nature of the English race. Mobile and rootless, American life had destroyed the old-fashioned neighborliness upon which the civic conscience of the older communities had flourished. Even the top layer of society suffered from the flux: there was no longer a "common stock of things taken for granted." Immigration had become the symbol of the broken continuity with the past.[53]

Lowell and Norton watched the end of their New England civilization, which was "obsolete as the mastadon." As the remnant of the old gentry, they still felt an obligation to raise the standards of the people. Self-appointed guardians, Norton and Lowell who had been editors and close to editors all their lives, never ignored politics. They, along with E. L. Godkin of the *Nation* and George W. Curtis of *Harper's Weekly,* were leaders among the first independent voters to resist party machines in the 1870's and 1880's. Protesters, determined to save America from herself, they tried to bridge the gap between past and present.[54]

A preacher of cultural values, Norton lectured and wrote that "in the midst of the barbaric wealth of the richest millions of people in the world" the *North American Review* and the *Nation,* "almost the only evidence of thought in America," struggled for a bare existence. While European countries had national ideals of beauty and imagination, in the United States the pursuit of money was the only end in itself. From the 1870's, Norton roused young Harvardians (and the young ladies in the Annex) from a fatalistic acceptance of America's defects. Agreeing with English critics that the American mind was dull and uniform, he called for "variety of experience and of thought . . . difference in tradition and conviction . . . collision of ideas" in the United States. But he did not know where to look. Admittedly he ignored what he designated as the small foreign communities in the city and in the country, partly because the immigrants assimilated too easily "humane democratic standards of thought." Mainly, however, he was so accustomed to regarding the foreign-born as a strange, undiscriminated mass that he was unable to conceive of attaining the desired variety of thought and tradition from the interaction of New England and immigrant cultures. To the well-bred, aesthetic Norton, the immigrant, with his inheritance of ignorance, connoted only the lowest and least intelligent classes, "destitute of ideas and of the power of initiative action."[55]

The notion of a democratic élite not only sustained Brahmins such as these, but widened the gulf between them and newer Americans. A modern "chosen people," they were too far removed from the corrupting temptations of vulgar, urban America to understand its growth. They had offered to serve as leaders and reformers, but their leadership seemed undervalued. In the decades to follow, new groups and individuals infringed upon the inherited prerogatives. Often, then, the Brahmins' egotism would block their otherwise tolerant perspectives about the strangers in their midst.

The next generation, reaching manhood on the eve of the Civil War, faced its trials without the long decades of mental conflict that a Lowell or a Norton had endured. Elder statesmen now, the Lowells and the Nortons, in the tradition of the Puritan elect, made way for their successors. In the 1880's and 1890's, the two generations, despite vast differences in age and experience, faced the same issues—religion, education, business, and politics—and reacted to the same groups—Negroes, Englishmen, Irishmen, and Jews. The problems of Lowell and Norton became still more the problems of younger men like the Adams brothers who wanted to serve their country as their elders had. And, as similarities and differences between the two generations of Brahmins appeared, the protagonists in two acts of this New England drama brought the crisis of their society into fuller view.

CHAPTER II

The Dissolution of the Democratic Ideal

The task of suitably putting our generation to bed and tucking them all nicely in, so as to rest in quiet for eternity, is one which much needs to be done by us, for I see no reason to suppose that our successors will concern themselves about it. As I watch the formation of the new society, I am more and more impressed with my own helplessness to deal with it, and its entire unconsciousness that I, or you, or George Washington ever existed. Therefore we had better do our epitaphs and do them quick.

—Henry Adams[1]

Of all the old New England families, the Adamses felt the most intense possessiveness about the destiny of the United States. As long as there had been a nation, an Adams had served her well-being. Although never popular, three generations of Adamses had prided themselves on moral altruism in the public offices of their country, as presidents, congressmen, and ministers.

The four able sons of Charles Francis Adams assumed that they too would share this unique pattern of careers. By their own admissions, they failed. Then, the eldest, John Quincy, "laughed at the idea of sacrificing himself in order to adorn a Cleveland cabinet or to get cheers from an Irish mob." Then, the youngest, Brooks, took the stand that it was time to perish for seldom could "a single family . . . stay adjusted through three generations."[2]

The other two brothers, Charles Francis, Jr. and Henry, weighed the "failure" and most plainly revealed the record of diffident Brahmins who set out to be the standard-bearers of the Civil War generation. As they lost their way in late nineteenth-century America, Charles and Henry surrendered the inherited ideals of their youth with extreme self-consciousness. The internal crisis of their lives transformed their New England souls and illuminated their attitudes toward those who were aliens.

In retrospect, the brothers felt that the Adams name had been an insurmountable handicap. At school, Charles could never forget that his grandfather was President of the United States. At the same time, the youngster Henry was astonished that the Irish gardener did not understand that Henry too would some day be president.

Ironically, however, these fortunate young New Englanders as children enjoyed no sense of well-being. Both recalled their physical timidity; and Charles condemned their father's puritanical deprecation of outdoor sports. The brothers had many complaints against the unedifying rigors of their formal education whether at the Boston Latin School, Mr. Dixwell's, or Harvard College. More important, the religious observances of the family—twice to the Unitarian church every Sunday—never seemed real to the boys. "The religious instinct had vanished" for them, and in later years Henry, particularly, resented New England's loss of "the most powerful emotion of man, next to the sexual."[3]

Although the charted course of the parents thus provoked in the children resistance rather than confidence and security, their New England inheritance gripped the offspring inescapably. Even in their querulousness, Charles and Henry never doubted that the thought and the moral criteria of Boston were better than that of any other in the world.

Growing up in a staunchly antislavery home, the brothers identified themselves with the patriots of 1776, and looked forward to doing their part for the nation. When the Civil War first challenged their New England virtues, Charles Francis Adams, Jr., physically afraid and mentally reluctant, nevertheless, against his parents' wishes, enlisted. It would not look right for the Adamses "in after years . . . to say that . . . not one at this day stood in arms for that government with which our family history is so closely connected."[4]

Military life liberated Charles from the haunting dread of failure; roughing it made him "more of a man" than ever before. At the same time, the war enhanced his awareness of his social importance. To his mother he wrote with amusement: "So . . . visitors see the best blood in America, in the person of your son, washing dishes, sweeping floors, wheeling coal etc., like a family servant." An officer in the First Regiment of the Massachusetts Volunteer Cavalry, he led "a body of picked men" of native stock and got along with them, feeling that they "were kith and kin." Through his war service, Charles Francis Adams, Jr. fulfilled a proprietary, almost aristocratic, obligation to the country; and, by the same token, made transparent the limitations of his social perspective. Young Adams did not bring to the battlefield the dedicated emotional convictions of his anti-slavery elders. After marching through the South, he disagreed with reformers who had crusaded for the equality of the poor black man. In 1864, Adams assumed charge of a Negro regiment, as "an interesting study," but this experience did not improve his opinion of Negro ability. Ashamed of the Negro's plight, Charles decided that clearly God had made the African hopelessly inferior to the dominant white race.[5] New England humanitarianism had already paled for this rising Brahmin generation.

Meanwhile Henry assisted his father, the Minister to the Court of St. James. English society, often chilly toward the young American, increased his morbid sense of inadequacy. Castigating himself again and again in a refrain of "failure," Henry nevertheless felt vicariously the stimulus and the excitement of his friends dying in the great cause.[6] Anxious to be part of it, he anticipated war's end as the moment of real action, when he would join the rest in controlling America's fate.

A student of the aristocratic views of Francis Bowen, François Guizot, and Alexis de Tocqueville, Henry took John Stuart Mill for his political and social guide and envisaged a limited republic controlled by the responsible members of society. Watching an Italian revolution in 1858, young Adams was astonished that it lacked "the Sicilian nobility and the gentlemen who ought to take the lead in a movement like this." For the Adamses the inherited duty was plain, to bring the country back to "its true course," that is, to ensure the victory for "the New England element." So Henry Adams sat in London and dreamed of "a national set of young men like ourselves or better, to start new influences not only in politics, but in literature, in law, in society, and throughout the whole social organism of the country."[7] Despite his sense of inferiority, this was a moment of promise for the earnest, over-refined youth. He and Charles did not yet know that the ideal of a democratic élite was foredoomed.

When peace came, after careful speculation, Charles chose the railroads and Henry the press as entries into the national life. Charles remained in the ancestral home, and Henry went to the federal capital to be "the champion and confidant of a new Washington." The brothers soon discovered how the machinery of government created by their ancestors was breaking down under the phenomenal industrialization of the country. Shocked and disoriented, the young New Englanders realized they were defeated as reformers before they started. The corporate forces of the railroads and the telegraph posed problems too great for their generation to solve. What was worse, the American people seemed indifferent to the vulgar "corruption" of the Grant administration; the reelection of the President confirmed the brothers' suspicion that the nation condoned any "success as all-redeeming virtue." The Adamses found that the nineteenth-century businessman had usurped their birthright as the moral guide of the people.[8]

As educated citizens, they still held to the position of the Independents with qualified support of reconstruction, free trade, civil service, and other reforms advocated by Lowell, Norton, Curtis, and Godkin.[9] The brothers nursed their grievances for another twenty years before acknowledging utter defeat. Only then did their lives, begun with similar aspirations, diverge so completely that their separate experiences represented very different variations upon the common theme of frustration.

From the worldly point of view, Charles distinguished himself in the last three decades of the century. Between 1869 and 1879 he was "the controlling mind" of the Massachusetts Board of Railroad Commissioners, and made a permanent contribution to the development of railroad arbitration in the United States. His undisputed knowledge of transportation led to his abortive work as president of the Union Pacific from 1884 to 1890, and on a more remunerative basis he was the head of the Kansas City stockyards. But Adams was an anomaly in the world of corporations, for he hated the business instinct and loathed the "coarse, realistic, bargaining crowd" of his associates.[10] In bitter afterthought Charles resented every minute he had dutifully spent as a man of action in industrialized America.

In 1916, Adams, as a retired old gentleman looking back to those years of practical living, forgot the intellectual curiosity with which he had once explored the economy of the United States. Yet, in the 1870's, he had pondered the ultimate social effects of the railroads upon modern civilization; like Norton, he had regarded with concern the universal assimilation effected by modern transportation. Adams too regretted that Paris and London were on the way to becoming "the stereotyped railroad centres of the future," and believed that soon no person or place would retain individuality. It was quite useless, of course, to reminisce on "the old quiet days of other years and another order of things." Rather he expressed the daring hope that a new compensating value might come in the distant future. The steam revolution would produce unparalleled emigration in this age of centralization and would inevitably draw the world closer despite differences in religion and nationality. With considerable imagination the young New Englander conceived the issue "to be, whether, in the process of time, a unity of end among men may be brought to override the prejudice of race."[11] Charles Francis Adams, Jr. in 1870 set his sights high; his desires for mankind soared above his skeptical reservations about the conduct of national affairs.

But Adams, the captain of industry and the philosopher of railroads, was even more the Brahmin who, during the same years, saw all he held dear vanish in the town of Quincy, Massachusetts. No one understood better the inevitability of the changes in that community, but he could not be stoical. Quincy was the "race-place" of the Adamses and there Charles Francis, Jr. was untouched by the enlightened universalism he had told himself might be the ultimate outcome of industrialization.[12] By 1892, when he recorded the destruction of the society of his youth, too much had happened to the Adamses and to Quincy to leave him the luxury of objectivity.

Adams saw three distinct parts to the story of Quincy's decline; in each, his family had experienced the complete impact of the fall. The first change for the worse had come in 1825. Until then, Quincy had been a felicitous farming community with a population predominantly of English blood. But in that memorable year the first railroad was built, and the granite quarries operated effectively. Native New Englanders left the fields for stonecutting or shoemaking and another race, of different blood and religion, took their place. The new men, Irish Catholic immigrants, grew steadily in number despite "the narrow but traditional prejudice against them and their faith." The change in the population revolutionized the old society. By 1840, four political elements contended for the "mastery of the Quincy town-meeting"—the old native farming stock, "conservative and generally disposed to show much deference to the opinions of the gentry"; the native "quarry-men" migrating seasonally from New Hampshire; "the foreign-born Catholics, who instinctively sided against all political traditions"; and the more intelligent, native "shoemakers." In the presence of these elements, concurrent with the spread of Jacksonianism all over the country, the downfall of the local gentry was merely a question of time. John Quincy Adams' gradual loss of favor with the townspeople, except among those of "old English descent," reflected the unsettling spirit which disrupted the old order of things.[13]

The downward trend accelerated in 1845, when the opening of the Old Colony Railroad marked the second phase. Quincy was becoming a suburb of Boston. The population increased "for the worse," Adams noted, and the town meeting became a noisy, unruly gathering, at which men wore hats and smoked and frequently appeared under the influence of liquor. The cleavage deepened between Irish and other townsmen; then, the elder Charles Francis Adams became the butt of social hostilities. Significantly, his son concluded that there was racial disparity between the immigrants who became Democrats and the natives who became Free Soilers under his father. "Quick of impulse, sympathetic, ignorant and credulous, the Irish race have as few elements in common with the native New Englanders as one race of men well can have with another."[14]

The chronicler of Quincy generalized sweepingly about the Irish Americans in verbs of the present tense because the issue was painfully contemporary. Charles and his older brother John Quincy were the Adams leaders in the community. The disorderly, democratic way of running the town since the 1840's had reached a climax in the early 1870's: the public debt of $8,000 in 1844 had risen to $112,000 in 1874. Reform was urgent, and John Quincy, who had been moderator for some years, succeeded in controlling his "tired, excited, noisy" fellow townsmen. He restored order at the meetings and brought the town back to the system of business by committees to prevent democracy from getting out of hand.[15]

For the next fourteen years, the brothers literally ran Quincy. How they delighted in the operations of the town meeting! "Its atmosphere—in the olfactory way pretty bad at times—came naturally to us."[16] Together they removed the town debt, passed a temperance measure, reorganized the public school system, and established both a public library and a system of parks. Visibly the town profited.

But by 1880 the years were numbered in which an Adams could dominate ancestral Quincy. The time was gone when "every man knew . . . by face and name and reputation every other man," and the farmers were practically extinct as a group. The great mass of people of varied occupation cared less and less for the old ways and traditions. When the members of the Irish labor union, the Knights of Labor, gained control of the town meeting in 1887, the assembly promptly voted the town out of existence. Quincy had become a commonplace municipality. Poignantly Charles Francis Adams, Jr. relived the day June 11, 1888 when the bells rang to proclaim the life of the newborn city. Amid the rejoicings Charles stood apart, the chief mourner of the "old political system . . . which had carried the people in safety through periods of sore trial, and brought them up into what they had become." Although "the change might be necessary," Adams felt that he had lost "a parent" and wanted to bury the ancient town "silently, tenderly, reverently."[17]

Almost simultaneously, even as his role of social, intellectual, and political arbiter to Quincy ended, Adams' business career dissolved. Dismissed from the presidency of the Union Pacific in 1890, he had lost his job like any ordinary American. He was bitterly conscious of undeserved failure. With the actual panic of 1893, he finally severed himself from these commitments of his youth: he was through with his civic stint both in the management of the railroads and of the town of Quincy. It was "awful" to leave Quincy, the "flesh of the Adams flesh," but he departed from the beloved "race-place" forever, to resettle in Lincoln, Massachusetts, a rural village still safe from the unbearable vulgarities of an urban municipality. For the rest of his life he never forgot that the Irish, who had thwarted his father and grandfather, had displaced him. Wistfully, he believed that the old Yankee farmers would have remained amenable to Adams leadership. In his anguish, Adams could not assess the steady advance of democratic living, and he misinterpreted the trials of his family.[18]

Retrospection became more than an amateur pursuit, as Adams discovered a new occupation—that of historian. He had once been asked to speak publicly about a Weymouth ancestor and to his own surprise had greatly enjoyed the experience. By the 1890's he felt that the study of the past was more satisfactory than his part in the present. On firm ground, he joined the company of academicians to determine the genesis of the New England town, "the one feature in the American polity which no one has as yet seen fit to criticize adversely." Holding his own in this historical dispute, Adams was indifferent to the various doctrinaire hypotheses of scholars. He rejected explanations which ascribed either Germanic or theological derivations for the remarkable Yankee polity; nor did he consider English towns, parishes, or vestries the original model. For Adams, whose family had grown up with the New England town, it was "autochthonous—the natural product of a foreign seed developing under new circumstances and conditions, religious, social, material, and political, local and general."[19] Unlike Charles' epitaph to

Quincy, written in the same year, his analysis of the origins of the New England town sustained an objective attitude toward the subject.

But although never impressed with the Anglo-Saxon authorship of his favorite political institution, in his last years Adams isolated the English roots of his heritage meaningfully. As he censured the present ways of the nation, "the old Anglo-Saxon respect for law" seemed "a thing of the past." And, more basic, the "pure English" ancestry of his father explained the personality of Charles Francis Adams, Sr. "Race characteristics went with him in the blood." By the same token, the political hostility of the Irish to the father had represented their "instinctive" dislike of the essentially Anglo-Saxon.[20]

While, as a historian, Charles Francis Adams, Jr. did at times deflate his past with realistic humor, admiration of his ancestors and of their presumed racial characteristics was an increasing solace to his vanity. After all, the New Englanders were a chosen people, and he, like James Russell Lowell, echoed the Puritan preacher: "God sifted a whole Nation that He might send choice Grain over into this Wilderness."[21]

Disillusioned with Irish immigrants, Adams repeated Darwin's testimony that the Anglo-Saxon emigrants alone—"the more energetic, restless and courageous men from all parts of Europe"—explained America's success. To their descendants in the west, not only of New England but even of Scandinavian and Teutonic stocks, he turned as the last hope of the nation. Evoking a rather pathetic "hereditary affiliation" to Wisconsin as a cradle of New Englanders, he urged its agricultural communities to preserve the ideas of the Founding Fathers. After the demise of his Quincy, Charles Francis Adams, Jr. distrusted the people in the crowded eastern cities; only the farmers of old Yankee and seemingly related backgrounds might preserve the covenant of the democracy and safeguard the future American race.[22]

Out of harmony with the times, Charles Francis Adams, Jr. no longer suppressed his lack of faith in human progress. Disavowing the principles of the Declaration of Independence, he renounced the base of the American system, which assumed "a common humanity

. . . absence of absolute fundamental racial characteristics." He, who had warred against the South, capitulated to the former enemy; he scorned the ingenious pre-Darwinian society of his youth for believing that the Negro "was simply God's image carved in ebony . . . a potential Yankee who had . . . never had a chance." More disastrous, his elders' same misguided humanitarianism had claimed that America was a "modern 'melting-pot,'" which converted any alien into a citizen. In the last fifty years, New Englanders had sadly and dangerously misplaced their confidence in "the educational influences and social environment" of the United States.[23] All too plainly, the democratic ideal had broken down.

By 1905, Adams felt that his generation had done its work and he was happy to be on the retired list. His disappointments in public service had destroyed his frail belief in the ability of all men, irrespective of race, creed, or color, to meet the test of democratic citizenship. Nevertheless, when asked to support the Boston Immigration Restriction League, he hesitated to be so "radical." Although "restriction would be an admirable thing under a law skillfully drawn and conscientiously and liberally administered," he doubted that the immigrant would receive fair treatment "at the mercy" of indifferent governmental agents. Charles Francis Adams, Jr. concluded that the question of immigration was "too big and too intricate . . . to meddle with."[24] By no coincidence, he reacted like his father, who earlier had refused to join the Know-Nothings despite the trouble the hostile Irish immigrants had caused him. The son's attitude toward restriction was characteristically independent and critical, for he had not entirely relinquished the values of a New Englander grown to manhood in the 1850's.

By a very different route his brother Henry reached a more complete impasse with the inherited New England purposes. On his return to America in 1868, Henry Adams, unlike Charles, had turned his back on Quincy and Boston. Wartime friendships with English literary and intellectual leaders had stimulated his distaste for the narrow range of Boston society. Washington became a magnet to the compulsive young man, who offered his talents to the country. Although two years as a journalist during the Grant administration shocked him, he did not give up.

Temporarily submitting in 1870 to a professorship of history at Harvard College and to the accompanying editorship of the *North American Review,* Henry continued to play a private game of politics. But his brief fling with political engineering ended dismally in 1876; his plan to be a maker of presidents collapsed when Carl Schurz deserted the naïve, politically inconsequential Adams coterie. At the same time, academic success did not satisfy his ambitions, and the seven years in Boston proved a "laborious banishment" from the capital.[25]

In 1877, Henry Adams and his bride gravitated to Washington "by a primary law of nature," fervently hoping to serve the nation there. In the next few years these proper Bostonians created an exclusive center, intellectual and international in tone. Delighted to escape the priggishness and materialism of Boston, Henry regarded himself as a democrat and a radical.[26] With their intimate friends, the John Hays and Clarence King, the Adamses settled down to watch the process of government and to find the meaning of democracy.

What they discovered, Henry revealed anonymously in the novel *Democracy.* The cultured heroine, Mrs. Lightfoot Lee, like the author, was restive and discontent in the United States, but she meant "to get all that American life had to offer, good or bad." She "wanted to see with her own eyes the action of primary forces; to touch with her own hand the massive machinery of society; to measure with her own mind the capacity of the motive power." Democracy she accepted categorically as a faith, yet with all the qualms of a New England Brahmin. It should raise the general level of intelligence in the masses, but perhaps *instead* the social experiment might fail and destroy America itself "with universal suffrage, corruption, and communism." And while she knew that party politics were foul, she wanted to believe that "underneath the scum floating on the surface . . . there was a sort of healthy ocean current of honest purpose." Courted by an attractive Midwestern

Republican Senator, she learned that political virtue or vice in the Adams sense did not exist. She refused to marry the politician, who justified compromise and bribery in public affairs; but Madeleine Lee was upset by the knowledge that most Americans, indifferent to moral conflict, would not understand her rejection. This novel of 1880 reflected Adams' growing sense of isolation from the aims of both the political manipulators of the government and of the rest of the American people.[27]

Nevertheless he had not yet been nervously shattered by his experience with democracy. In his major creative work of these years, the *History of the United States,* the New Englander transcended his despair with the materialistic operations of the country. The *History* was an act of faith, conceived in defiance of all the facts around him, and cemented by Henry's desire to stick by democracy as long as he could. The common hopes and ideals of the Brahmin group lay in his questions for America. "Could it transmute its social power into the higher forms of thought? . . . Could it take permanent political shape? Could it give new life to religion and art? . . . Could it produce, or was it compatible with, the differentiation of a higher variety of the human race? Nothing less than this was necessary for its complete success." Henry, like Charles, adapted the Darwinian thesis to the older Puritan evaluation of America: as, in former times, the New Englander was dedicated to the moral "evolution of a race." The questions were unanswered in the *History* but its eager, moving tone invited affirmation.[28]

As a Harvard professor, Adams had been immersed in the Teutonist doctrine and method, but the *History* bore no sign of Anglo-Saxon racial interpretations. Although in his seminars he had presented the continuity of democratic institutions according to the theory of Teutonic origins, he had never been content with the demonstrations of the great English scholars Stubbs, Kemble, Freeman, and Maine. In a brilliant monograph, which none the less lacked definite proof, the young historian had explored the alluring hypothesis that the early Anglo-Saxon institutions contained both the idea of the territorial state and of the federal principle. Even while fascinated with the Teutonist thesis as a refreshing alternative to the Romanist tradition, he rarely responded to the inferences of Aryan racial superiority. Indifferent to German thought and literature and rebellious of English influences upon American society, he had no strong desire to trace the political institutions of his own country back to those of the Black Forest or of the Saxon village. When he resigned from his professorship, he gave away his Germanic law collection and never took its hypothesis seriously again. Adams later concluded that his Anglo-Saxon apprenticeship to history had been "a *tour de force*" of his youth.[29]

Therefore, even though the theme of the *History* was the unfolding of the American national character (and in that respect the work conformed to the "institutional" pattern of Teutonist historians), Adams did not use Teutonist conceptions of race. He was interested in ethnic studies, but his book expressed no doctrinaire judgments of the groups which made up the American people.[30]

Instead the author idealized the immigrant of the pre-Civil War period. He thrilled to the conditions of economic and social mobility which "reached the lowest and most ignorant class. . . The penniless and homeless Scotch or Irish immigrant was caught and consumed by it; for every stroke of the axe and the hoe made him a capitalist, and made gentlemen of his children." With the knowledge of what had turned the European peasant into a new man within half an hour of landing in the United States, Henry Adams bowed to the newcomer, who had seen "what was invisible to poet and philosopher,—the dim outline of a mountain-summit across the ocean, rising high above the mist and mud of American democracy."[31]

The *History* was, however, a swan song to the American dream, a vision belonging to the Henry of 1870, "a strangely different being" from the Adams of 1890. In it he had not given way to the fears with which he had probed the workings of government nor had he passed judgment upon the pernicious influences of industrialization. Negatively, however, his paean for the Scotch and Irish immigrant was associated with the past and did not encompass the present immigrants. In his second novel, *Esther*, Adams designated New York of the 1880's, "the sink of races."[32] Before too long he would cease being an avowed democrat who hated the effects of democracy.

Henry Adams had lost faith in the criteria of his parents long before he admitted it. In the accents of an old man (similar to those of Norton), he had announced at Harvard's class day exercises in 1858 that the future of the world depended on the moral order, not on political arrangements. In a dour mood, the college senior had attacked the smug, money-making, Godless society of his relatives and friends. But, until he found himself outside the destiny of the democracy, his hunger for new spiritual values did not show a religious cast. Only then, in the 1880's, did he and his wife struggle to recover the instinct for the supernatural, which Boston had shelved so comfortably. *Esther* evinced their groping desire for a religion of the heart, and their inability to achieve it in any organized form. In the 1890's, after he had brushed all his deepest hopes and plans, the "cinders of a misdirected education," into the ash-heap, Adams found a way out.[33]

By 1892, twenty years after he had set out to reform America, Henry Adams was a "failure" in the sense that he had always dreaded. Only once in his life—as the class day orator of Harvard 1858—had he been elected to any public office, and no president had called upon him to serve the nation. Rejecting honors proffered by Charles W. Eliot and Seth Low, he complained that his countrymen had not appreciated the *History* or his other literary productions. Depressed since his wife's suicide in 1884, Adams was tired of the United States, and saw only its defects. More bitter than Norton, he proclaimed that the people had no gods, no faith, not even in money of which they had no understanding; they used it only to make more or to throw it away. "Drifting in the dead-water of the *fin-de siècle*," Henry Adams was suddenly shaken out of his morose torpor; like many other Bostonians, he had the "shock of finding one's self suspended . . . over the edge of bankruptcy" in the depression of 1893. With the repeal of the Silver Act, all his fears of the last twenty years were realized. His lone stand for the eighteenth century was over. "All one's friends, all one's best citizens, reformers, churches, colleges, educated classes, had joined the banks." America's submission to the gold standard meant acceptance of finance capitalism and with it the protective tariff, the corporations and trusts, the trade unions and socialistic paternalism.[34] The class into which Adams had been born would be stamped out. In fact, his failure as an individual paralleled the death of a society.

The year of division came, for Henry as for Charles, in 1893. In permanent retreat, he had an "aching consciousness of religious void" and found some repose at the shrine of the Virgin Mary. Such worship, which had seemed idolatrous to young Charles Eliot Norton in the 1850's, had lost its censorious impact. Beginning with the study of Dante under James Russell Lowell and culminating with an absorption in stained glass windows under John LaFarge, Henry Adams turned steadily toward the symbolism of the Middle Ages, emotionally and aesthetically comforting to the thwarted descendant of the Puritans. Under the aegis of Mary, he plunged into a universe which not only was a sharp contrast from the hateful nineteenth century but also reversed the spirit of the beloved eighteenth century. The democratic dogma of his ancestors foundered in the medieval absolutism which united "Church and State, God and Man, Peace and War, Life and Death, Good and Bad."[35] Released from the ancestral ideal he found so dead, Henry Adams sought a warmer refuge than the Protestant churches he found so cold—although he never took communion outside them. Ironically, his medieval religion of the heart fed Adams' hatreds of the present, particularly his anti-Semitism.

Thus, it was no accident that the Jews rather than the Irish became the special focus of Henry Adams' xenophobia. Of course, he had felt the traditional Brahmin superiority to the Celts, and his wife preferred Protestant maids; but Henry had moved away from Boston and did not suffer Charles' personal sense of displacement because of the Irish. They were unimportant, merely an "ubiquitous bore." Only in old age did Henry Adams sympathize more closely with his fellow-Brahmins. "Poor Boston has fairly run up against it in the form of its particular Irish maggot, rather lower than the Jew, but more or less the same in appetite for cheese."[36] Even then, his disdain for the Irish differed from his consuming venom for the Jews, who had become the object of his wounded vanity.

When Henry was growing up, Boston still had only few Jewish

residents and he like Lowell probably never noticed them. In his youth his library contained a copy of Richard Cumberland's, *The Jew; A Comedy in Five Acts.* The portrayal of Sheva, the brother, was designed to reverse the hostile image of Shakespeare's Shylock and to dispel anti-Semitic prejudice. At Harvard, he read Milman's *History of the Jews,* a sympathetic and tolerant account even though it stereotyped the Hebrew as a sordid character in pursuit of wealth. But, like Henry Lee Higginson, in 1858 Adams first met Jews in Germany, and was interested mainly in their numbers. There, in a Gymnasium, Henry was provoked by a "grinning, tactless Jew boy" and boxed his ears. Later, he claimed that he had been haunted in the Berlin days by "the derisive Jewish laughter" which had permeated the entire city and the university.[37]

Yet, as late as 1880, Jews appeared in Adams' *Democracy* as upper-class Americans with no ethnic stigma. The Schneidekoupons were descended from the kings of Israel and were prouder than Solomon in all his glory. The brother was a rich, versatile amateur, conniving in Washington politics; his activities were typical of other citizens in the nation's capital. The sister Julia was acceptable even to the inner circle of Washington parties. Significantly, Madeleine Lee, the idealistic heroine, paid tribute to the fluidity of American society created afresh by each generation with no one excluded, not even those who said "Abraham is our father."[38]

Adams himself was socializing with Jews in London and on the continent in 1879, and soon his neutral tone disappeared. Early in the 1870's, he had become intimate with his old teacher, James Russell Lowell. The poet found Henry responsive to his snobbishness, and wrote from Bruges that the German passengers on shipboard were "rank Jews, pronouncing schän and mäglich." The summer after *Democracy* was written, the Adamses visited Lowell in Madrid. There Henry complained that "the hotels" were "bad; the streets vulgar, and the people simply faded Jews." In London too, when Lowell was airing his Semitic obsession, the Adamses were close to him. The older and the younger Bostonian agreed that "the Hebrew" was "pervasive and irrepressible."[39] But the time lag between their New England lifetimes made for an important difference in

point of view. While Lowell feared the rising Jews, he felt identified
with them positively and negatively; even in the 1880's he idealized
them as victims of persecution. In contrast, Henry Adams departed
from this frame of thought and conjured up a Jewish mind, the evil
spirit of the modern age.

The late 1880's inaugurated a maniacal bitterness in Adams' attitude. In traveling between Harrisburg and New York, the presence
of immigrant merchants on the train produced a violent complaint
that these German Jews had become "the aim and end of our greatest triumphs in science and civilisation."[40] The protest heightened
in the crisis of 1893, as he conducted a personal vendetta for himself
and his dying group against capitalistic America.

His anathema fell on all who shared in money-making; "Jewish"
became an adjective for greedy, avaricious, and materialistic, and
"Jew" interchangeable with the *nouveau riche* American, the British
businessman, capitalist, or goldbug. Similarly, art dealers, theater
managers, and publishers were, by the nature of their occupations,
apt to be repulsive Semites. Since the taint of finance afflicted even
an Adams (living on inherited income), he complained wittily that
he himself was getting more Jewish every day. So aware of the
ubiquity of industrialism, why did Henry, like his brother Brooks,
place the main onus of shame and responsibility upon one group?[41]

Out of their forced identification with medievalism, Henry and
Brooks created in the Jew a logical villain for the capitalistic society.
The "imaginative" man of the twelfth century, familial and martial
in his loyalties, had been innocent of finance, like an Adams, and
had required another to perform these sordid services. Mont-Saint-
Michel had rested upon the degradation of the Jewish moneylenders,
who had been outside the orbit of the "imaginative man." Claiming
that the Virgin Mary had shared the people's prejudice against the
Jew, the brothers fixed on the Jew as the archetype of the loath-
some, industrial man of their day.[42] In need of profound solace,
Henry Adams had turned to the cathedrals and made medievalism
a text for his war with the industrialized democratic society of his
time.

Obviously there were overtones to the use of the words "Jew" and "Jewish." In 1893, the Adamses for the first time in their lives knew what it might be like to lack financial security. For a while they were not at all sure that the family "could keep solvent until relief came." Although they did not go under, like many other New Englanders, they had received a terrible fright. John Quincy died of the shock a year later, and Charles turned to his ancestors for stability. Henry and Brooks passively awaited the end of the family in the belief that "a type must rise or fall according as it is adjusted to its environment." An Adams, Henry saw, was as conspicuous in late nineteenth-century America as any lowly Jew who had just arrived. He, who had not found a career suitable to his aspirations, envied and resented the adaptation of the Jewish immigrant "fresh from Warsaw or Cracow." Even "a furtive Yacoob or Ysaac still reeking of the Ghetto, snarling a weird Yiddish . . . had a keener instinct, and intenser energy, and a freer hand than he—American of Americans." With unexpected crudity, he observed that, since God had not succeeded in drowning out the world, there were "said to be four-hundred-fifty thousand Jews now doing Kosher in New York alone." Fantasizing personal competition between his family and the Jews, Henry Adams did not limit his animosity to the few Hebrews who were part of the financial hegemony of the world.[43]

When, in the last years of his life, Adams felt completely *déclassé* and uninfluential in the affairs of the nation, he resorted to the compensations of an aristocrat. As far as he could see there was only one power left to the Brahmins, and he meant to keep it: "Our sway over what we call society is undisputed. We keep Jews far away, and the anti-Jew feeling is quite rabid." Their presence on boats and trains or in places he loved, like Paris, were disturbing encroachments upon a would-be private world. In his psychopathic rivalry, he was determined that the Jew should at least remain a social outcast. There were exceptions to the rule, however, and he still claimed a few Jewish friends, who were either anti-Semitic or removed from their ethnic origins.[44] The author of *Democracy,* who had included the Schneidekoupons in "society," was unrecognizable in the Henry Adams of later years.

Not surprisingly, Adams differed from most of his countrymen in his attitude toward the Dreyfus Case. He did not take the side of the French Jew, and, for a few years, refused to take the matter seriously. He permitted himself "the extravagance of Drumont," the leading French anti-Semite, and responded vicariously to the mood of rioters on the streets of Paris. But, by 1899, he was forced to admit the Dreyfus Affair represented the "moral collapse" of "soldiers and civilians alike," indeed of France itself. Henry could not make up his mind whether he was for or against the defendant, but in the end he decided that whether justice was done to the individual was less important than the honor of France. American and English partisans of Dreyfus were meddlers. His blind spot weakened his moral position on the Dreyfus Affair; Henry Adams preferred to consider the whole affair a "Jew War."[45]

A displaced person in industrialized America, Adams felt himself a curiosity as much as any Jew; only the Jew made him "creep." Stimulated by his despair with social and economic trends, Adams' anti-Semitism did not remain a symbolic protest against capitalism. And if such anti-Semitic remarks recalled a perverse child, still his warped view was more than an idiosyncrasy. Although this anti-Semitism was based on intuitions and built up to a literary mythology rather than to a "scientific" racism, the pragmatic effects upon Adams' thinking were almost totalitarian. The honor of the state outweighed considerations of justice in the Dreyfus Affair. Describing the theological symbolism of Mont-Saint-Michel and Chartres, Adams enjoyed the fall of the synagogue before the dominant Church of Christ, and in his medievalism found relief from his distorted rivalry with the Jews.[46]

Charles Francis, Jr. and Henry had started life on the same path and, although they took separate roads, in old age the cycle of their intellectual wanderings led them to similar destinations. These Adamses were never sure they could measure up to their past and did not find their burden any easier in the hectic postwar era. Resistant to the provincialism of Boston, they hated even more the *nouveaux riches* and the rising masses in capitalistic America. Insulating themselves through the study of their ancestors or through new aesthetic and religious experiences, the Adamses deviated further than Lowell and Norton. In the end, still dissatisfied, the brothers resented the new status of others, whether Negro, Irish, or Jewish. Differing in temperament and experience, each yielded to xenophobia in his own way. As they ceased to believe in the principles of 1776, their Brahmin ideals and visions degenerated into mere prejudices.

The Adamses had suffered a common reaction. From the middle of the nineteenth century, many New England families were dazzled, indeed blinded by the cultural luster of their society. Lowell, Norton, and the Adamses expressed the subtle, internal changes of mind and heart, which made it difficult for their group to have faith in the future. Lowell outlived his time; in the 1870's and 1880's, he resisted his alienation from America and his attachment to England. The more skeptical Norton was an uninhibited Jeremiah to an optimistic, materialistic nation, but he too strove to elevate it to higher levels of culture and morality.

The Civil War came as the climax of dreams which New Englanders sought to realize; the aftermath of disillusion produced the first lost generation of Americans. Growing up in the shadow of a great tradition, the Adamses paid a price in self-consciousness and oversensitivity. What had been a naïve nostalgia in Lowell and Norton became self-deprecatory retrospection in the sons of Charles Francis Adams. Their withdrawal from a life of action left them only a lonely snobbish preeminence which they knew to be a farce. Their ultimate passivity and helplessness had more than personal significance, however; it marked the end of a dynamic society. In the 1890's, the Adamses articulated the deepest fears of Brahmin New England which no longer knew the meaning of its existence.

CHAPTER III

Brahmins and Irishmen in the 1880's

Let them come, then, as the waves come, and cause the absentee
English landlords to mourn over their deserted glebes. It is very
easy for every man of them to have a farm which they can soon
call their own. . . If politics are necessary to the existence of
Irishmen, they can get plenty of the needful in this country, in
some parts of which they vote so soon as they touch the soil. Our
Celtic friends are good at voting, they vote early and sometimes
often, and as a general thing can be relied upon for the whole
Democratic ticket. With all that drawback, we say the cry in Ireland should be, Young men, leave Erin for the American shore.
                    —*Boston Evening Transcript,* 1880[1]

New England Protestants will do well to remember that the Catholic population gains on them every year, as well by natural increase as by emigration. New England families have dwindled in
numbers generation after generation through all this century, and
it will be folly to provoke collision till the race returns to its pris-
tine vigor, and promises a good supply of recruits for the war.
                    —Francis Parkman, 1890[2]

As Brahmins entered the 1880's, they already knew the drawback of being born into a declining society. A steady increase in
divorces and suicides as well as a lowering birth rate reflected the
internal tensions of their society which Lowell, Norton, and the
Adamses expressed as individuals of two generations. They felt
trapped in their external relations between the "half-taught plu-

tocracy" of American capitalists and the "ignorant proletariat" of the foreign-born.[3] Nevertheless the idea of excluding the inferior immigrants did not yet seem even a partial solution.

Old New Englanders were still too close to the past to act positively against their own traditions. But as new relations between Yankees and Irishmen distorted the older patterns of existence, the possibility of stopping the emigration of Europe's poor to America would seem less revolutionary. By the end of the decade, new political, sociological, economic, and intellectual conditions would crystallize. The restrictionist attitude would emerge and a later generation would seek the reversal of America's traditional immigration policy.

At the outset, Yankees were accustomed to immigrants. For forty years, to their own satisfaction, they had surmounted the obstacles created by the presence of the Irish. These and the more recent French Canadians were the mainstay of the lucrative textile mills. The conviction was still held that immigrants were essential to the New England economy; in 1882, Boston's most conservative newspaper ridiculed the notion that the United States would ever suffer from overpopulation.[4]

But the Irish were not just cogs in an economic machine designed to guarantee to prospering Bostonians a leisurely pursuit of culture. Through the 1880's, successive levels of conflict between the two groups showed that the Irish had developed a group consciousness. Educational, philanthropic, and political spheres of influence all reflected this growing assertiveness which challenged Brahmin domination. The inexorable collision would alter radically the democratic habits of thought which had originally glossed over the community's discord.

The Civil War had brought temporary unity and sympathy between old and new members of crusading New England. The Know-Nothing fever had waned, and citizens of Irish derivation had warmed to the good will of the natives. Yet in the opinion of Catholic historians twenty years later, the Church had overestimated the harmony brought about by war.[5] There had been no riots and no burning of churches; but the estrangement was just as real, if less violently displayed.

Yankee memoirs recorded the impact of this division upon younger members of the native society. Eleanor, the daughter of Rev. Edward Abbott, never forgot the distinctions of the Cambridge of her youth. Two horsecar lines ran parallel at a short distance from each other: one took the Irish laborers to work; the other transported the proper gentlemen to their duties. Children learned that a Brattle Street lady and her Mt. Auburn Street washerwoman did not travel in the same vehicle. Paradoxically, the young shared an intimacy with the foreigners, who were their nurses and cooks, while at the same time learning from the parents an inward remoteness from the people who had come "from a mysterious green island far across the sea . . . bringing many of their strange customs with them." Parents enforced such divisions by forbidding their offspring to play near the marshes where the humble neighbors built their alien settlements.[6] Native children therefore became the conscious legatees of the enduring, irreconcilable cleavage in their society.

With no particular malice the restricted boys and girls made a game of preying upon the children of the foreign-born and sought occasions for open war. The battles between the defenders of Brattle Street and the ragamuffins of Mt. Auburn Street needed no provocation beyond the habitual desire to attack the marsh dwellers. Similarly, the snowball fights on Boston Common (of which so many Brahmins later boasted) dramatized the keen sense of difference between Beacon Hillers or Latin school boys and North Enders.[7] Thus youthful aggressions laid the groundwork for adult antagonisms.

A righteous snobbery developed early in life. Charles Francis Adams, Jr. was frankly relieved that his father (despite the belief in democracy) had not expected him to go to school with the children of the laborers who tended the family place at Quincy. After the Civil War, fewer and fewer of the sons and daughters of the proper families attended the common schools, which had become increasingly public by 1850. When Judge Robert Grant went to the Boston Latin School in the 1870's, and still later when he sent his own sons there in the 1890's, friends frowned on this gesture to the democratic precept of education. Some parents feared an exposure "to crime or contagion," particularly before the level of high school. Well-bred New England youngsters sensed the real meaning of the separation from foreign-born contemporaries, and a Yankee girl naturally drew her skirts away from the contaminating contact of a "Paddy" in the public school classroom.[8]

More and more, being an American had assumed a limited definition in the minds of adult Brahmins. Their children never doubted in the 1870's that it applied only to those who "came from approximately the same class of homes, and knew, in short, 'their knives and forks.'" Although Phillips Brooks once noted that the Boston Latin School provided "a blessing no private school can give," it was at his behest that Endicott Peabody founded Groton. This model of the great English schools climaxed the growing trend toward an aristocratic standard of education for old New England.[9] Private schools not only marked the existing gulf but also inevitably widened the chasm between the Brahmins and the naturalized Irish Americans.

By the 1880's, however, the submerged conflict between the "Anglo-Saxon" employer and the "Celtic" employee, which was the normal condition of the relationship, was about to erupt in a political revolution. The Irish were no longer poor, ignorant peasants; in their maturity they resented the old New Englanders' claim that only descendants of the Puritans were truly American.[10]

By the same token, as Catholics, the Irish were offended by the unequal status publicly accorded their religion. Massachusetts had quietly aided private Protestant benevolent societies until Catholic groups requested similar distributions. A long struggle attended the efforts, finally successful in 1879, to have Catholic priests included as chaplains in the charitable and reformatory organizations of the state; and even in the 1880's, Catholic inmates had to attend Protestant services as well. The Bay State did not admit any obligation to respect, let alone preserve, the faith of Catholic wards.[11] In the institutional sphere, New England leaders acquiesced only slowly and reluctantly to Catholic demands for equal treatment.

As in the 1850's, the upper-class natives generally regarded the needs of the Irish from their own point of view. Even Edward

Everett Hale, who recognized the shortcomings of Boston toward these immigrants, occasionally lapsed into insularity. In the 1870's he urged that Protestant churches conduct neighborhood centers to enlighten rejected aliens and "to teach the Irishmen why his race has been kept down and by what sure training it shall rise." A lady writer for the *Atlantic* was confident that if only the Irish were dispersed all over New England, they would gain from "our own people" the "unconscious education" necessary to transform them into good Americans.[12] Brahmins at the top of the New England social hierarchy had set a tone of indifference to the thoughts and feelings of the newcomers which became common among other Yankees.

The patronizing attitude of the old stock affected the children of the foreign-born virulently through the schools. Cardinal O'Connell remembered the attitude of the Yankee spinster "schoolmarms" in Lowell, Massachusetts. He "sensed the bitter antipathy, scarcely concealed, which nearly all these good women . . . felt toward those of us who had Catholic faith and Irish names. For any slight pretext we were severely punished. We were made to feel the slur against our faith and race, which hurt us to our very hearts' core."[13] In effect, the teachers left an indelible impression of hate upon the children of New England's first immigrants. Thus, even through the public schools, native antipathy reached the Irish and added directly to mutual misunderstanding.

The imperious rule of old New Englanders in their inherited communities drew to a close, as the more recent Americans entered state and municipal politics. Early in the 1870's, the Celts had taken over the police and fire departments of Boston and the mill towns; by the late 1870's, Benjamin Butler, the Civil War general, who was a demagogue in Brahmin eyes, sought the favor of the rising Irish citizenry. As the 1880's opened, their power in Boston was still indirect, though Patrick Maguire and Michael Cuniff chose mayors, aldermen, and councilmen for the city. But, two years later, Irish leaders were strong enough to defeat the "Boston aristocrats" in the Democratic Party. The entire state of Massachusetts succumbed to the challenge of the changed party machinery, and Benjamin Butler won the gubernatorial election of 1882. Proper Bostonians were aghast. Butler would give the rum dealers of the state a free hand; he had broken with "the sound traditions" of New England, as "the slums of the cities emptied themselves at the polls to pay him appropriate honor." By contrast, to Martin Lomasney, then an ambitious young politician, Butler was the champion of the oppressed Irish, the defender of their rights.[14]

At last, in 1884, Boston had an Irish Catholic mayor. Hugh O'Brien (formerly chairman of the Aldermen) first succeeded the Puritans in their own Hub of the Universe. At the end of this fateful decade, Irish politicians controlled the government of sixty-eight Massachusetts cities and towns. Although Republicans still dominated state elections and Democratic candidates for state offices were of the old stock, no political aspirants could ignore the Irish machines in the future.[15]

There was now a reversal of roles in the two major groups of Boston. To the descendants of the Founding Fathers the Irish were at best usurpers. And the Irish, as outsiders for almost fifty years, had suffered not only from the direct shafts of the Yankee Know-Nothings but also from the subtle patronage of the Brahmins. There would be little meeting of minds in the contest to control the public good.

Coincident with the Yankee defeat in politics, the Catholic Church inaugurated more aggressive plans for parochial education. In 1880, Archbishop Williams announced that he would withdraw Catholic children from the public schools wherever and whenever practicable. Having suffered humiliations from the teachers of the older stock, the Irish planned to educate the young in the more secure atmosphere of their own kind and in accordance with their own religious beliefs. But natives, who observed the campaign to gain public funds for parochial use, were determined that Yankee pocketbooks would not assist. Associated with the rising force of Irish politicians, this practical contingency was disturbing to those who could not understand the Catholic position. Since few Irishmen could afford the embryonic parochial system, as late as 1907 only two-fifths of the children in the Archdiocese of Boston attended; the problem would remain academic for a long time. Still old New England seethed at the very idea of removing a large segment of the foreign-born children from her educational surveillance.[16]

Yankee concern culminated in legislative proposals, first in 1888 and again in 1889. Both bills required the state to establish local boards of education for the inspection and supervision of all private schools in Massachusetts. The ostensible motive of ensuring proper standards of instruction did not hide the real purpose of the bills—to expose the Catholic pedagogy to the public eye. A furor of anti-popery comparable to that of the earlier Know-Nothingism found special partisans among some public schoolteachers, Evangelical ministers, English skilled workers, and single-minded feminists.[17] The vague, amorphous fears of the new political force in the New England community were aggravated and distorted by the grievances of these particular groups.

Such nativists warned New Englanders to protect their "fair heritage, left . . . by . . . the Pilgrims and the Puritans," but few Brahmins joined the anti-Catholic bigots. Lacking the monomania or the special interest of the various nativists, they had more complicated reactions to the problem of Catholic education; there were multiple facets to this controversial issue.[18]

Some Brahmins defended the parochial point of view because they associated it with essential Christian piety. For Puritan descendants, the old hostility to Catholicism as a religion had been softened by a real attraction since the 1850's. For example, they no longer shared their ancestors' disapproval of the celebration of Easter and Christmas. Thomas Wentworth Higginson, a staunch Unitarian, even declared that Catholicism represented the "highest point" of Christianity, while Protestantism "marked its decline." Significantly, many Brahmins were becoming members of the Church of England or of Rome.[19]

Others were conscious of the sterility of the rational tradition. The Congregational minister Joseph Cook, who was not happy about parochial education, favored Bible reading in the public schools. Julius Ward, a free-thinking pastor, had suggested that Catholics sit on the Boston School Committee to determine a common fund of religious belief for the children. At the hearing on the school bill, the

Unitarian Rev. Cyrus Bartol admitted that the piety which dominated his Puritan ancestors was sadly lacking in the present Godless
schools. Bartol could not bring himself to favor sectarian indoctrination in the Boston system but he was dissatisfied with the mere intellectual instruction of the future citizens. Accepting the Catholics'
attitude, he declared himself "glad of all the religion which you can
get into the parochial schools."[20] Deeply concerned with the spiritual
growth of the next generation, these New England ministers regretted the loss of faith in their flocks and admired Catholic religious
conviction.

Still other Protestant ministers who regarded the public schools as
a training ground for citizenship alone, opposed the discriminatory
legislation for different reasons. The Rev. Minot J. Savage and the
Rev. Francis E. Abbott asserted that Catholics could rightfully object
to the watered-down Bible reading in Boston classrooms. The present curriculum was not secular enough for Savage who had wanted
to let "the distinctively religious institutions devote themselves to
looking after religious needs." Moreover, to Abbott, the real peril in
the growing Catholic power lay in the counteraction from Protestants. The school bill brought to fruition his worst fears that the
Evangelical sects could subvert the fundamental republican principle
of religious freedom.[21] Nevertheless, although these ministers of
rational Protestantism sought rabidly to preserve the separate functions of church and state, still as spiritual leaders they too disapproved
of the Massachusetts formula of religious compromise.

With broader understanding of the position of Catholics, men
such as Thomas Wentworth Higginson, Charles W. Eliot, Edward
Everett Hale, Edwin D. Mead, and Francis A. Walker opposed the
school bill on the grounds of civil liberty. Walker, a member of the
state board of education, during a similar experience in New Haven,
Connecticut, had already stated his opinions explicitly. He had objected to compelling a Jewish child to bow his head in Christian
worship, a practice which could not "be justified except upon the
ground that he has no right to be a Jew, a ground . . . repulsive to
the ideas of the present age." Nor did the schools have the right

"to make thousands of Catholic children listen to the reading of the King James version . . . which their priests and bishops tell them is an unsanctified version, and fraught with danger to their immortal souls." Mead, the editor of *The New England Magazine,* an outspoken critic of the Catholic clergy and of the parochial system, still denounced as religious persecutors the suffragettes and ministers who advocated the school bills.[22]

Higginson reminded Bostonians that as a child he had watched the burning of a Catholic convent and as a young man had witnessed the Know-Nothing parades. A mature "Protestant of the Protestants," he urged his fellow citizens to learn the lesson and permit no law invading the equal rights of Protestants and Catholics to send children to private schools of their own choice. Moreover, these distinguished citizens recognized that the Brahmins had the most to lose by the passage of the school bill. Hale, a trustee of the Roxbury Latin School, saw the unpleasant position of parents who sent their children to private academies.[23] Ironically, the discriminatory legislation, if actually applied, would have affected more Protestants than Catholics, and upper-class citizens saw the meaning of civil liberty for themselves as well as for others.

But the question of parochial education had a deeper significance for Brahmin society. Eliot, a consistent advocate of the public school system for *all* children, minced no words in analyzing the social problem: this restrictive legislation would only increase "the breach" between the Protestant and Catholic population, which had "widened greatly during the past ten years." Moreover, under the circumstances, the religious differences between the two groups, if intensified through public contention, would perpetuate political alignments along the present disagreeable lines. Likewise, Mead declared that just because "many of our Roman Catholics" were "still essentially 'foreigners'" constituted "a reason why they above all others should be kept long in the public school." Eliot did not then deny that he looked "with some apprehension upon what is likely to be the result in those Massachusetts communities where Catholics are in the majority, or are rapidly approaching a majority."[24] Eliot not only believed idealistically in the democratizing influence of American schools but hoped prudently to stave off the expansion of parochialism.

Other Brahmins took their cue from him and proselytized for a united front on the school question. The editor of the *Boston Daily Advertiser* politely appealed to the Catholic Church to show that it was American first and Roman afterward by sustaining the free educational system of the United States. Now the suggestion seemed more natural that Catholics as well as Protestants should sit on the state board of education. In the emergency of the times even violent anti-Catholics recognized the same logic as Eliot and suppressed their deep-seated prejudices for the joint cause. Francis Parkman, who had always been contemptuous of immigrants and had earlier scorned the power of the American environment to assimilate the foreigners, soon upheld the common schools as the crucible from which young Americans would evolve irrespective of their origins.[25] Brahmins showed discretion in protesting the nativist attacks upon the Irish Catholics; on the practical level, there was no wisdom in antagonizing further those who now held the balance of political power in the state.

The school bill had evoked a significant variety of protests among the Brahmins. In the tradition of their fathers, the majority still believed that the separation of church and state must apply in the educational institutions of a democracy. Opposed as well to those who would ignore this principle by financial support of parochial schools, wealthy New Englanders, like their predecessors of the 1850's, would not, on principle, countenance nativistic counterattacks.

Brahmins also rejected the legislation with a tardy sense of reality. The school bill had forced them to a belated realization that their obtuseness could endanger irreparably any potential harmony in the divided community. Their leaders had been slow to invite the newer citizens to share the administrative responsibilities of education. Old New Englanders guiltily acknowledged that their schoolteachers had given the impression that it would be just as well for Catholic children to lose their faith. Civic-minded, they denounced parochialism on democratic grounds, but hoped to meet its challenge by a "better

feeling throughout the community, and especially by the improvement of the public schools themselves."[26]

Native ambivalence toward religion also affected Brahmins' response to the school question. Lacking strong belief in the religious
tradition of their fathers, many became interested in the ritual of the
newcomers. Some, who did not themselves turn to the Roman or
Anglican churches, tended to envy their spiritual impact. Other
Yankees, who disliked Catholic dogma, still valued the Church's re-
straining influence on the foreign-born. The Rev. Joseph Cook, for example, believed that the Church was "the chief barrier against com-
munistic and socialistic inroads from the howling sea of an ignorant
and unprincipled population."[27]

Although the Brahmins had remained loyal to the tradition of
civil and religious liberties, the implications of parochialism shook
the self-controlled leaders of Boston far more than the explosive
nativists. Since in the minds of the young lay the dominion of the
future, they wondered whether or not the intellectual and social
values of their New England would continue to flourish. This trial
had already begun in the Hub of the Universe, where Patrick
Maguire's opposition to civil service reform and Hugh O'Brien's
closing of the Boston Public Library on St. Patrick's Day were painful deviations for the old-timers. The triumphant remarks of Irish
politicos did not ease Brahmin fears. Mayor O'Brien boasted that
the "old Puritan city of Boston" had become "the most Catholic city
in the country."[28] If the Irish now segregated their children from
the rest of the community, the next generation would be even more
detached from New England traditions than their immigrant parents had been.

Walking in the Boston Public Garden, James Russell Lowell saw
two Irishmen look at George Washington's statue, and was appalled
when one asked whom the figure represented. Were such to solve
the new problems of American life rather than a Lowell who had
been brought up "among the still living traditions of Lexington,
Concord, Bunker's Hill, and the Siege of Boston?" Convinced that
this heritage would be lost through parochial education, the Brah-

mins would have preferred some impartial means of supervising Catholic instruction. Instead, upper-class Yankees, most of whom favored private schools for their own children, adopted the view that the withdrawals of the foreign-born for sectarian instruction affronted New England's democratic tradition.[29]

In this dilemma, old New Englanders looked back to the relatively homogeneous society of their forbears as the example of ideal democracy, untainted by class distinctions. In the present divided community, they regarded themselves more than ever as "the better half of the people." The image of the independent voter conjured up an educated citizen of Yankee stock, increasingly antagonistic to the Irish-born electorate.[30]

The more conservative citizens even interpreted the instability of labor relations after the Civil War as another form of Irish subversion. When the Celts suffered a setback in a municipal election of 1875, Francis Parkman was delighted. It signified a defeat for the lowly and socialist elements which 200,000 Irish immigrants had contributed to Boston's population. The Rev. Cook shuddered at the "blasphemous" radical talk of the Irish Knights of Labor in 1880. And since universal suffrage had brought New England to the terrible plight of political control by foreigners, many proper citizens and their wives resisted the movement for woman's rights. Presumably the Founding Fathers had erred in the voting principle; those who thought "Patrick" was bad enough, did not want to add "Bridget" to their troubles. Parkman observed that if women received suffrage, the bad politicians would not reach "the better class of female voters," but would penetrate only "the marshes and malarious pools of society."[31] Afraid of an unknown future dominated by parochially schooled Irish Americans, some New Englanders began to resist the extension of the democratic principle as it might apply to workers or to women.

As Brahmins and Irishmen tended increasingly to view each other with resentment, the question of Irish Home Rule exposed the fundamental dissidence of Boston society. Traditionally, New Englanders had defended the Irish victims of British imperialism, for, like other Americans, they had espoused European causes for national liberation. Even in the early 1880's, the solid citizens of Boston received Parnell in their homes and contributed generous funds to suffering Ireland.[32] But in the next few years the Anglo-Irish conflict helped bring the complicated relations of Bostonians with the Irish American group to a new breaking point.

James Russell Lowell was one of those who had supported Irish nationalism since 1848; forty years later he decided that this nationalism made Irishmen impossible as Americans. Since his antislavery writings of the 1840's, he had been aware of the plight of the oppressed Irish. Although he, like other Brahmins, suffered from their intrusion in New England, nevertheless his past humanitarianism influenced Lowell's attitude toward them even in the postwar era.

Discussing Irish agricultural reform in the 1870's, Lowell expected the possession of land would "cure" the peasants of "one of the worst diseases . . . their belief . . . laws are their natural enemies," thus indirectly reducing the criminal proclivities of Irish immigrants. During a walk with William Dean Howells through "squalid Irish neighborhoods" of Boston and Cambridge, Lowell chided the young Midwesterner for bearing "a grudge" against the newcomers. Even Celts with a socialist tinge did not upset him. Having once seen "the Irish mobbed in Boston . . . for the very same reason that the Chinese are now hounded by the Irish in California," the tolerant New Englander thought "it a good sign that Kearney can address his countrymen in Faneuil Hall and talk . . . much nonsense." In 1880, Lowell's attitude was one of *noblesse oblige,* and he still believed that "the solidity of our social framework" could withstand any Irish deviation.[33]

But while Minister to the Court of St. James, from 1881 to 1885, Lowell had to deal with Irish Americans who exploited double citizenship. Despite long sympathy with the Irish cause, he felt that he could not, as a government representative, protect Irish Americans from the penalties of England's Coercion Act. When Celtic nationalists scorned his official policy, he became vexed with those citizens whose "wild and whirling words" harmed "something more than the cause of Irish peasantry." The Irish Americans were harming America itself, "whose citizenship they put off or put on as may be most convenient."[34]

Lowell no longer condoned the actions of the Irish as the failings of a maladjusted abused people. He regarded their attacks upon him as impertinence to a superior, to one who knew what was right and wrong for his country. Their insults evoked the response of an aristocrat:

> Through veins that drew their life from Western Earth
> Two hundred years and more my blood hath run
> In no polluted course from sire to son;

Why, he demanded, ignoring the record of Irish American soldiers in the Civil War, should an eighth-generation American be boycotted by "Irish fellow-citizens (who are kind enough to teach me how to be American), who fought all our battles and got up all our draft riots?" Hurt by the recriminations of a few extremists, Lowell never regained his balanced perspective toward the Irish. Repeating Parnell's "distinction between 'the American people' and 'the Irish nation in America'" he declared that Irish Americans could never be true patriots to their adopted land.[35]

Brahmin reactions to the Anglo-Irish problem also reflected the advance of Hibernian political power in New England. Home Rule had become an oratorical expedient of politicians which often annoyed Yankee candidates for public office as well as the Minister to England. In 1887, Lowell's cousin, A. Lawrence Lowell, added a new argument to oppose Yankee support of Irish nationalism. As a matter of foreign policy, he worried lest England resent American intervention in the Irish land question. Although recognizing the justice of the Irish cause, Brahmins no longer sided with these victims of Britain. New England experience with the Irish "legislators, mayors, laborers, cooks, Democrats and Catholics" had revealed "the difficulties of the Irish problem" in a glaring light. Profoundly fatigued with the "various annoyances" of their immigration, Bostonians did not want to be reminded of the Irish pursuit of national fulfillment.[36] Now that Irish immigrants had become influential in

New England life, Brahmins identified themselves with old England in the tangle of Anglo-Irish relations.

Twenty years after the Civil War, Brahmins had completed their retreat from the Anglophobe position of their fathers. Painfully the Lowells and the Nortons had insulated themselves from the present social unpleasantness, by turning toward an English way of life. But for younger members of the group, rapport with England involved no such conflict; they were more English than Yankee in education, in religion, and in social and political opinions. Dr. Oliver Wendell Holmes perceived with amusement that "as the New England characteristics" were "gradually superseded by those of other races, other forms of belief, and other associations," a New Englander would "feel more as if he were among his own people in London than in one of our seaboard cities."[37] For many, their Anglophilia aptly differentiated them from the latecomers.

But Boston was still the Brahmins' home and there, as a concomitant to their Anglophilism, they controlled private society more rigidly than ever before. They drew back from the Irish Bostonians much as Henry Adams excluded Jews from his personal orbit. Although Hibernians sat in the City Hall and the State House, old New Englanders rarely dined with them. By the same token, "the better class" did not open their doors to Celtic aspirants in business or in professional fields. It was with genuine surprise that a proper Bostonian noted the infiltration of Irish names in *Transcript* obituaries of the 1890's. Despite politics, the Irish still figured mainly as "good servants"; one Boston lady who grew up in that era, remarked that only late in her life did she realize that there was other than this single class of Irishmen.[38] In the end, the contest for political and educational control of New England strengthened existing social barriers and prevented understanding between the two groups.

As Brahmins ceased to be the undisputed arbiters of the public good, they became less confident of the Americanization of the newcomers. Emerson's pleasure in watching the emigrants "go to school" in his country was a thing of the past. In 1878, an *Atlantic* editor reported the disappearance of the belief in "that wonderful perfection and vitality of character" that had enabled Americans "to receive from all other countries the most incongruous and unfavorable materials, and assimilate and transmute them all into the texture and substance of a noble national life." Ten years later, Lowell decided that not even emigration to America could right what was wrong with Irish peasants, as their trouble was "something too deep for railways or transplantation to cure."[39]   In defeat, the Brahmins resorted to ethnic criteria to explain the deterioration of American society and politics.

The earlier belief in the ability of all to become good Americans was fading rapidly. Thus far the Celts had not proved to be the flexible material envisaged by Emerson and Hale, which New Englanders could remold in their Yankee image. Recalling colonial days, James Russell Lowell concluded that men of English blood with "hereditary instincts" for democracy had created American manhood. He began to wonder whether it would survive the onslaught of "millions of newcomers alien to our traditions." Reluctantly he questioned the assumption that superior Anglo-Saxons could transform any alien stock. But his younger kinsman, A. Lawrence Lowell, raised the same doubt with a new belligerence. Desperately he asserted that Brahmins must not only dominate the Irish but "absorb" them: these newcomers could not remain Irish and be American at the same time. Yet the idea of absorbing the Celts seemed impossible in the face of actual relations between the groups. The Irish now comprised a social entity reacting implacably against their own experience and that of their parents and grandparents. How would the differences between the Celts and the Anglo-Saxons be resolved? It seemed that a racial problem confronted New England.[40]

More significant than A. L. Lowell's effort to restate the old assumption, was the fact that he did not yet spontaneously propose an alternative solution—the restriction of immigration. But he and other New England intellectuals were receptive to new interpretations of the nature of their heritage to support their own less confident view of newcomers in the Hub of Irish politicians, Catholic clergy, Yankee nativists, and dispirited Brahmins. In a fresh conception of the Anglo-Saxons, this New England group would forge one vital link in the chain of restrictionist thought.

CHAPTER IV

The Anglo-Saxon Complex

. . . the work which the English race began when it colonized North America is destined to go on until every land on the earth's surface that is not already the seat of an old civilization shall become English in its language, in its political habits and traditions, and to a predominant extent in the blood of its people. The day is at hand when four-fifths of the human race will trace its pedigree to English forefathers, as four-fifths of the white people in the United States trace pedigree today.　　　　—John Fiske[1]

The climate of the United States has been benign enough to enable us to take the English short-horn and greatly improve it . . . to take the English race-horse and to improve him . . . to take the English man and improve him too, adding agility to his strength, making his eye keener and his hand steadier, so that in rowing, in riding, in shooting, and in boxing, the American of pure English stock is today the better animal.
　　　　　　　　　　　　　　　　　—Francis A. Walker[2]

Believing that a distinctive American nationality was in the making, early Brahmins had deliberately pushed their Old World origins into the background. But to many New Englanders of the 1870's and 1880's "the American" was already recognizable by definite traits. Citizens of Yankee stock were likely to attribute such traits to English roots and to believe that they were maintained from generation to generation, in a swiftly changing nation, by qualities derived from Anglo-Saxon forbears.

As industrialization accelerated after the Civil War, Brahmins more often wondered whether the Anglo-Saxon caliber of the population would prevail against whatever characteristics the hordes of newcomers might inject. Thus far, the nation had absorbed extraneous elements; but continued success of this democratic experiment would certainly depend upon the predominance of the Anglo-Saxons in numbers and leadership. What would happen if the Anglo-Saxons could no longer assimilate, and thus Americanize, the strange breeds now crossing the Atlantic? Might the newer people not be a menace—to the Anglo-Saxons as well as to American culture in general?

By the 1880's, Anglo-Saxonism provided the same arguments, tinged with different sentiments for English-speaking groups; already its tones had changed to cover the shifting moods of the New Englanders. In the early part of the century, the time of conscious emancipation from England, many wanted to repress English origins and influences. And in the democratic pitch of the 1840's, liberal Yankees left the Anglo-Saxon cult to Southern slaveholders or British empire builders. But when, by the 1850's, Boston society lost its unity, the distinction between the practical Anglo-Saxon, solid in building nations and adventurous on the high seas, and the imaginative, gay Celt who lacked the capacity to create or sustain successful political institutions, underlined the New Englanders' superiority over the Irish immigrants.[3] Derived from both the philological and ethnological studies of European scholars, the Anglo-Saxon became the archetype of the most desirable branch of the Teutonic race.

As upper-class citizens lost the balance of power in their divided society, English antecedents became the measure of all good things. In the 1870's even the names of the streets in Boston's newly made Back Bay—like Berkeley, Clarendon, and Dartmouth—were copies of English originals. Increasingly, other Yankees followed Brahmin leadership in turning away from the social flux of the present to a more congenial Anglo-Saxon past. A Vermont University professor observed in 1886 that "the American of the present day . . . would rather know who was his grandfather in the year 1600, than to know who will be the next president." In search of "this ancestor," the Yankees would gladly "cross the Atlantic to England."[4]

This preference for English roots stimulated many native historians to justify Anglo-Saxon prestige. If Yankees could prove the superiority of the species, then the existence of the old stock would serve an ulterior purpose in preserving the democracy of the United States. Therefore, at the same time that young scholars, influenced by Darwin and Ranke, sought to make history an objective science, they included a nationalistic meaning in their interpretation of the American life.[5]

Henry Adams, in his Harvard seminar of the early 1870's, set out to prove that modern democratic institutions had migrated with the Germanic tribes of the Black Forest to Britain and thence across the Atlantic with the English emigrants of the seventeenth century. Teacher and students read with excitement the Germanic texts and the old Anglo-Saxon charters, and sought their parallels in Massachusetts townships. The cooperative product of this seminar, *Essays in Anglo-Saxon Law,* was a triumphant saga routing the course of republican institutions from their ancient homeland. Significantly, for young New Englanders the Teutonic thesis then provided an affirmation of the modern democratic organization of government, not yet given up for lost in the 1870's.

The influences of Adams' courses were as varied as the views of his students who were distinguished in later life. The pioneer of the new science of history inspired an intellectual curiosity which, for some, transcended the limiting dogma of the subject. Although Henry Cabot Lodge, Barrett Wendell, and A. Lawrence Lowell rigidly adhered to the concept of Anglo-Saxon superiority, others like Edward Channing, Henry Osborn Taylor, and George Woodberry did not fully conform to the developing Teutonist orthodoxy.[6]

Henry Adams had been independent of the main stream of historical scholarship in the United States because he had not accepted as sacred the dicta of the British Teutonists. The direct growth of Teutonism in this country during the next few years depended upon the simultaneous activities of John Fiske and Herbert Baxter Adams. Their common mentor was Edward A. Freeman, the bombastic Englishman whom Henry Adams and his wife had privately ridiculed. Freeman's infatuation with the heritage of Anglo-Saxon abilities permeated the thinking of most American scholars in the next decade.

John Fiske, originally Edmund Greene, an enthusiast in the fore-guard of new ideas, was the most important popularizer of the Anglo-Saxon legend. Born into a comfortable middle-class family, of respected old stock on his mother's side, he grew up in the quiet town of Middletown, Connecticut. By 1855, he had identified himself completely with his maternal relatives by dropping his father's surname. A precocious youth at Harvard, he became a student of James Russell Lowell; and the New England poet and gentleman became Fiske's ideal. Determined to enter Brahmin society, he remained in Cambridge, although his criticism of Buckle and his radical espousal of Darwin and Spencer had shocked the solid citizens of Boston so much that not even Charles W. Eliot dared to give him a permanent post at Harvard. In 1872, the first year of Henry Adams' seminar, Fiske began to investigate the same field, as he catalogued the American room of the college library. The study of early Americana appealed to his innermost predilections. The first act of his new research became a genealogical quest: he was pleased to inform his mother that the Fiskes' English lineage went back to the fourteenth century.[7]

Immersing himself in Freeman, Kemble, Stubbs, and Maine, the young evolutionist related his background of linguistic studies and Spencerian premises to the development of the Teutonic peoples of the Aryan race. Ten years earlier, when philology had dominated his thoughts, Fiske had avowed jokingly that Yankees were more Celtic than Teutonic; now, with relief, he joined Freeman in reviewing the Anglo-Saxon march from the Black Forest to New England. Although vague about the ethnological facts, he assumed the existence of an Aryan folk-moot as the original seed of Western political institutions. When his secret hope of succeeding Henry Adams at Harvard vanished, John Fiske made a career of remunerative public lectures. Nation-wide, to large and small cities, he carried the story of the vital principle upon which American democracy rested—the New England town meeting.[8]

In the year of Henry Adams' resignation from Harvard, another descendant from the same Braintree ancestor took up the cudgels for the Anglo-Saxon cause at Johns Hopkins University. Herbert Baxter Adams was born in western Massachusetts "of sound Puritan stock." After attending the public schools and Phillips Exeter, Adams headed the class of 1872 at Amherst College. Product of a New England heritage and environment, he went to the University of Heidelberg for his Ph.D. Armed for academic battle under Bluntschli and other German professors, he nevertheless later showed more interest in the works of his British colleagues. His correspondence included only a scant number of letters to and from his German professors; by contrast, "the number and eminence of the Englishmen who visited the Johns Hopkins University and with whom Adams corresponded" was large. Instigating cooperative efforts between English and American historians, he announced that a *"united English effort in the direction of historical science"* seemed peculiarly appropriate, for "the history of the two countries" was "one. The whole tenor of . . . researches at Johns Hopkins University" was "to show the continuity of English institutions in American."[9]

This preference for the English school of Teutonists affected the training Adams gave to a host of graduate students in the 1880's and 1890's. Under his editing, the pages of the Johns Hopkins *Studies* overflowed with erudite monographs which combined the comparative method of Freeman and the evolutionary notion that "free local institutions" sprang upon American shores from a "germ" just as the English wheat had been planted here. Following the pattern of Maine and Von Maurer which Freeman confirmed, Herbert Baxter Adams urged the study of local institutions as "the primordial cells of the body politic."[10]

In search of English antecedents, he encouraged the study of local history everywhere north, south, west, as well as east;[11] but the Johns Hopkins group also found New England the richest field for proof of the Teutonic basis of democracy. Despite weighty footnotes, their story was substantially the same as that which John Fiske related so engagingly to throngs of American adults in popular lectures.

In the last two decades of the century, the academic concord between English and American historians was so close that Freeman and Fiske both came to rely on the Johns Hopkins *Studies* for refinements of the Teutonic thesis. This Anglo-American entente, also symbolized by Freeman's blessing of both Fiske and Adams, was more significant than the specific historical writings of either man.[12] Together, Yankee and English minds had drawn upon the Germanic body of scholarship to herald not only a common heritage but also a desired future.

English historians traveling in the United States or writing for American readers played upon the new sympathy between old and New England. In 1881 and 1882, Freeman shared with receptive Boston audiences his special feeling of communion for New England, the last home of his forbears, where the primitive tribal assembly of his Baltic ancestors lived again in the town-meeting government. At the same time, he hastened to add that he rejoiced in the entire United States as another English nation.[13]

But Freeman and his associates were conscious that many citizens of the United States, particularly in New England—the precious third England—were not Anglo-Saxons. The historian to whom the everlasting "ties of blood and speech" surmounted geographical and political barriers, was maudlin in his disappointment with the actual population in the land of Hawthorne. ". . . alas, alas . . . in the oldest of the wooden houses where I went to find New England Puritans, I found Ould Ireland Papishes-Biddy . . . instead of Hephzibah." Another English historian, Goldwin Smith, claimed that nothing stood in the way of reconciliation of the two Anglo-Saxon nations but the "dynamite and blatherskite" of the Irish, who intimidated both the press and the politicians. Even James Bryce, who was more tolerant of ethnic diversity, regretted the disappearance of old New England where "the most purely English part of America is now becoming one of the most Celtic."[14] Ideologically and socially, the rise of the Irish Americans in politics was as embarrassing to English intellectuals as to Boston Brahmins.

British observers of the Yankee democracy were outspoken against the foreign element in the population of the United States. Although it was indelicate to criticize the principle of universal suffrage,

Freeman remarked that "the English heart" of America was strong despite the lavish grants of citizenship. Pointedly he asked, "You receive all strangers, but do you assimilate all strangers with equal ease?" He admitted that the High and Low Dutch and the Scandinavians, the Teutonic kinsfolk, could pass the test of assimilation. But, "I tremble" to speak of Aryan settlers who are not Teutons. In public he conceded that it was feasible to absorb the Celts slowly and to make them citizens in the third generation of their residence; in private he desired to eliminate from the English-speaking world all the Irish along with the still worse Negroes and Jews. Like Goldwin Smith, Freeman abhorred non-Aryans and would never have granted them citizenship in the Anglo-Saxon community.[15] Thus, earlier than American Anglophiles, these English intellectuals had arrived at the more sinister potentialities of Teutonist racism.

Naturally the British admirers of old New England were dubious about the American immigration policy. Goldwin Smith was surprised that the republic had transformed so well the "victims of English misrule . . . fugitives from the military system of Germany," but he suspected the importation of socialism by "immigrants radically alien as a race, socially and morally, to American civilization." With a different emphasis, Herbert Spencer, in a visit to the United States in 1882, feared that the Anglo-Saxon group was dying out from overwork. He explained to Fiske that the heterogeneity of races on different levels of social and political culture might prevent the proper development of the American people.[16] Thus, by 1882, British historians and social scientists, respected by the Brahmins, were questioning the assumption that all stocks could be assimilated and were urging the end of America's traditional welcome to European immigrants. That pattern of prejudice forecast the shape Brahmin resentments would take later in the decade.

But in the early 1880's the American Teutonist historians interpreted present-day ethnic groups according to the existing social attitudes. Therefore, these historians were not anti-Semitic. James K. Hosmer's popular history of the Jews expressed an inherited New England view much like that of James Russell Lowell. Hosmer, who grew up in western New York, was a true son of his father, an old New Englander who had carried from Massachusetts the strong humanitarian convictions of an antislavery minister. Though, as a historian, he applied the comparative method of Teutonists which universalized the Jewish people as a generic type and thus regarded the Jew of New York, Chicago, or St. Louis as one in "body and soul" with the "Jew of London, of St. Petersburg, of Constantinople, of the fenced cities of Judah in the days of David," Hosmer's concept was broad and free of malice. He singled out Goldwin Smith's criticism as "unjust" to the Jewish character, and was unsympathetic with Europeans who feared the Hebrew businessmen of their countries. This old-fashioned New Englander thought Yankees could compete with Jews for practical shrewdness. Any "real down-Easter . . . honed for a few generations on the New England granite" ought to "hold his own" with "Abraham or Jacob or Moses." At the same time, like a refrain from the older religious tradition, he added, "would that we might be as sure" to "match them in" the "higher spheres" of "Hebrew genius."[17]

Nor did it occur to Herbert Baxter Adams to apply the Teutonic thesis literally to non-Ayrans. He worked sympathetically on educational and social problems with rabbis as well as priests and ministers. He insisted that a University position "must be created" for Charles Gross, the eminent medievalist, and a Jew.[18]

On the other hand, English distrust of the rising Irish Americans corroborated the deepest suspicions of academicians who had either social or intellectual ties with New England's past. Echoing Lowell and Parkman, Fiske glorified the local farmers who had left their villages and towns to go west or to cities, and damned the incoming Irish or French Canadians as "a class of people very different from the landholding descendants of the Puritans." Like Norton, he had a rural retreat: his place at Petersham, New Hampshire, was delightfully free of the Irish and Negroes. What a contrast the earlier natives presented: they had not looked like peasants and the conformity of manual labor and domestic service in all homes had there prevented social barriers. Fiske, the would-be Brahmin, lamented the class distinctions which had altered the former democratic character of New England.[19] Often escaping to England, he idealized a bygone world;

he replaced the image of criminal, free-drinking, alien factory workers with the picture of responsible, home-loving Yankee farmers.

Fiske's dismay with the present New England population permeated the writings of others who were not on the local scene
in the 1880's. Hosmer, who had lived elsewhere after the Civil
War but took pride in his descent from an old Concord family
and in his education at Harvard College, while a professor of Washington University at St. Louis, Missouri, described the tragic deterioration of the Teutonic town meeting due to the presence of
Celts. The Irish and the French Canadians were by race "uncongenial" to this institution. Favoring "a closer interdependence among
the great branches of the English-speaking race," Hosmer deplored
the dilution of the old stock. This conceptualized opinion of New
Englanders was also implicit in the interpretation of American
immigration by Edmund J. James, a Middle-Western Teutonist-
trained political and economic scientist who was then teaching at
the Normal University in Illinois. In an influential essay appearing
in the new *Cyclopaedia of Political Science,* he repeated the prevailing
sentiment: "Institutions which were successful with the well-trained
and thoughtful New England community" could not work with
the present "mixed and ignorant population." Deeply rooted in the
emotions of the old New England group and spread by its intellectual advocates, the Teutonist theory had found its first American
victim in the Irish group.[20]

But the implication of English critics that the United States must
restrict either suffrage or immigration did not meet with the approval of American Teutonists in the early 1880's. Even the New
Englanders, although as apprehensive as their English friends, were
unprepared for this fundamental reversal in democratic thinking.
Phillips Brooks, the Episcopalian leader, *"our* Bishop" to Bostonians,
whether they joined the Episcopal church or not, was an accurate
gauge of upper-class Anglophile sentiment. Proud of his Puritan
ancestry, he felt insecure about his country in much the same way as
Norton, whose open pessimism the Bishop disapproved. Brooks too
was troubled by "the lack of national character" in the United States.
Yet how could it be otherwise, he decided, in an unstable society

which allowed the presence of foreigners. Nonetheless, the community's leading preacher did not suggest any radical departure from
the traditional immigration policy. Instead in 1880, he prayed, for the
new people, which was slowly being born out of the "strange meeting of the races." Eight years later, when his misgivings were even
greater, Brooks insisted that the United States, "swarming with the
disturbed elements of all the world," was "yet not too much for
faith."[21] The question was the most profound one which these
Brahmins faced in the ninth decade of the century; this "yet"
foretold that a breaking point was imminent. How long would
New Englanders cling to slight faith in an American people of unpredictable character?

In 1882, educated Yankees accepted through tradition the economic
and political validity of free immigration. Henry Cabot Lodge, who
five years before had been a Harvard graduate student in Anglo-
Saxon studies, nevertheless welcomed 1881's 700,000 immigrants and
boasted that over a million newcomers seemed to be on their way.
To the citizens of Nahant, Massachusetts, an old coastal village which
Cabot Lodge loved as his "ancestral acres," the politician emphasized
that these immigrants included "in ever-increasing numbers, the
best elements, both mentally and physically, of the laboring population of Europe." Going further than Lodge, a Yankee statistician,
Worthington C. Ford, concluded that immigration had made the
American "a race . . . pre-eminent for its vigor," well nurtured on
the free institutions of the democracy.[22]

Brahmins were still able to dismiss warnings lest the Irish immigrants "transform this Germanic and Protestant country." These New
Englanders counted on the efficacy of free institutions to assimilate
"the foreign element."[23] The Teutonic myth then offered a vehicle
for their will to affirm the social principles of the past, which the
Anglo-Saxons would impose on the new Americans.

In the terminology of Freeman, Fiske defined the American people, not as Anglo-Saxons, nor as Anglo-Americans, but as "the English race," a phrase enveloping the citizens of England and the
United States in one happy family. The dominant Teutonic characteristic of this English race was "a rare capacity" to absorb "slightly

foreign elements." The Americans had "absorbed considerable quantities of closely kindred European blood," yet remained "in . . . political habits and aptitudes . . . thoroughly English." Even as the present English race was a compound of Teutonic, Norman, and Celtic strains, Fiske blandly predicted the continuity of the Anglo-Saxon destiny: soon four-fifths of the world would "trace its pedigree to English forefathers." But these British idols had encouraged inward doubt as to the limits of American assimilation, and Fiske agreed that one of the immediate effects of foreign emigration was "political and social deterioration." Nevertheless to Spencer, the evolutionist, he pointed out the compensations: immigration fostered "an ever-increasing differentiation in the interests and the employments of the people, coupled with an ever-increasing development of integrating power on the part of the Government" and thus resulted "in the provisions for public education, sanitation, and transportation" and protected "the public from unjust demands of capitalistic combinations and labor organizations."[24]

Fiske in 1882, like Lowell in 1885, tried to justify the existing immigration policy. New Englanders still shared, if uneasily, the social assumptions of the past. And the arguments of conservative economists like Charles F. Dunbar and J. Laurence Laughlin gave additional support to the traditional point of view. Until common faith in the economic and social values of immigration was destroyed, New Englanders would not accept the idea of restriction.[25]

By the end of the 1880's, one of their own people, Francis Amasa Walker, a leader among contemporary historians, economists, and other social scientists, satisfied the incipient desire to justify the end of the free immigration policy. In a relatively short life (1840–1897), he had a distinguished career as a Civil War general, lawyer, journalist, economist, statistician, and college president. In public service his breadth of action and tolerance for new ideas made him a force among his friends and among younger scholars. Walker established a theory which bridged the gap between the Brahmins' new inclination to stop the flow of European immigration, and their economic and democratic inhibitions against the idea of restriction.

The product of generations of English colonial stock, Walker grew up in a respected Yankee family. His father, Amasa, after a successful career in the manufacture of boots and shoes, retired to the life of a scholar and became a well-known economist. In the 1840's, he was an active Democrat, peace advocate, agitator for the secret ballot, and supporter of the underground railway for fugitive slaves. The son therefore inherited the tradition of service to the New England community. Spending his youth in the small town of Brookfield, Massachusetts, Francis Amasa attended the Leicester Academy before graduating from Amherst College in the class of 1860. As an undergraduate, he showed his father's aptitude for economics; but at the end of the Civil War he experimented with teaching and journalism before becoming Chief of the Bureau of Statistics and Deputy Special Commissioner of Internal Revenue and Commissioner of Indian Affairs in Washington. In 1872 he accepted an appointment as professor of political economy and history in the Sheffield Scientific School at Yale. By 1876, his ability was recognized among New England Independents in politics to the extent that the critical Henry Adams wanted him to edit a Boston newspaper for the Adams coterie. From 1881 until his death Walker was the second president of the Massachusetts Institute of Technology. Like his friend Fiske, he became part of Brahmin society; he belonged to the parish of Phillips Brooks and joined clubs in which "the lights of Boston" shone.[26]

In a life of varied interests, Walker had developed as an economist. At first, like his father, the young theorist was impressed with the function of immigrants in the American economy. Laborers had "come . . . from every part of the world." Some had "brought with them small amounts of capital, and . . . have been all the more welcome on that account." But, however they had come, "were it with but a bundle on a stick," there had been "room and work enough for all," and, despite "periods of distress," there had never been "any real excess of labor." This increase of population did not cause a decrease of wages in the United States. Moreover, should wages go down at a later stage of the nation's development, even then the newcomers, although socially uncongenial, would contribute to the productivity of the country.[27] In 1875, he accepted immigration as an unquestionable material good for the United States.

But, in the very same years in which he defined the role of the foreign-born in the economy, Walker initiated a survey of aliens from a very different and disheartening point of view. His direction of the census of 1870 brought the realization that the ethnic composition of the American people was undergoing a radical change. Among the natives, he discovered to his horror, "the rate of growth characterizing the eight preceding decades of the nation's history" had suddenly dropped. He disagreed with optimists, like Dr. Edward Jarvis of Concord, Massachusetts, who dismissed the "very extravagant and even wild statements" that before long "the foreign element" would supersede the old stock. Acknowledging the Civil War losses of the native population, Walker sought a more basic explanation for the visible decline in the national birth rate. The drop had started when Yankees had left agricultural for manufacturing pursuits; but the first effects of this exodus from country to town "were covered from the common sight by a flood of immigration unprecedented in history." Ominously, he predicated that "social forces and tendencies, not heretofore felt or at least not heretofore recognized, in our national life" were "beginning to affect powerfully the reproductive capabilities of our people."[28] According to the trend of the censuses, the native birth rate would continue to decrease from decade to decade. Therefore he attached a social meaning to the factor of immigration entirely inconsistent with his current study of its economic value.

With deep-felt concern for the future of his own stock, Francis A. Walker analyzed the foreign-born in the early 1870's. Lamentably, industrialization had subjected Irish and German newcomers to occupations in the East and had created "the miscellaneousness, the promiscuousness, and . . . the tumultuousness, of the immigration . . . since the days of the Irish famine." There had been no happiness either for the immigrants or for the communities they marred, because the aliens came ill-prepared "for the experiences of their American life." Many a "wretched beer guzzler" and follower of the city bosses would have been better off on the western frontier, if the government of the United States had helped these European peasants to utilize the agricultural knowledge of their past. Far from being indispensable to American industry, the supply of half-taught peasant labor had encouraged only the early, coarse types of manufacture and had probably prevented the growth of finer, precise work.[29] Fearful that the newcomers were potentially more important in the composition of the American people than the Yankees, he had begun to dislike the conditions which offered opportunities for immigrants. Industrialization, which was precipitating the present ethnic upheaval, had proved a mixed blessing to the United States.

Personally, Walker felt the terrible alienation between the native and immigrant groups. Even the second generation of Americans of Irish and German extraction were really *"home-made foreigners"* and, "though born among us, our general instinctive feeling testifies that they are not wholly of us. So separate has been their social life, due alike to their clannishness and to our reserve; so strong have been the ties of race and blood and religion with them; so acute has been the jealousy of their spiritual teachers toward our popular institutions—that we speak of them, and we think of them, as foreigners." Walker, who in the next decade defended the religious rights of all strangers in the New England community, regarded the Irish as the most adversely adjusted group in America. But the study of the census of 1870 offered one minor consolation: contrary to popular belief, these "American Irish" did not have a higher rate of increase than "the American German."[30]

The fecundity of the foreign elements in the United States became an obsession. The census of 1880 confirmed his suspicion that in all urban communities, especially in his own, the marriage rate among natives was lower, and many of them put off getting married. Worse still was "the close restraint put upon reproduction within the married state." As a result, immigrant groups would supply more and more of the American citizenry. Confronting the differences in "race-characteristics and religious adherence" between the newcomers and the older portion of the population, Walker translated his anxiety into racial criticism of newer Americans.[31]

The Teutonist formulations appealed to him in his discomfiture. From Fiske's text, he praised the mechanical inventiveness inherited from Anglo-Saxon forbears.[32] The shabby, squalid homes of tens of thousands of Irishmen and French Canadians now blighted New England villages. The newcomers lacked the English capacity for mechanical ingenuity. Determined to make up for this loss of talent among the common people, Walker advocated manual training in the public schools. Presumably industrial education would also instill in the sons of the foreign-born a sense of decency and good citizenship. With similar purpose, he proposed to teach the daughters to sew and cook in the New England way; then the filthy dwellings of the immigrants would become clean and their foreign foods, so "provocative of a craving for strong drink," would become unpalatable.[33]

The growing power of organized workers in the 1880's further stimulated Walker's rejection of "the foreign element," despite his willingness to admit the validity of the labor movement. As the first president of the American Economic Association, he agreed with more radical members that economic theory must change to accommodate the changing industrial relationships in the United States. Although a free trader himself, he acknowledged that the doctrine of *laissez faire* had been the medium of an aristocratic economics; and, however much individuals favored it "as a general rule of conduct," he supported "the abandonment of *Laissez-Faire* as a principle of universal application." Walker acknowledged that every class in the economy had a right to protect itself. Theoretically, employers could not be the natural trustees of laborers; and, as the labor unions said, "the masses of the people" were "the only proper and safe guardians of their own interests."[34]

But even though repudiating the traditional position of employers as guardians of their workers, Walker was unprepared for the actual consequences of organized labor's views. In the 1880's, the strikes of skilled workers, "the fortunate portion of the working population," were prompted by "ambition" rather than by "misery." Uncomprehending, he blamed the seeming irresponsibilities of the present unions upon the millions of immigrants, "bred under other institutions." How "different" they were from the law-abiding, reasonable, native employees, who appreciated their employers' factory and market problems. "Nor in vain have our people for generations been endowed with the franchise and invited to the discussion and decision of public questions." Indeed, the very formation of trade unions was "alien" to old Yankees. They had inherited the English pioneers' ability to assert themselves individually in economic as well as political action. Had vast numbers of foreigners not migrated to America, Walker doubted that labor organizations would ever have had much influence in the United States. And even worse than the trade unions, the terrifying Knights of Labor had arisen to destroy the master class entirely. He urged his colleagues to "assert themselves against those who come into our land to trouble it." Although he repudiated the idea of a "proscriptive Know-Nothingism," he nevertheless abused the contemporary industrial movement as un-American. By 1887, Walker had decided immigration was a questionable asset for his country.[35]

Yet Walker knew better than to attribute the prevailing notions of socialism, communism, and anarchism entirely to European immigrants. As a friend of the Adamses and a vigorous critic of Edward Bellamy and Henry George, he was aware of the native roots of anti-capitalist thinking. Essentially, his conflict between the emerging democratic theory of economic relationships and their awful realization in the forms of strikes, boycotts, and alien labor leaders, was still another aspect of the dilemma of the upper-class Independents of the 1880's. Just so, Brahmins resented the rise of new capitalists controlling the destiny of the United States; just so, these Yankees reacted to the threat of New England Catholic parochial schools. Walker, emotionally involved on all these levels, found his defense of the new economics less worrisome when it applied to "our own people" rather than to "the offscourings of Europe." Yet in reflective moments he did not envisage an anarchist threat from the foreign-born. Likewise on middle ground, Walker did not seek the protection of the American businessman as a primary objective. Rather he conceived a balance of power between employers and employees which would permit the national economy to function for the benefit of all citizens.[36] As in other experiences of Independents, the difficulty was that they could not understand the demands of the masses of Americans, old and new, for new rights and opportunities.

Like many Yankees, Walker turned from the contemporary ruptures in the *status quo* to the past triumphs of the Anglo-Saxons in America. Especially his own New Englanders, advancing beyond other Teutons and far ahead of laggard Slavs and Celts, were a select group: they had mastered the virgin land of a continent and maintained their virility for two hundred years.[37] Thus, the industrial strife of the present incited him to rationalize the native superiority to non-Anglo-Saxon latecomers.

Walker had been the Director of the United States Census Bureau since 1870. From that time the presence of immigrants had troubled him in myriad ways and, by 1890, made a mockery of his liberal stands. Constantly the implications of the census figures reminded him that the challenge of the foreign-born was not ephemeral. The peculiar genius of the Yankees was still alive but the changed economic and social condition was steadily reducing their numbers in the total population.

The climax of his fears for the survival of the English stock in America came after the count of 1890. This census revealed that five and one quarter millions had migrated to the United States from 1880 to 1890. More determined than ever, Walker knew he must penetrate the indifference of his countrymen to this catastrophe before the real American people became extinct. His first appeal was to the young economists: they, who justified radical shifts in economic thought, must realize that in America the new relations between employers and employees were complicated and intensified by the ever-increasing influx of aliens. His youthful colleagues must protect the "political and industrial experiment" by reassessing the national immigration policy in every aspect, to decide whether its present volume and character required stringent restriction by law. As Teutonist historians were saying that only Anglo-Saxons were fit for the privileges of democratic citizenship, so Walker added that the foreign-born generally lacked the capacity to share in the developing equalization of the rights of capital and labor in modern industrialized society.[38] Although his speech was circumspect, his tenuous allegiance to the older view of immigration had ended.

Walker continued to lead the way in dramatizing the subject of immigration. By 1891, he evolved the argument which would most conclusively lead New England's upper classes to favor restriction. Based upon population statistics from 1850 to 1890, its hypothesis had brewed in Walker's mind since 1870: the arrival of foreigners in the United States had caused a "shock to the principle of population among the native element." When the newcomers had poured into the Northern states, they came ill-equipped to maintain and even to understand the high standard of living in these communities. "Life" in the Yankee world, ". . . even at its hardest, had always had its luxuries; the babe had been a thing of beauty, to be delicately nurtured and proudly exhibited; the growing child had been decently dressed, at least at school and church; the house had been kept in order, at whatever cost, the gate hung, the shutters in place, while the front yard had been made to bloom with simple flowers; the village church, the public schoolhouse, had been the best which the community, with great exertions and sacrifices, could erect and maintain." The foreigners had changed all this, with "houses that were mere shells for human habitations, the gate unhung, the shutters flapping or falling, green pools in the yard, babes and young children rolling about half naked or worse, neglected, dirty, unkempt." Overwhelmed, Walker asked, "Was there not in this, sentimental reason strong enough to give a shock to the principle of population?" Moreover, there was as well "an economic reason" for the subsequent native decline in numbers. Unwilling "to engage in the lowest kind of day labor" with the aliens, Americans "shrank from the industrial competition" and were "even more unwilling to bring sons and daughters into the world to enter into that competition."[39]

As in his earlier reflections, Walker felt obligated to vindicate the virility of the old stock. New England became the habitual setting of his sad tale of the Yankees' self-denial in refusing to reproduce. He described the demoralization of the homogeneous, classless town which Brahmins had idealized during the last forty years. Those who had already absorbed the myth of their inherited Anglo-Saxon communities could take to heart his account of the unborn, native citizens lost to democratic society. And not a few New Englanders would resent the vitality of the foreign-born, who were less restrained in martial relations then sensitive Yankees.[40]

According to Walker's principle of population, Irishmen, Germans, French Canadians, and Scandinavians who had come during the nineteenth century, instead of constituting an addition to the American people had disastrously replaced the older Yankees.[41] This was the death blow to the popular, optimistic assumption of the 1870's and early 1880's that the Anglo-Saxons could absorb the inferior peoples who migrated to the United States. The happy ideal of assimilation, which Fiske had spread over the land, disintegrated under Walker's cogent proofs, and, for old New Englanders, immigration became a matter of racial preservation.

At that time a few members of the American Economic Association shared Walker's desire to justify a radical change in immigration policy. In 1888, while he was still its president, the Association acted as judge in an essay contest on "The Evils of Unrestricted Immigration" sponsored by the nativist magazine *America*.[42]

Of the men in the American Economic Association who affected the intellectual development of the restriction movement, the most important was Richmond Mayo Smith. Born in Troy, Ohio, in 1854, Mayo Smith was proud of his descent from seventeenth-century settlers of Massachusetts and Connecticut. In the class of 1875 at Amherst, like Walker and Herbert Baxter Adams, Smith had imbibed the orthodox New England values. After studying under the Teutonist historian John W. Burgess and at German universities, he joined the faculty in history and political science at Columbia University in 1873. Six years later he gave the first course in statistics in any American college and came into Walker's orbit.

Thereafter the two scholars exchanged ideas closely, and Walker's influence upon the younger man was evident. As late as 1887, Mayo Smith had dismissed the arguments of labor leaders favoring restriction as "mostly mere demagogy." But, one year later, the idea was conceivable. Of the influx of strange elements into the Bay State, the junior statistician now wrote: "One-half of the people of Massachusetts can no longer speak of the constitution as the work of the [Founding] Fathers except in an adoptive sense; and it is scarcely possible to conceive of the Fathers adopting the mass of Catholic Irish and French-Canadians and beer-drinking Germans who make up the foreign-born." Although minimizing both the hazard of politics and the excess of crime and vice among immigrants as typical of "the lower classes," he asked whether our national institutions and character could stand the strain imposed by "this infusion of foreign blood." By 1888, for Mayo Smith as for Walker the economic advantages of immigration had receded markedly before the social consequences.[43]

Significantly, nevertheless, Mayo Smith felt impelled to explain restriction on grounds other than the deterioration of the American character, and concluded that it was "expedient . . . to add to our previous inquiries a further one . . . to consider whether we any longer need the immigrants." In addition, he drew upon Walker's argument that foreigners with their lower standard of living had an unfair advantage over native workers. Accordingly, Smith pointed out the disastrous competition to the older American working classes: "the Irish drove the New England girls out of the factories of Massachusetts and now the French-Canadians are driving out the Irish." Furthermore, since the United States was fairly well built up, a large labor supply was not necessary. This declaration of a Columbia University professor appealed to the *Boston Daily Advertiser,* which was wavering between the veiled desire to end the flood of aliens and the habitual belief in the material advantages of immigration.[44]

Edward Bemis of Springfield, Massachusetts, another Amherst graduate, and a Johns Hopkins economist, was deeply impressed by Mayo Smith's repudiation of the economic values of immigration. Exposing, in the *Andover Review,* Boston's corruption by Negroes and Irish Americans, Bemis complained that Irish and German emigration had changed for the worse in the last thirty years. He too found the burden of assimilation overtaxing, and became the first scholar to suggest publicly a literacy test as the method of selecting future immigrants.[45]

For social scientists like Bemis, Mayo Smith, and others identified with the old New England society, Walker's fully developed thesis with its two-edged sword of racial and economic attack upon the traditional free immigration, soon had a devasting cogency. In 1892, Walker altered his rationalization in one significant respect by suppressing his hostility to the Irish Americans. Retracting much of his harsh description of the alien invasion in the native villages since the 1850's, he admitted that after a time the Irish had improved their standard of living and worked hard for the decencies of life. And if their houses were not as attractive as those of the native manual laboring classes, at least these newcomers dressed their wives and children for church. Even more telling, he observed that, despite some immediate political disadvantages, the republic had borne up under the strain of these immigrants.[46]

Walker had not suddenly forgotten his diatribes of 1874 against "the American Irish" and "the American Germans." Abruptly he had repressed his true, explosive sentiments. With the help of modern transportation, other peoples from southern Italy, Russia, and Hungary had discovered America. They provided a more convenient target than the descendants of the first foreign-born who had political status in the community, and on them fell the onus of all the complaints which New Englanders had accumulated in the last forty years. Now Walker demarcated Teutonically another line of inferiority, that of "old" and "new" immigrant groups. If the latter dregs of humanity were to replace the Anglo-Saxons, the future American character would be that much worse. Having established this politic distinction, Walker had crystallized his defense of immigration restriction and provided a complete formula for future restrictionists.[47]

It remained for Richmond Mayo Smith to examine, through the same lenses of Yankee gentleman and Teutonist scholar, the sociological implications of immigration in a full-length study. Assuming that "the ethical consciousness" of the national community attained a fixed nature by 1783, he had four criteria by which to measure American character in 1890: first, political ability, inherited from England and manifest in self-government; second, social morality derived from the New England Puritans and maintained through the spirit of equality and the absence of privileged classes; third, economic well-being of the masses; and fourth, desirable social traits such as the Anglo-Saxon love of law and order, humanitarianism toward the helpless, good humor, and national patriotism.[48] The sociologist of New England origin, like the Brahmin group itself, attributed all the virtues of the American people to their English ancestry.

Consistent with these Anglo-Saxon assumptions, Mayo Smith divided the population into three groups: the descendants of the original "colonists," who had settled by 1783; the immigrants, or their children, who had come to the United States since 1790; and Negroes. Dismissing colored Americans as hopelessly incapable of the native "capacity for political and social life," he judged the white newcomers since the Revolution by their ability to conform with his static ideal. Acknowledging that many members of the various ethnic stocks had become as good Americans as the children of the Puritans, nevertheless he classified post-1790 settlers as "the foreign element," a very different category from the descendants of the seventeenth- and eighteenth-century citizens.[49]

Face to face with contemporary migrations, Mayo Smith found that "the process of assimilation" had become increasingly difficult since 1850. With useful ambiguity, however, he did not distinguish between the physical absorption of the foreign-born and their Americanization in living. Any deviations from the "ethical consciousness" of the nation derived from the alien infiltrations. To show that assimilation was not as successful as formerly, he repeated the complaints of upper-class New Englanders. The foreign-born had the habit of voting in blocs, which resulted in Irish ardor for Home Rule, German pride in the Fatherland or German views on liquor consumption, and unAmerican "outbreaks of anarchism and socialism." The prevalence of crime, pauperism, and illiteracy among these Europeans also reduced the endurance of the Anglo-Saxon social traits, advanced by the generations of native Americans.[50] All these deteriorations of the original Yankee ethos proved unequivocally that the new blood would alter the American character for the worse. Like Walker, Smith concluded that French Canadians, Hungarians, Poles, Italians, and others were repeating the evil propensities of the Irish, Germans, and Scandinavians.

Trained in the scientific method of history, political science, and economics, this pioneer sociologist did not relate his strong judgments upon people to the changing conditions of their existence. Convinced of the values of the Anglo-Saxon tradition, he followed any avenue leading toward restriction; at the same time he was aware that the traditional policy was the consistent practice of the nation. As if to assuage the national conscience, Mayo Smith asserted that freedom to migrate was not the right of an individual and that the United States was justified in selecting elements which would contribute to the harmonious development of "our civilization."[51]

By 1890 a handful of academicians, sharing a mutual faith in their Anglo-Saxon origins, agreed that the United States could no longer assimilate the mass of extraneous groups who were arriving with even greater momentum than formerly. Circuitously, intellectuals questioned and finally shattered for themselves the economic justification for welcoming European immigrants to the United States. Through Walker, the New Englanders' fear of being displaced had become an hypothesis adaptable to racial and economic considerations of immigration; through his associate, Mayo Smith, a more detailed text for restriction was available to Brahmins who were ripe for that point of view. Yet the two-hundred-year-old welcome to Europe's poor and oppressed was still part of the American law and the task of convincing the influential majority lay ahead.

CHAPTER V

Founding the Immigration
Restriction League

Wide open and unguarded stand our gates,
And through them presses a wild motley throng—
Men from the Volga and the Tartar steppes,
Featureless figures from the Hoang-Ho,
Malayan, Scythian, Teuton, Kelt, and Slav,
Flying the Old World's poverty and scorn;
These bringing with them unknown gods and rites,
Those, tiger passions, here to stretch their claws.
In street and alley what strange tongues are these,
Accents of menace alien to our air,
Voices that once the Tower of Babel knew!
                                —Thomas Bailey Aldrich[1]

By 1890 older Brahmins were on the verge of an intellectual
decision in favor of immigration restriction. But, fundamentally
conservative, they were still restrained by precedents. It would take
a new generation, less influenced by the heritage of the past, to
break with the old immigration policy.

The mature men of the 1880's had "scientific" proof that the
Anglo-Saxon stock was indispensable to the democratic civilization
of the United States. The Teutonist rationale encouraged the conviction that ideas and acts which shocked the values of the older
community must be alien and un-American. In this state of mind,
superior to the evils outside it, educated New Englanders viewed

the turbulence of the industrial struggle in the last two decades of the century. The Brahmin group and those identified with it had to face more than the new Irish political power and the parochial school crisis; strikes, riots, and anarchists were also visible symptoms of a strange disorder in modern society.

Dislike of the foreign-born mounted after the Haymarket bomb: America was not for Anarchists whom "a beer saloon serves . . . for forum and church." Some outraged citizens advocated organization of an armed militia to meet any potential mob. Others suggested a limitation on foreigners' property rights. All citizens of foreign birth became the object of native scrutiny and the burden of proof rested upon them to disown any sympathy with anarchism. The Rev. Cyrus Bartol even blamed political party managers for tolerating radicals among the immigrant masses; "these riotous enemies of society" were "not an indigenous growth." Conscientious and puzzled citizens assured themselves that the strike, as a weapon of organized labor, was "an American anomaly." Violence was not the method of a people accustomed to the ballot. Educators and ministers asked what would happen to the children of today's voters, as barbarian hordes hurled themselves "upon our civilization." Determination grew that the European savages must not conquer "the Anglo-Saxon race," and plans to preserve the American ideals of the past became an urgent necessity.[2]

However, no sustained sentiment for restriction developed in the old New England group as a result of the anarchists' action at Chicago. On the contrary, the *Boston Daily Advertiser* still claimed on May 25, 1886 that "free and unrestricted immigration" was "one of the most important factors of the system of protection to home industries. Desirable immigrants" were "consumers as well as producers, and every one" who came "to remain and identify . . . with our institutions" contributed to the American economy.[3]

New England's solution to the social and political threats was good leadership and enlightened voting. The daughter of Massachusetts' Senator Dawes believed that the bad men had gained control of Boston because "the better citizens" had deserted their duty. The withdrawal of the upper class from political affairs was so noticeable that Henry Cabot Lodge's entrance into the political arena in 1882 evoked public praise. Increasingly it was necessary to remind New Englanders that "young men, zealous for reform, have been found to make some of the best municipal officers."[4] The exhortations of James Russell Lowell and Charles Eliot Norton to Harvard graduates were commonplace. The educated men of the dominant generation must preserve the country, and the younger generation in the schools and colleges must be prepared for the same civic responsibilities.

The tradition of community service received additional stimulus from Teutonist academicians. They taught American history, Herbert Baxter Adams reported, "not so much to make historians as to make citizens and good leaders for the State and the Nation." Father to a generation of scholars, he spread the New England gospel of civic obligation throughout the country. In the next few decades, university professors trained at Johns Hopkins not only studied the problems of the past but promoted adult education courses in good citizenship.[5]

At Boston, Teutonist intellectuals joined other conscientious men who wanted to understand and weather the social crisis. By the mid-1880's, a plethora of clubs—the American Institute of Civics, the Citizens Association, the Citizens Club of Boston, and others—had sprouted. In 1889, the most articulate of these organizations was the Massachusetts Society for Promoting Good Citizenship. In contrast to predecessors which pursued only specific legislative causes, this Society weighed social problems with the future in mind. Both in a political and an intellectual sense, its membership was miscellaneous, ranging from its radical president, Edward Everett Hale, to conservative businessmen like Samuel B. Capen and Dr. C. F. Crehore. All were representative cultured natives. One of the group, Mellen Chamberlain, the director of the Boston Public Library and an amateur historian of some repute, held up Josiah Quincy, the aristocratic mayor of their town in 1821, as a model of the good citizen. Quincy had been "not of the people, but with the people . . . always! If he never indulged in the illusions of hope respecting the perfectibility of popular government, he never indulged in the illusions of despair."[6]

The old Federalist mayor, who had disagreed with the majority of his electorate, was a consoling ideal for disconcerted New Englanders, vulnerable to the acts of Irish politicians.

Like similar clubs, the Massachusetts Society wanted to purify corrupt local government. In a democratic country where universal suffrage was a *sine qua non* and even a valuable safety valve, the only solution to the contemporary evils was education.[7] The Society worked to edify three different groups in the community: the immigrant children who would some day have the vote; the native adults of the better classes; and, finally, their children who would have to deal with the democracy of the future.

To meet the varied levels of such an audience, Society promoters wrote and publicized books and pamphlets on the history of American institutions and sponsored public lectures on civic questions. Its Committee on Studies, an important agency for spreading ideas, included John Fiske, Albert Bushnell Hart, Davis R. Dewey, and Edwin Mead, all of expressed Teutonist views.[8] With true New England enthusiasm for the efficacy of education, these intellectuals blazoned nursery and forum with the Anglo-Saxon standard of citizenship.

By proper indoctrination of foreign-born parents and children, the Society hoped to counteract the violence injected into American life by immigrants, unacquainted with the Anglo-Saxon respect for law and for "the republic of the founding fathers." The Committee on Studies recommended Anna L. Dawes's text for American boys and girls and for the adult foreigners whom "we are month by month trying to assimilate . . . to whom our institutions are strange and incomprehensible."[9]

For the most part, however, the task of inculcating the young newcomers remained the challenge of Edwin D. Mead who, in 1883, under the auspices of the Old South Meeting House, had inaugurated a program for the children of the North End. Guided by the Rev. Edward Porter, an able antiquarian, Irish and Italian youth examined their "home" surroundings and learned the meaning of Bunker Hill, Copp's Hill, the tomb of the Mathers, and the Old North Church. But the results of this instruction which linked "grandfathers and great-grandfathers with broad historical movements," were disappointing; the education of Boston's foreign-born youth was hindered and vexed by "rowdy, rogue, and priest." Mead concluded that "like every missionary" he had dealt "with much hard and unpromising material."[10] The inappropriateness of the "ancestral" tone of the enterprise escaped him; a generous reformer, he nonetheless felt the old impasse which lay between the upper-class natives and the alien masses.

Others like the prosperous Capen, who opposed all private schools and looked to the public system to unify "our heterogeneous population," did not expect even simple decency from the poor children of Boston. A more intellectualized prejudice led Crehore, the Society's active secretary, to fear that the pressure of so many different ethnic groups might make the task of the public schools insuperable. Not an up-to-date Teutonist, he urged secondary schoolteachers to read Robert Knox's *Races of Men,* the book which forty years before had certified Dr. Holmes's faith in the superiority of the Anglo-Saxon over the Celt. Reminding the local pedagogues that "Celt, Saxon, Latin, Indian, Mongol, and Negro must, at least, till immigration ceases, remain separate races among us," Crehore wanted students classified according to racial categories in order to ascertain their moral character.[11] Such xenophobic sentiments reflected the assumption that there were Anglo-Saxon standards of behavior.

Of more immediate and direct concern to the leaders of the Society was the passivity of their own group in the midst of municipal corruption. It was shocking to find, after an election in 1888, that "hundreds of the class who have the most at stake in our free institutions, who were born here and know their worth, have failed to exercise the right of suffrage." As an antidote, the intellectuals urged their contemporaries to read the *Political Science Quarterly,* the *Johns Hopkins University Studies,* and the *Publications of the American Economic Association,* along with the *Nation* and *Forum.*[12] In the literature of the modern social scientists, the New England Independents in politics and reform found sympathy for their position reinforced by the compelling logic of Teutonist scholarship. For additional enlightenment, the Society presented public lectures on political and social problems: housing for the poor, city government, practical politics, and representative government were characteristic topics.

Twice in 1891 and once in 1892 the Society considered the influence of the foreign-born upon "the elements of the political citizenship." Immigration became the subject of discussion. Horace Wadlin of the Massachusetts Bureau of Statistics of Labor observed that now only one-third of Boston's citizens were of native parentage; "instead of a Puritan Commonwealth, as in times gone, we have become a country somewhat alien in sympathies." Although perplexed by the changed population, he held steadfastly to the idea of Americanizing the newcomers. It would be easier, he observed "to shut the door, but how can we go on in our progress if we do?" In contrast, Henry Cabot Lodge thought the time had come to exclude the illiterate foreigners, to sift them from "intelligent and thrifty immigrants."[13] In the short period from 1889 to 1893, the Massachusetts Society for Promoting Good Citizenship had traveled far down the road to restriction. But in these years most of the members were still content to listen to the pros and cons of immigration.

At the same time, however, the older generation queried: "Whose country is this, or rather, whose was it?" Phillips Brooks joined the Sons of the American Revolution in 1891, because it was well to "go in for the assertion that our dear land at least used to be American." Fiske and Winslow Warren lent their support to various ancestral societies to revive real "Americanism" as "the antidote to the bane of foreign immigration which, in spite of much good it has brought, has also poured in upon us a vast deal . . . hard to absorb and amalgamate . . . which can be met in no better way than by the enforcement of those American ideas . . . inherited from the Revolution." Patriotic organizations of old stock Americans might safeguard the nation and make possible the assimilation of the new elements of the population. And even more, the formalizing of Yankee kinship enhanced the appealing belief that "Americans of old British birth" were "the genuine type of Americans."[14]

Beyond this kind of group identification New Englanders did not organize themselves against a future of continued immigration;

although dissident in their hearts, they were immobilized by the past. Without taking action, however, they could protest against their burden of the foreign-born. Urgently, Thomas Bailey Aldrich voiced the native desperation. Aldrich, from New Hampshire, cherished his "Boston-platedness" more than a born Brahmin. In 1892 he surrendered his post as editor of the *Atlantic* and with it his cultural control of the genteel tradition in American letters. When, in that same year, the City Fathers authorized the closing of the Boston Public Library on March 17, Aldrich suffered bitterly: "Columbus didn't discover America; it was St. Patrick. He is in full defiant possession now, his colors waving everywhere, 'The Grane above The Red'—white, and blue." After attending a meeting of anarchists that spring, his social resentments increased, and "fellow citizens" there enraged him to greater vituperation. "These brutes" were "the spawn and natural result of the French Revolution." With the suggestion of action, the poet held "that jail birds, professional murderers, amateur lepers ('moon-eyed' or otherwise) and human gorillas generally should be closely questioned at our Gates." An aristocrat by choice, Aldrich predicted a sorry end for real Americans, because they let their politicians "coddle the worst elements for votes" and their newspapers *"would* appeal to the slums for readers." Disgusted with his native land, the poet thought "some sort of unnaturalized mongrel" would be more accurate an emblem for America than the eagle.[15] He finally launched a full, direct attack upon immigrants in the poem "The Unguarded Gates"; less restrained than most of his friends, Aldrich released a racial venom, prophetic of things to come.

But systematic action against the traditional immigration would wait for the next generation. In the troubled 1880's, the responsibilities of the native youth had become the major focus of all thinking citizens. Samuel B. Capen was vexed to find that "our young men . . . of American ancestry read novels" while the Irish American boys studied "history, biography and constitutional law" in the city libraries.[16] Neither the Massachusetts Society nor Capen was alone: the plea to the young men of the better classes was the universal cry on the lips of Brahmins and Teutonist scholars alike.

All over the country, the education of the native college man was a watchword in the cause of good citizenship. Its impact upon the students of Harvard College proved decisive to the cause of immigration restriction in New England.

Harvard College excelled in the new civic education of the 1880's. Most conspicuously among her faculty, Charles Eliot Norton, Barrett Wendell, Albert Bushnell Hart, Nathaniel Southgate Shaler, and Francis Greenwood Peabody, in the study of fine arts and belles-lettres as well as in physical and social sciences, exposed young men to the complex society which was contemporary America. And the university's president, Charles W. Eliot, recognized "the task of making the college a thing not of the past but of the future, not a nursery of tradition but a seminary of service."[17]

After the Civil War, although Harvard expanded in numbers, it became more Bostonian in character than ever. Students and instructors increasingly identified with the Brahmin group. "When the supply of eligible young men in Boston was decreased by the westward movement, the Boston mamas suddenly became aware that Harvard contained many appetizing young gentlemen from New York, Philadelphia, and elsewhere." And since Eliot's introduction of the elective system reduced the unity of the classes, various clubs—social, athletic, or quasi-academic—became the focal points of friendships and associations. Few Southerners now came. Neither the children of the newly rich nor the poor working students provided leadership. Thus, the college environment reinforced the narrow social habits of upper-class Boston.[18]

In the same degree, the Harvard faculty continued to be predominantly "an extension of the Back Bay." For students who either inherited or desired the New England way of life, professors like Norton and Wendell personified Brahmin ideals. Since 1872, Norton had needled the sons of American capitalists to rise above the materialistic pursuits of their parents, and in 1881 Barrett Wendell joined him in the job of humanizing Harvard boys.[19]

As an undergraduate of the class of 1877, Wendell had responded to "the ancestral spirit" of Lowell and Norton, and the sardonic personality of Henry Adams. Three generations removed from the pre-Civil War culture, Wendell was temperamentally insecure, easily depressed and driven with the ambition which young New Englanders seemingly born too late for the great tradition still felt. He had difficulty in settling upon a career. Struggling to be a writer while he taught English composition, he wanted his American novel to be "as true a passage in the great book of human life," as Homer's Greece or Shakespeare's England. Frustrated by the aridity of his own fiction, he saw that the creativity of his elders had been born of the faith which neither he nor his society shared. All the more he impressed his students with the necessity of cultivating the imagination and a sense of beauty; like Norton, he related college studies to "actual life and conduct." Feeling the inadequacy in his own life, this littérateur who publicized his snobbishness knew as well as Henry Adams that private "society" did not give "our time significance." The social facts of 1893 which did were hard for Wendell to contemplate. Willingly he would have trusted "our future to such native guidance as has governed our past. But the floodgates" had opened. Europe was "emptying itself into our Eastern seaports; Asia overflowing the barriers we . . . tried to erect on our Western coast; Africa sapping our life to the southward. And meantime the New England country" was "depopulated, and the lowlands drained by the Mississippi . . . breeding swarms of demagogues."[20]

Wendell consoled himself that his forbears had at least "tried" to set ideals "for other folk to live by." Through his survey of literature he conveyed the meaning of the culture of his ancestors. Attributing its genius to the growth of a homogeneous society of pure Anglo-Saxon stock which left Elizabethan England, he proclaimed the superiority of the seventeenth-century emigration to all successive migrations. Irrespective of the subjects he taught, Barrett Wendell exemplified the Brahmin Anglophile personality, for whom New England voiced the "experience of English humanity."[21]

Nathaniel Southgate Shaler, beloved among colleagues and students, also fostered the belief in this native superiority. Born in Newport, Kentucky in 1841, he regarded himself as a New Englander by adoption. Although always welcome in Boston homes, he never felt completely one with the society of which he became a part; and reserving a slightly critical attitude toward the community, prided himself upon being immune from Yankee bigotry toward Catholics. Intensely sensitive to Brahmin exclusiveness, this warm Southerner was the friend of lonely and humble students, for he never forgot "the time when he too had been a stranger in a strange land and had somehow got the impression that a man from outside of New England did not count, indeed that the rest of the country was in a way superfluous."[22]

In reality, however, Shaler was not entirely foreign by New England standards. He could trace his family back to England. He had Yankee forbears and, as a youth, had met New England relatives. Moreover, his father had graduated from Harvard in 1827, and he in 1862. After fighting on the side of the North, Shaler returned to Cambridge in 1864, to spend the rest of his life as a geologist. In short, his credentials both in ancestry and in environment fitted him for Boston society.

Despite his early indelible sense of isolation in Cambridge, Shaler was at home "in the essentials." The contemporary New Englanders too were taking their stand against religious persecution. Moreover, Shaler was as obsessed as any Brahmin with ethnic variation. A son of the South whose first memories were of his Negro nurse, he felt keenly "the Negro problem." But though never losing his guilt for America's "evil past" in connection with slavery, he felt more acutely "the fear that must come upon any one who will see what a wonderful thing our modern Teutonic society is."[23] Like latter-day New Englanders, he was sure that the exotic black people could not reach the high level of the native civilization. Strongly motivated by extreme consciousness of "race," Shaler, as much as Barrett Wendell, measured all ethnic groups by the superior Anglo-Saxon American.

Naïvely, Shaler, the physical scientist, prided himself upon his ability to identify people of different nationalities with unfailing accuracy. Abroad in the 1860's and 1870's, he observed the faces of a picked lot of Englishmen and, far from discovering certain assumed modifications in the lineaments of old stock Americans, he recognized the familiar features of his Southern friends in the faces of the Britishers. Likewise he delighted in the "strong likeness between the Duke of Argyle and a respected old carpenter in Cambridge, Massachusetts." As a Teutonist, Shaler looked in Germany for "points of resemblance in the Anglo-Saxon and Teutonic character," while in France he sought out "national differences." Yet in another trip in 1882, he found the Tuscan as good a spade as the Irishman and lacking in servility, without "the droll land pride of the French peasant, and the cloddy quality of the English laborer." Nevertheless, this approval of the Tuscans ended on a patronizing note of wonder at their lack of "inventiveness." Although the future of mankind was probably safer "in the hands of many races, rather than in the hands of but one," Shaler could not suppress his pride in the quality of the English."[24]

During the 1870's and 1880's, sharing the old New Englanders' dislike of the new immigrants whom industrialization had brought into their land, Shaler wrote Norton that the residents of Pennington, Virginia were "all that is left of the yeoman, simple, devout, careless to gain, they know nothing of our modern improvement in human nature." On local walking tours, he admired Northampton, Massachusetts, "a well-balanced town" still unsullied by foreigners and factories, where the women were so "beefy" that they looked almost English. Shaler found a "painful contrast" between such folk and the workers in the "manufactories" in Framingham, Massachusetts. To be sure, ordinary Yankee farmers were "rather lean," but so "free from marks of drunkenness" and "well to do in every way." In contrast, "the factory hands" were "another race, so far as a glance would tell, much inferior in bodily condition to the country man." Like the Brahmins, Shaler attributed the outward deterioration of Yankee villages to the shiftless Irish; but surprisingly he held up the French Canadians as more promising Celts than their predecessors, who have "threatened to overwhelm us for so long." Still, as early as 1873, he concluded that all such newcomers would sorely "try the digestion of our New England civilization."[25] Aware that Anglo-Saxon Americans were "losing that breeding power," long one of their most distinguished characteristics, Shaler, who had seen "the wonderful influence of New England," was disturbed "to think of its yeoman class being swept away by any other stock in the world."[26]

During the social and political upheaval of the 1880's, he eagerly joined the "good fight for better government," and his service as vice-president of the Massachusetts Society for Promoting Good Citizenship was the public counterpart of his deeply felt obligation to the students of Harvard College. But Shaler saw certain dilemmas in the education of the young. He sought to maintain the savage virility of their forbears in the bloodless, overeducated youth often produced in modern civilization. And, conscious of his own prejudice, he wanted to overcome human biases by education. How to develop "the capacity of sympathy" toward strangers with whom one felt no sense of kinship was the most fundamental aspect of "humanizing" the college man. Shaler deliberately invited all kinds of students to his home and assisted the poor Russian Jewish boys who commuted from Boston.[27] At the same time, however, this well-intentioned, impetuous man was unable to overcome his own prejudices and, as the 1880's drew to a close, the geologist who welcomed every Harvard son to his door, was among the first to urge the closing of America's gates.

In 1888, Shaler wrote an article for the nativist magazine, *America*. This enlightened man recalled his ambulatory survey of European peasants and stated categorically that the United States could not compensate "the inheritances of a thousand years or more" in the Old World; and that in facing the immigration policy, Americans must get over the accepted idea that " 'a man is a man for a' that.' The truth is that a man is what his ancestral experience has made him."[28]

Five years later Shaler expressed his theory with less diffidence; it was impossible to develop in the European peasant any political capacity or "individuality of mind." Unlike the American working population who evinced their intelligence in devising and utilizing mechanical inventions, the Italians, for example, showed no desire to change either "the faith or the tools of their forefathers." Harking back to the seventeenth-century migrations of "our English race,"

Shaler insisted that the first stock alone, by tradition and practice, qualified for democratic society. Not only were the foreigners unfit for citizenship, but also the laws of heredity showed that their descendants would "remain laggards in the way of progress." Without the original settlers, Shaler doubted that the American commonwealth could have been founded; what was worse, could it be preserved amid the flux of alien peasants? They could not be Americanized in one generation, and to would-be optimists Shaler suggested that they consider how long it would take to force an American "into the characteristic mould of body and mind of the peasant." The political and social strains of the 1880's intensified his intellectual estrangement from the foreign-born and solidified his judgments against them. Although his beliefs on mankind did not enter directly into his lectures on geology, his convictions became well-known to his students.[29]

History offered a more direct route to collegiate minds than literature, fine arts, or geology. Toward the end of the nineteenth century, Harvard was bursting with the activity of Teutonist historians of such excellence that Herbert Baxter Adams of Johns Hopkins thought their work rivaled that of any German university. Offering an extraordinary range of courses in the study of political institutions of the western world, Harvard scholars focused upon the relationship of the various nationalities to their institutions. Since history remained a popular subject with undergraduates, even after the last compulsory course was abandoned in 1879, the contemporary academic emphasis on the character of nations inevitably permeated students' minds. Through the study of native institutions, the traditions and the problems of the United States were connected with the character of the American people. Although the department never held to a single line of interpretation, Albert Bushnell Hart was then the professor most likely to influence the average student.[30]

Hart was to become a college personality comparable to Norton, Shaler, and Wendell. Born in Clarksville, Pennsylvania, of a family who had gone west from New England, Hart was proud to trace his ancestry east to Connecticut, thence to England. After a boyhood in Ohio, he came to Harvard in 1876, as if it were Oxford or Heidelberg. The next four years were crucial in his development. Most impressed with Charles Eliot Norton, who widened the horizons of a student's life and strengthened his principles "by . . . precept and example," Hart later recalled that Norton made the young "see things as they are, with a view to making them better." He also felt the spell of James Russell Lowell and considered him "the first citizen of the Republic" in the 1880's.[31] Under the tutelage of Ephraim Emerton, a recent German Ph.D., the young Midwesterner found his life work. Back from Germany with a doctorate earned under Von Holst, in 1883, Albert Bushnell Hart was a confirmed Teutonist. He settled down in the Cambridge academic community as an instructor in complete harmony with the old New England perspective, its ideals and its prejudices.

Despite the elective system, Hart's History 13 which dealt with the United States from 1789 to 1860 became a voluntary undergraduate "must." Emphasizing the English origins of American institutions, explicit reading on the character of the Anglo-Saxon race was assigned. From Richard Frothingham's *Rise of the Republic,* the students learned that, by the time of the Revolution, the Anglo-Saxon traits of the American people were fixed. The unique quality of their self-government sprang from their "love of liberty" which existed without "the infection of wild political and social theories." Bringing the story of the nation up to contemporary times, Hart included such topics as "comparison of races" and "immigration." His concurrent articles stated his general attitude toward newcomers in America: the ignorant foreign-born had ruined good city government in the North just as surely as the poor Negroes had in the South. Refreshing himself with an example of an old New England town still extant in 1893, he described the success of Barnstable. This "virile little commonwealth" on Cape Cod was still "American America"; the one Negro and the one Irishman at the town meeting seemed "caricatures of their race."[32] By the 1890's, Hart, who helped to shape the minds of so many Harvardians, had accepted the Brahmin view of an American.

But as Fiske had earlier, Albert Bushnell Hart still expected the nation to absorb the foreigners. Unfortunately, the price of their assimilation was high; it would create an urban "type of character" very different "from that found in country regions." And since the children of the present newcomers and their descendants would some day rule the cities, Hart wanted to make the best of a bad situation by improving the education of these future citizens. He did his part in the Massachusetts Society for Promoting Good Citizenship; and, like Herbert Baxter Adams, expended much of his career in writing and editing textbooks and bibliographies.[33]

Hart committed himself to the task of acquainting his students with the social and political problems of their country, not as incidental materials of history but as vital issues which they might decide as adult voters before long. Introducing pioneer studies in sociology and statistics, he wrote and lectured about the growth of cities, civil service reform, the right of suffrage, and the disposition of the public lands. In the same way, he encouraged student research in topics of public concern such as Boston politics, Key to the Publication of the Census, the Social Question, Rights and Duties of Citizenship, and the History of Riots.[34]

His discussion course, English 6, clarified by debate disturbing public issues. Initiated at the suggestion of Francis Parkman in 1879, this course weighed such complex matters as parochial schools, free trade, free silver, the Knights of Labor, and the eight-hour day. The problem of immigration restriction appeared almost annually from 1884 to 1893. Hart provided all arguments and sources. As late as 1887, there were more positive reasons offered for the continuance of a liberal immigration policy; the negative arguments were limited to the scant debate in Congress over the contract labor law in 1885, and to Edmund J. James's article of 1883, which had protested the emerging role of Irish politicos in New England. By contrast, in a debate of 1891, Hart's references for the restrictionist defense were more cogent; Richmond Mayo Smith's book and articles, Jacob Riis's picture of tenement squalor, and Henry Cabot Lodge's advocacy of greater restriction both on the floor of Congress and in the *North American Review* represented the immediate reactions of sociologists and statesmen, while the anti-restriction data relied upon the writings of laissez-faire economists like Charles F. Dunbar and J. Laurence Laughlin.[35] The case for the restrictionists gradually infiltrated the total presentation of the immigration issue. But although the restrictionist point of view was increasingly prominent by 1891, still, in the college debates as in public lectures of the Massachusetts Society for Promoting Good Citizenship, there was the presumption that the conclusion was by no means clear cut.

One other channel in the Harvard curriculum awakened the undergraduate to the political and social evils of contemporary America. In 1881, the Rev. Francis Greenwood Peabody gave a course in practical ethics known as "The Social Question." Relating ethical theories and moral reform, Peabody analyzed problems like temperance, divorce, prisons, labor, and charities. In this examination the presence of foreign masses in the slums loomed large. Peabody used Hart's essay on the growth of American cities to emphasize the impact of immigrants on the urban population. Another Unitarian minister, the Rev. John Graham Brooks, urged Harvard students to join study groups with working men and to attend the meetings of the Associated Charities. From such experiences, upperclass youth could better understand the influence of the Catholic Church and "be brought immediately face to face with the problem of immigration with its ramifications in socialism, intemperance and cheap labor."[36]

The exhortations of these religious educators marked the beginning of the important movement which would transform oldfashioned, pre-Civil War philanthropic social service into the new forms of the early twentieth century. But Peabody, in the 1880's and 1890's, concentrated upon the inward spiritual needs of educated men rather than upon alleviations of the urban problems. He acquainted his sheltered students with the specific ills of modern industrialized society to inspire service to the community as the ultimate goal of privileged citizens and as an essential religious experience. Although immigration was part of the background of his lectures, as the foreign-born did figure in "The Social Question," restriction did not enter the framework of his ideas.[37]

The civic tutelage of Norton, Shaler, Wendell, Hart, and Peabody, all Harvard bred, affirmed the old purposes of the college, to make gentlemen and useful citizens. More important, after the Civil War, the students responded sensitively to the new accents in which these rising professors put the old obligations.

As New Englanders became self-conscious and diffident in their commitment to the nation, the college men mirrored the constant, forced convictions of their elders that, as Moorfield Storey told the class of 1866, "the duty of educated men" was to seek public office. From 1872, the Ivy Day orators in the despairing tones of Norton, attacked American hostility to thought and the low state of art. So Curtis Guild, in 1881, urged his classmates to resist "the money-getting selfish side of our nature," rather to imitate the English not only in dress and manners but in patriotic leadership as well. And in 1883, Arthur Richmond Marsh added that since the poor copy the rich in attaining the false rewards of materialism, "why should we complain that men are Socialists, Communists, Nihilists, Irish Leaguers? Why should we wonder at strikes and riots, murders and the destruction of property?"[38] Dedicating themselves to elevate the country, these Harvard students mimicked the fears and tensions of the older generations.

Like their parents, the young graduates were confused by the nature of democracy. The Rev. Phillips Brooks explained in a baccalaureate sermon that, even as they were "stepping forth unquestionably into the ranks of privilege," respect for privilege was rapidly disappearing in the United States. They were about to enter a strange new world, in which "the angry hosts" were "crowding on to . . . attack on those who for so long held the favored places of the world. The chartered and hereditary right to govern" was "going everywhere."[39] Instead of inheriting the role of leadership, in modern democratic society these young men would have to fight to perform their duties among corrupt, foreign-born politicians and win electorates who did not instinctively respect the better classes.

Reflecting his father's experiences as a member of the Common Council and as an alderman of Boston, Curtis Guild was the first commencement senior to rail against "the swarms of ignorant peasants" who joined "our own uneducated classes." As a consequence of unrestricted immigration, the United States resembled Rome in the years of the downfall of that ancient republic; the modern counterpart to the plebs was "the ignorant mob misled by crafty demagogues, . . . Irish Molly Maguires, German Socialists, French Communists, and Russian Nihilists." Disgust for the advancing Irish also appeared in an English A theme of 1885; even the student complained of the corrupt party of Boston's Mayor O'Brien which included "all the Irish-Catholics and rum-sellers . . . in this 'Athens of America.'" The feeling grew among these children, who had never voted, that the safety of the democracy hung "in perilous balance" while two million illiterate voters controlled the destiny of the United States. The class day orator in 1887 thought that the times and conditions demanded true heroism on the part of his group who stood "among the gathering races facing problems which have questioned them in vain . . . Men can flee no further to escape them, the outer verge of civilization has been reached, and we must stand and meet the issue here."[40]

As the ninth decade drew to a close, the idea of restricting the United States democracy to the fit seemed valid to a small group of Teutonist scholars, and a few Harvard undergraduates agreed. One young man concluded an outline of an English theme on Immigration with the category "the Right to Restrict it." A student-run debate in the Harvard Union also introduced the new self-conscious claim (which Mayo Smith had just stated) that the nation had "the right" to chose its own policy on immigration. Finally, three young men of the class of 1889—Charles Warren, Robert DeCourcy Ward, and Prescott Farnsworth Hall—friends from school days at G. W. C. Noble's in Boston, regarded the question of immigration with more than academic intensity.[41]

Charles Warren was the descendant of a famous colonial family and the son of Winslow Warren, a member of the class of 1858 and a typical Mugwump. Winslow Warren was one of many solid citizens, like John Quincy Adams II and Gamaliel Bradford in the 1870's and 1880's, and like Josiah Quincy and Curtis Guild in the 1890's, who struggled to participate in local, state, and national politics despite Hibernian obstacles to reform. At the time of his son's college career, he became the Democratic Collector of the Port of Boston.[42]

In the same years, son Charles, as an undergraduate, was probing the political implications of New England life for one born into the old pattern of public service. A serious youth, he copied into his notebook for Norton's Fine Arts 4 that the incentive of moral conduct was "the effect we shall produce on the world and the goods we shall hand down to the future generations." Taking Hart's course in the constitutional and political history of the United States in 1887, he concentrated on the nature of representative government. In a student debate, he argued for "the formation of an independent political party" to meet "the best interests of the country." And, in his senior year, in a paper on "Plato's Republic with Reference especially to the Functions of the State Therein and its Relation with some Modern Questions," he deduced that the contemporary state needed social regulation to prevent the domination of the political majority.[43]

The climax of Warren's undergraduate thoughts was clear in his speech at commencement in June 1889, "The Failure of the Democratic Idea in City Government." Expanding upon the conflict between the majority of numbers and the majority of interest in urban communities, he objected that the immigrant voters had the power to vote for taxes which others had to pay. Moreover, the desire of the poor to receive jobs from political parties would ensure the continuation of degenerate municipal government. He expected that in a crisis the corrupt authorities would probably "be suppressed by mobs in the street and not by citizens at the polls as they should have been." He generalized upon the city's foreign-born with Teutonist finality; they were "poor ignorant men bound by all the old ideas of bureaucratic and autocratic rule" with no knowledge of "the relation and duties of the offices" and of "questions of Party" in America.[44] Warren's remarks were derived from no direct experience with foreigners, but rather were the ideological culmination of four years at Harvard which corroborated the practical lessons his father learned in the Democratic party of Massachusetts.

The second member of 1889's restrictionist band was Robert De-Courcy Ward, the son of a Boston merchant, Henry Veazie Ward, and Anna Saltonstall. As an undergraduate, Ward took the average eclectic course with some emphasis on German literature, biology, and European and American history. As a senior, however, he studied "The Ethics of Social Reform" under the Rev. Peabody with lasting effect. In 1891, Ward observed that "all the great questions . . . the liquor question, the public school question, the problems connected with prisons and reformatories, and many more," were "tied up with the one great problem of foreign immigration." These matters would remain insoluble, "so long as our ports are open to the ignorant, the depraved and the vicious of all nations." After graduation, he continued advance study in Professor Shaler's department, and the influence of the older man became apparent. Now Ward made a point of observing steerage passengers here and talking to peasants abroad. After watching "a good looking lot" of Irish, Scandinavian, and Russian Jewish emigrants land in East Boston, he "could not help feeling that it would be far better for the country if many of them could be sent back." It appeared that the social evils, intensified by the numbers of the foreign-born, did not upset Ward as much as the strength of "the foreign element" in the United States. The national census of 1880 had listed 15,000,000 immigrants in the country and the Massachusetts census of 1885 classified over 63 per cent of Boston's population as foreign by birth or parentage. Since few native children attended the same schools as the foreign-born, the public schools could no longer accomplish the task of Americanization. Well-versed in the intellectual justifications of restriction, Ward could not understand the indifference of the American people to the dangers of free immigration.[45]

The third member of the Harvard triumvirate was Prescott Farnsworth Hall, the son of Boston merchant Samuel Hall and Elizabeth Farnsworth. Describing his background, Hall's widow later recalled that "his . . . was one of the old-time families which spent winters in Boston and summers in Brookline." At college he showed an interest in German thought and literature, Wagnerian music, and in modern philosophical trends, but took no specific courses which related to the subject of immigration. After attending Harvard Law School, he practised his profession for a time, but eventually made the cause of restriction his life work. The origin of Hall's mania about aliens remained elusive. He was, however, like Henry Adams and Barrett Wendell, an unstable New Englander, contemplative, subject to depressions;[46] he became violent in his prejudices and later seized upon ideas whose abnormality extended beyond any inculcation at Harvard.

The young men reflected their elders' insecurity in the nation of their ancestors, with an important difference. Four generations removed from New England's prime, these Brahmins entered adulthood in the 1890's with the conviction that neither the economic nor the social promises of democracy seemed to work in the divided society of rich and poor, native and foreigner, educated and illiterate, Anglo-Saxon and scum of Europe. With their parents' emotion and their professors' ideology, youths like Warren, Ward, and Hall could easily ignore the old belief that immigration was materially advantageous to the United States; and even if it were, these students of Norton would have rejected vulgar financial considerations. As observers of the Mugwumps, the new generation saw that neither civil service reform nor educational activities in the community had solved the terrible problems which New Englanders had lived with since the Civil War. Mindful of the census, they thought their elders' fight for good citizenship against the low elements was futile if the Anglo-Saxon Americans continued to die out. The heirs of the independent voter tradition answered Henry Cabot Lodge's exhortation to use their liberal education in the service of their country, not as petty critics but as positive doers. These three Harvardians of the class of 1889 resolved to save the nation by preventing any further inroads upon Anglo-Saxon America by strangers. With the help of Warren and Hall, Ward rounded up a few congenial classmates, who agreed that the gravity of the social problem demanded organized action. In the spring of 1894, a handful of Brahmin young people formed a committee which became the Immigration Restriction League of Boston.[47]

CHAPTER VI

Early Years
of the League

If to this particular nation there has been given the development
of a certain part of God's earth for universal purposes; if the world
is going to be richer for the development of a larger type of manhood here, then for the world's sake, for the sake of every nation
that would pour in upon that which would disturb that development, we have a right to stand guard over it.

—Phillips Brooks[1]

In the beginning, the founders of the Immigration Restriction
League sought the advice and encouragement of their seniors in the
Boston community. The response was sympathetic, yet discreet.
John Murray Forbes, the eminent railroad capitalist, welcomed the
project with strictly private enthusiasm. "The issue," was real and
"must soon dwarf all other political questions." Forbes envisaged
a "struggle" to keep "our voting power and our reserves of public
land out of the reach, for twenty years at least, of the hordes of half-
educated and wholly unreliable foreigners now bribed to migrate here,
who can under our present system be dumped down on us annually."
However, "in these panicky times" he would contribute only confi-
dentially to the League treasury. Forbes wanted to "avoid even the
appearance of leading" the cause.[2]

Other distinguished citizens were also cautious. Elijah A. Morse
of the House of Representatives gave a silent nod of approval but
claimed that he could "do more . . . from the outside" than as a

member. In turn, Colonel Henry Lee of Lee, Higginson and Co., Francis A. Walker, still president of the Massachusetts Institute of Technology, and George Edmunds, formerly Senator from Vermont, begged off from serving as president of the new organization.[3] These advocates of immigration restriction not only were sensitive to the general unpopularity of the idea, but were too busy to carry the responsibility of pushing this radical movement.

After considerable canvassing and rejection, the young organizers persuaded John Fiske to accept the presidency. Although he hated practical details of club work, for the next few years he led these New England restrictionists. Other solid citizens became vice-presidents: Henry Lee, Robert Treat Paine, the Honorable Henry Parkman, and the Honorable Leverett Saltonstall lent the prestige of their names. George S. Hale, a prominent corporation lawyer interested in local charities, followed their lead, and Samuel B. Capen represented the Municipal League of Boston. George F. Edmunds also agreed to be a vice-president for the League's task was "of the utmost importance to the welfare of the country." Most fittingly, Nathaniel S. Shaler and Richmond Mayo Smith, who had rationalized the idea of restriction for the young, joined the roster of backers.[4] In these initial years, the Immigration Restriction League was the mouthpiece of older New Englanders who had wearied of the burdens of humanitarianism.

But reform-minded Brahmins of the generation coming of age were the conscious agitators and performed the work of the executive committee. In addition to the three founders—Robert DeC. Ward, Prescott F. Hall, and Charles Warren—the active participants included Joseph Lee, the son of Henry Lee, Robert Treat Paine, Jr., the son of Robert Treat Paine, John Farwell Moors, Alpheus S. Hardy, James A. Bailey, Jr., G. Loring Briggs, and Frank A. Farnham. Although the core of the group, schooled at Harvard College, belonged to the Mugwump-Democrat-Free Trader element of the community, as a whole by 1896 the membership of 670 was politically heterogeneous.[5]

The small clan had a mission to save the nation from foreign infiltration, but in the discharge of their duty they intended to be free from racial prejudices. Immigrants, wrote Robert DeC. Ward, should not be excluded "on the ground of race, religion or creed." In fact, the League showed its broad-mindedness by including a Catholic on the executive committee, Thomas Ring of the St. Vincent de Paul Society; and when the notorious American Protective Association precipitated the anti-Romanist riot of 1895, the executive committee protested against Catholic persecution. Identified with generations who had rejected nativist baiting in the 1850's and in the 1880's, the League at the start did not condone crude group bigotry. Although hesitant heirs of the mid-nineteenth-century democratic thought, the young leaders began with the assumption that the majority of the American people would never accept the idea of restriction, if it was "based simply on the desire to keep America for the Americans."[6]

The immediate job before the League was to rouse indifferent thinking people to the present dangers of free immigration. It was not the League's "object . . . to advocate the exclusion of laborers or other immigrants of such character and standards as fit them to become citizens." But somehow "public opinion" must be made to recognize "the necessity of a further exclusion of elements undesirable for citizenship or injurious to our national character."[7]

By 1895, the League had prepared a variety of articles, pamphlets, and letters, designed to attract the attention of newspaper editors, lawyers, and ministers. In addition, the executive committee promoted speeches on immigration before civic, business, and labor organizations. On the one hand, Hall spoke at the Mystic Valley Club and Curtis Guild at the Boston Boot and Shoe Club; Richmond Mayo Smith, Robert DeC. Ward, and Davis R. Dewey debated with W. L. Garrison at the Massachusetts Reform Club. On the other hand, Robert DeC. Ward talked before the Firemen's Protective Union and the Waiters' Alliance. Early the League leaders adopted the strategy of extending their appeal beyond the lethargic upper-class citizens.[8]

For the most part, however, the crusaders at Boston concentrated their efforts upon analogous groups in other parts of the country. Aiming for a national membership, the League cultivated New

Yorkers like Henry Holt, the publisher, and James R. Burnett, a leader in Good Government Clubs; by promoting the interest of such, it hoped to induce the growth of local restrictionist groups in other cities. By November 1894 there were counterparts in New York, Philadelphia, Albany, San Francisco, Chicago, Milwaukee, and Brooklyn, and in the states of Alabama and Montana. To coordinate the activities of these autonomous clubs, the executive committee elected Prescott F. Hall as General Secretary of the Association of Immigration Restriction Leagues.[9]

Some of these branches depended upon the Boston League for their impetus. In Milwaukee a few Harvard alumni, like Francis Keene (class of 1880) and Wyman K. Flint (class of 1891) galvanized restrictionist sentiment among friends who enjoyed their New England ties of blood and education. When John Fiske visited the group in 1895 he was pleased with the esprit at lunch, "a surprise party of eight chaps to talk about immigration restriction. . . Jolly party, beer and fun." Looking east, the Milwaukee League issued circulars which echoed those of the parent organization. St. Louis also proved receptive: there an active New England Society had fostered pride in the descendants of native pioneers. At Washington University two prominent New England Teutonists, Fiske and Hosmer, had intensified the Yankee identification. In 1895, the Western Restriction League of St. Louis announced its association with the Boston group. On the other hand, a Brooklyn League began independently in 1893, under the direction of Edward C. Brennan, a young Republican, who wanted to protect local labor unions.[10] More important, the Brahmin clique of restrictionists watched over these budding outposts, whether or not they were closely related; all received pamphlets and circulars from Boston and constituted channels by which to spread the intellectual rationale for restriction over the United States.

Very much in the pattern of teaching at Harvard College, the executive committee planned an educational program for the American public. One of the League's first publications was a bibliography of articles which presented views for and against the prevailing immigration policy; at the same time, however, an editorial comment indicated that Mayo Smith's *Emigration and Immigration* was the best interpretation of the subject. Like a debating club, the League coterie developed manifold arguments for restriction without emphasizing their relative importance.[11] Despite this semi-conscious ambiguity, which enabled the League to approach a wider audience, the leaders themselves valued the economic, social, and intellectual aspects of the immigration question differently.

The economic import had many ramifications for these restrictionist intellectuals, most of whose families had already wrested solid fortunes from the nation's resources. The young men were contemptuous of industrial profiteering. With particular animosity toward steamship companies and railroads, which transported immigrants, the group protested repeatedly in the next twenty-five years that "this Pipe Line Immigration" (Francis Walker's phrase) had made a business of bringing the worst members of the European community to American shores. Thus, unlike earlier immigrants, the present newcomers did not come of their own free will but were passively conveyed here, the victims of an artificial selection.[12]

Such New Englanders also liked to claim that immigration had not created economic and social mobility for the native working classes. Rather, as Walker and Mayo Smith had contended, the Irish had eliminated the Yankee girls from the local factories only to be pushed out themselves by the French Canadians who, in turn, would now be displaced by still lower groups. Immigration would remain a problem, the League foresaw, until organized labor recognized its stake in the issue. Anxiously the executive committee pursued the unions and tactfully explained that "the better class" of employees was still desirable. Only "the horde of illiterate, unskilled laborers ... almost entirely in the cities of the Atlantic States" was "a menace to the labor as well as the national interests."[13] The appeal to the skilled workers was ingeniously snobbish, for it merged their interests with those of the middle and upper classes in the fight for restriction.

On the same basis the League tried to make capital out of the great depression of 1893, which had brought a slackening in emigration to America. But the restrictionists feared lest the return of prosperity renew the old cycle of aliens swarming across the Atlantic. In any case, some immigrants still came and, by the League's standard, they were inferior to native workers. In 1895, the Report of the Commission on Unemployment in Massachusetts provided useful ammunition. Headed by Davis R. Dewey, a Johns Hopkins Ph.D. and protégé of Francis A. Walker at the Massachusetts Institute of Technology, the Commission attributed unemployment "in a considerable measure . . . to ill-responsible, ill-advised and ill-adapted immigration."[14] With this document in hand, the League pressed all the more firmly for speedy restrictionist legislation in the conducive atmosphere of economic depression.

Despite their emphasis on unemployment, the League youths refused to exploit it by relating the restriction of immigration to the end of free lands in the West. Yet some restrictionists had already questioned the wisdom of allowing the foreign-born to share in the remaining public lands. Richmond Mayo Smith who stated early in 1888 that there was plenty of available land, only a few months later changed his mind. Like Henry Cabot Lodge, he asked why the public lands should be divided "among strangers"; they should be kept as a safety valve for Americans and their descendants. In 1892, Francis A. Walker declared that a shortage of land was a new destructive condition in the American economy. "No longer can a continent of free virgin lands avert from us the social struggle which the old world has known so long and so painfully." Since the newcomers could not afford to buy farms from the homesteaders at prices determined by the agricultural value of the land, the deteriorating existence of the immigrants in the cities would pose a constant problem. Both Smith and Walker complained that the foreign-born would no longer undergo the cleansing experience of Americanization upon the Western frontier.[15]

By contrast, the passing of the frontier seemed a specious consideration to the League. Since most foreigners of "the objectionable races" gathered in the Eastern cities instead of going west, immigration was really a sectional curse. Moreover, economic specialists differed in their predictions as to when all the public lands would be used up. Sweeping aside the whole controversy, Prescott F. Hall ignored the matter of available acreage in the United States. "If immigrants be undesirable, the fact that there is land enough for many times the population . . . would be generally conceded to be an inadequate reason for admitting them."[16]

The same premise lay behind his response to the teasing criticism of protectionists. For the League, free trade and free immigration were mutually exclusive spheres of thought. Hall pointed out that there was "all the difference in the world between a bale of foreign goods and a batch of foreign people." At least "the goods" were "clean" and "inert." But foreigners came in "removed as far from American citizenship in their political and social habits as the language they speak." Interbreeding "with the native American stock or the earlier and better immigrants who came over before 1880," the newcomers could only "dilute the Yankee gumption . . . pollute the Yankee blood." How could real Americans look with complacency upon such people becoming the mothers and fathers of the next generation?[17] Neither exhausted lands nor tariff rates, but the future of their own group was the prime object moving young New England restrictionists to action in the 1890's. The League's conception of the immigration peril was not a matter of economics.

But just as economic conditions sometimes served the aims of the League, other startling social phenomena seemed to dramatize expediently the need for restriction. When irate Southerners lynched eleven Italians awaiting trial in a New Orleans prison in 1891, New Englanders joined others in blaming the victims. Although Lodge denied that the killing involved any "race feeling," less politic Bostonians openly impugned these Italians as members of the Mafia, a secret society which embodied "two thousand years of Southern Italian and Sicilian civilization." Phillips Brooks suggested that "the fiery folk" learn to behave or else not come to America "to murder and be murdered." To the League's satisfaction, this episode, like the earlier bomb-throwing in Chicago and the riots in the Pennsylvania coal mines, encouraged the impression of the recklessness of foreigners to the detriment of all immigrants.[18]

Nevertheless, educated New Englanders knew well that the mass of immigrant stocks despised "the Molly Maguires in Pennsylvania, the Anarchists in Chicago, the Mafia in New Orleans, and . . . a similar organization among some of the Poles," and took no part in them. Although the League sought public attention in 1894 by urging the deportation of the English "Anarchist Mowbray," Prescott Hall admitted that the danger to the state did not come from "the few educated cranks" among the foreign-born. Restrictionists welcomed flagrant acts of violence and radical activities among immigrants; as Albert Shaw, the editor of the *American Review of Reviews* suggested, "un-American" outbursts should awaken the natives who consented "to spoil their breed of pedigree stock by allowing the introduction of the refuse of the murder-breed of Southern Europe." In this spirit the League played up the distress and alarm which occasional riots inspired.[19]

But since large blocs of immigrants predominated among the victims of the urban slums, the very passivity of the foreign masses seemed to justify a restrictive policy even more tellingly than the violence of a few aliens. The directors of the League, acquainted with the valuable weapon of statistics, focused upon the behavior of the foreign-born as shown by the Massachusetts Bureau of Statistics of Labor, the Reports of the Superintendent of Immigration, and other agencies. Ferreting out quantitative evidence of crime, delinquency, pauperism, and illiteracy among the newcomers, the Brahmin reformers isolated these statistics cogently. For example, the League assumed that illiteracy would be permanent because of the foreign-born, and ignored Horace Wadlin's conclusive demonstration that "neither native, foreign born, nor aggregate illiteracy" was "increasing in Massachusetts so fast as her population."[20]

With respect for scientific verification, members of the executive committee went to Ellis Island in 1895 to examine six shiploads of immigrants, which included Germans, Bohemians, Finns, Russians, Hungarians, Croats, and Ruthenians, one thousand human beings in all. Applying a reading and writing test to them, the New England interviewers found a "close connection between illiteracy and general undesirability" of the newcomers. According to the committee's sampling, the requirement of a literacy test would limit the

numbers admitted to the United States from the southern and eastern countries of Europe. Actually the total emigration from these
sources had decreased sharply in these years and even as late as 1900
the majority still came from the northern and western countries. But
the inferiority of the "new" immigrants was already the main theme
of the restrictionists.[21]

From the first pamphlet in 1894 the League emphasized that the
predominant nationalities in the migrations of peoples to America
had changed for the worse. Most willingly these disillusioned New
Englanders clung to Walker's distinction between "old" and "new"
immigrants. Had not the waning of the Brahmins come with the
admission first of the Irish, then of the French Canadians, who had
discouraged the old Yankee stock from reproducing itself at the
former high rate? As the first small wave of southeastern Europeans
broke over the American shore, Walker's thesis seemed more omi-
nous than ever. Prescott F. Hall observed that, "in proportion as still
lower and more degraded immigrants come, the process applies to a
larger portion of the people already here." To his fellow Americans
he posed the essential question. Did they "want this country to be
peopled by British, German, and Scandinavian stock, historically
free, energetic, progressive, or by Slav, Latin, and Asiatic races, historically down-trodden, atavistic, and stagnant?"[22]

This academic distinction between "old" and "new" ethnic groups
in the United States was an essential ingredient in the restrictionist
formula even when it contradicted experience. As one young man
who had gone to Ellis Island years later recalled, the Ruthenians
were "as nice people as you could desire" but just the same "the
country could not assimilate any more people."[23] The force of the
Walker thesis operated upon Brahmin xenophobia intractably. Instead of connoting the traditional Teutonist pride in the ability of
the English-speaking group to absorb different strains of people,
assimilation now threatened the survival of the old New England
element in the face of invading aliens.

No one understood more shrewdly the ramifications of restrictionism than Henry Cabot Lodge, the main political sponsor of the
League's undertaking in 1894. Lodge was born in 1850, well after

the first waves of Irishmen had transformed provincial Boston into
an industrial, divided community, but as a child he had still felt in
persons and places the remnants of the eighteenth-century society.
The son of a rich China trade merchant, of a long line of old New
Englanders including the extreme Federalist, George Cabot, in
young manhood Lodge was mindful of his heritage. In the 1870's
he looked up with avowed hero worship to Henry Lee, James Russell
Lowell, and Thomas Bailey Aldrich, as symbols of New England's
great tradition. Early he evinced a conservative temperament in
harmony with his background.[24]

After graduating from Harvard in 1872, he became one of the
first candidates for the Ph.D. in history and found in Henry Adams
a new guide and friend. Under this sophisticated mentor, Lodge
experimented dually with the professions of history and politics and,
at the same time, bolstered his personal needs with intellectual props.
Like Adams, he scoffed at the social Anglophilism of the times;
his resistance to the stranglehold of English culture and manners
gave him a continuity with New England leaders of the 1850's that
suited the ambition of the able young Bostonian.[25]

Nevertheless, in marked opposition to this assumed independence
of spirit, Lodge's deeper pride in his English origins expanded in the
Adams seminar on Anglo-Saxon institutions. His Ph.D. thesis on
Anglo-Saxon land law extolled the Teutonic virtues of the English
people with no originality. In England, ". . . the purity of the race,
the isolated condition of the country, and the very slowness and
tenacity of intellect . . . gave a scientific development to the pure
Germanic law hardly to be found elsewhere. Free from the injurious
influences of the Roman and Celtic peoples, the laws and institutions
of the ancient German tribes flourished and waxed strong on the
soil of England." In 1880, Lodge extended this image of Anglo-Saxon
genius in a popular textbook study of the English colonies in America. Later, his politic tributes to the town meeting and the two-party
system appealed to the vanity of his native constituents.[26] In fact,
his interpretation of the United States was permanently colored by
Anglo-Saxon premises.

Like Henry Adams, he was fascinated with the exploits of his ancestors in the unfolding of American history. With more obvious partiality for his forbears, however, Cabot Lodge betrayed his aristocratic predilections in a biography of great-grandfather George Cabot. At Harvard, Lodge criticized his student Edward Channing for debunking their common ancestor, Francis Higginson. Without Adams' skepticism as a tool of scholarship he differed still more in defending the conservative concept of democracy of the Federalists. In the end, Adams suggested to President Eliot that the course in American history could be more fairly offered if both Adams and Lodge gave their separate versions.[27]

Despite these intellectual differences Lodge joined the Adams clique of Independents, intent on providing a reform president to end the corruption of the national government in 1876. While Adams retired from political contests after that fiasco, Lodge became even more serious. Renouncing his short-lived academic career, he became a State Representative in 1879 and soon left the camp of political idealists. Placing party before principle at the Republican Convention of 1884 (which nominated Blaine), Lodge shocked many of his friends deeply; some proper Bostonians never spoke to him again.[28]

Lodge, the traitor of the New England intellectuals in the 1880's, began a slow climb up the political ladder. Determined to be a statesman in a nation which no longer favored Brahmin leadership, after a few setbacks he was elected to the House of Representatives. Seven years later, in 1893, he realized his ambition to be a Senator from Massachusetts. He maintained a dual consciousness as gentleman and politician: he was both the old New Englander par excellence and the elected spokesman of new New Englanders. This divided allegiance created inconsistencies in his service and in his thinking.

Having renounced the Mugwumps, Lodge became a strong protectionist for his state's textile, shoe, and leather interests. In the same years he became a staunch advocate of immigration restriction. In 1898, he argued that the cotton textile industries of New England had not advanced with the general prosperity of the country. Threatened by Southern competition, New England needed protection because of the wage differential. He inferred that labor was not cheap enough in Yankee factories despite the migration of foreigners. Therefore, regarding the subject of immigration, he could safely ignore the importance of the alien labor market to the economic well-being of his section. By pressing the validity of a high tariff to support the businessman, Lodge could more consistently seek immigration restriction to shield the wage earner. And, to insure prosperity, Lodge probably agreed with Governor Greenhalge's statement that at present Massachusetts did "not appear" to need further immigration.[29]

But for all his eloquent praise of the American businessman on the floor of the Senate in 1894, Lodge spoke in typical New England Independent accents before the Massachusetts Republican State Convention in 1896. The question of immigration was "of greater importance to the future of this country than either tariff or currency." He would not "be deterred from dealing with it because . . . the capitalist who is building a railroad cannot get his labor as cheaply as if the gates were not shut." Immigration was "not a money question"; it involved much more: both "the quality of American citizenship and the wages of American labor." Like most latter-day Brahmins, Lodge had no sympathy for the nation's plutocrats; on immigration he did not respect their preference.[30] Essentially, he spoke from the heart when he set out to push the unpopular cause of restriction with the Republican Party.

From the late 1880's, he, like many Brahmins, was haunted by the instability and restlessness of democratic society. In a plea for true Americanism, Lodge described the American idea as "a free church in a free state, and a free and unsectarian public school in every ward and in every village, with its doors wide open to the children of all races and of every creed." Deriding "any political divisions resting on race and religion," he condemned the attempts "to divide our people according to origin or extraction."[31] Yet Lodge's protest had a confused, forced quality, because he was deeply troubled by the diversity of the American people which had posited parochial schools, votes of foreigners, and loyalties to the Old World.

Even though he revered the past, the political and social ideals of the 1840's seemed anachronistic. The study of history and science demonstrated "ineradicable differences between the races of man." Speaking for his generation, Cabot Lodge "questioned the theory that opportunity was equivalent to capacity." He did not believe "that a people totally ignorant or to whom freedom and self-government were unknown could carry on successfully the complex machinery of constitutional and representative government which it had cost the English-speaking peoples centuries of effort and training to bring forth."[32]

In the last years of the decade, Lodge ignored his former welcome to European immigrants. In 1888, he singled out the pauper, the criminal, the diseased, the vicious, the anarchist, the communist, and the polygamist (all of whom the nation was ready to exclude), and he added ambiguously that "the general flow of immigration should be wisely and judiciously checked." By 1891, he spoke of extending the restrictions to the "new" immigrants "from races most alien to the body of the American people"; for this purpose, Representative Lodge introduced a bill which included a literacy test to exclude those who could not read and write their own language. Lodge who, three years before, had wished to appear impervious to the varied ethnic origins of his fellow citizens, now made a study of "The Distribution of Ability in the United States." Defining immigrants as those who arrived after the adoption of the Constitution, Lodge "classified by race and occupation all persons of foreign birth who have gained distinction in this country." The evidence, based upon *Appletons' Cyclopaedia of American Biography,* showed, accordingly, that Great Britain, the major source of emigrants in these decades, had contributed "three-fourths of the ability furnished from outside sources." After this research, Lodge launched further attacks upon the "new" immigrants, and continued to work for the adoption of a literacy requirement.[33]

Finally, on March 16, 1896, Lodge delivered to the Senators an impassioned lecture on the dangers of free immigration. In the best intellectual tradition, he acknowledged there was "no such thing as a race of original purity according to the divisions of ethnical science." But for practical purposes one could speak of "artificial races," like the English-speaking people, the French or the Germans, who had emerged over a long period of time through "climatic influences, wars, migrations, conquests, and industrial development." In the case of English-speaking people he observed that there had been little mixture of blood in England or the United States; and what there was of different elements in the present stock derived from the same Germanic race. With academic plenitude he examined the virtues of the various Teutons and judged their superior qualities to be fixed and determined. Now strangers in their midst threatened the moral quality of this homogeneous people of the United States. To describe the process of ethnic deterioration, Lodge turned to "a disinterested witness of another race"—the French sociologist LeBon —and repeated "if a lower race" mixed "with a higher in sufficient numbers . . . the lower race" would "prevail." Clearly, there was "a limit to the capacity of any race for assimilating and elevating an inferior race."[34] Thus beneath all the complaints made against the times, lay Lodge's real fear: the descendants of the Puritans were doomed in their native land. For him, as for Francis A. Walker, the essence of the immigration problem was racial.

Although the League leaders as Democrats and Independents were part of a political tradition which he had rejected, Lodge was only superficially an anomaly in their company. Sharing the "race-pride" of Brahmin society, he believed the old New Englanders to be a chosen people, who had created special values.[35] Despite his own compromise with the outside America, Lodge still felt that his civilization was on trial. He had a profound satisfaction in seeking restriction; in this cause he believed himself faithful to his superior Puritan ancestors. For him, as for the League he encouraged, restriction in the 1890's was a crusade: the survival of his own kind was a fight for the best people and the best things in American life.

At the same time, Lodge made restriction serve his pragmatic needs in politics. He aimed to impress skilled working classes with the fact that they suffered economic deprivations from the continuous arrivals of foreigners with a lower standard of living. He utilized Teutonist racial theory to discredit the recent immigrant groups in comparison to their predecessors. But the New England Irish, who were most important to Lodge's career, did not qualify technically as Teutons, nor did they stand out as superior immigrants in the experience of Boston Brahmins. Yet, with considerable delicacy Lodge, who had earlier freely insulted the Celtic group, from 1891 upheld the role of the Irish in building the United States. In the eloquent speech of 1896 he pointed out how "the Irish, although of a different race stock originally," had "been closely associated with the English-speaking people for nearly a thousand years. They speak the same language, and during that long period the two races have lived side by side, and to some extent intermarried." A wary cognizance of the ethnic elements in his community influenced Lodge's public interpretations of the Irish for the rest of his life, and in a later period affected his known views of French Canadians and Italians. Yet Lodge, who often did not know which foot to stand on, united his divided loyalties in the crusade for restriction. On its behalf, he appeared both the faithful Brahmin and the friend of American labor.[36]

At first the association with Lodge embarrassed the League because of his political ties; but in time it was admitted privately that his devotion to the immigration problem proved that he was "one of us."[37] They were right. Among such New Englanders—whether Mugwump, Democrat, or Republican—the advocacy of restriction went deeper than differing political and economic opinions. Also, restriction might prove the tool by which to identify the interests of the older immigrant groups with that of the Yankees.

In 1895, after consultation with Lodge, with Assistant Commissioner McSweeney, and various Congressmen, the League drafted a bill which required all European immigrants to show a knowledge of reading and writing for admission to the United States. Cautiously, Lodge and the restrictionists had settled upon the literacy test as the best legislative device to accomplish their ends at the moment. Realizing that Walker's alternative of a ten-dollar head tax upon every immigrant would discriminate against the poor too openly, the executive committee found the test "a simpler, more practical, more effective, more equitable, and more American method of keeping out those immigrants who are undesirable." An educational basis of admission seemed reasonable; the Massachusetts State Constitution already contained such a reading and writing requirement for voting. Moreover, the bill had the strategic usefulness of not discriminating against any group by name, nationality, religion, or race. The passage of a literacy requirement would keep out "people we wish to exclude" and add another category "to the excluded classes" in immigration legislation.[38] It would slow down the migrations to America and, as a neutral measure, operating fortuitously, would appear devoid of racial bias.

In another respect, the legislation, far from neutral, was all too transparent. The Senior Senator from Massachusetts, George F. Hoar, wanted to add an amendment giving the Secretary of State general power to admit immigrants seeking asylum from political oppression or from war, but his junior, Henry Cabot Lodge, suppressed this humanitarian proposal.[39]

In 1895, Lodge sponsored the literacy bill in the United States Senate; Representative Samuel McCall of Massachusetts backed it in the House. Sympathetic New Englanders supported their Senator publicly in 1896: Prescott F. Hall, Robert DeC. Ward, John F. Moors, and Davis R. Dewey went to Washington to testify at a hearing of the House Committee, bringing letters of approbation from Francis A. Walker, Henry Lee, Samuel B. Capen, James R. Dunbar, John R. Leeson, and other distinguished Bostonians. At home local newspapers printed Fiske's brief statement that the literacy test could not "possibly exclude any immigrants whom it is desirable to have in the United States." Albert Bushnell Hart approved the legislation: "the republic" was "entitled to protect itself against enemies to its welfare, whether they" came "in the steerage of a passenger ship or in the gundeck of a war ship."[40] After the strenuous efforts of Lodge and McCall, the bill passed both houses, only to be vetoed in March 1897 by the President.

Grover Cleveland recognized the implicit intentions of the bill. He observed that its supporters had not demanded "further restriction of immigration on the ground that an excess of population" overcrowded "our land." Rather they had claimed that "the quality of recent immigration" was "undesirable." To this opinion the President rejoined, "the time is quite within recent memory when the same thing was said of immigrants who, with their descendants . . . now numbered among our best citizens."[41] Analyzing the allegations of Boston's Immigration Restriction League, he denied its racial distinctions between the old and new Americans.

Undiscouraged by Cleveland's veto, the restrictionists were hard at work again in January 1898. At Lodge's request, the League prepared two notices: one pointing out the interest of the American Federation of Labor in the matter; the other reminding Republicans of their commitment in the 1896 party platform. On January 17, 1898, the Senate passed the literacy bill only to have it lie on the Speaker's table in the House of Representatives for many months. The Spanish-American War had intervened from April to July. When, in December, the House still refused to consider the literacy bill because it was occupied with "colonial questions arising out of the Spanish War," the League's first period of political endeavor abruptly came to a close.[42]

The cause had not yet interested most Americans, although an articulate minority of nativist societies and some labor unions sympathized. The proposal to stay the European migrations to the United States was radical, and the Brahmins, like the intellectual advocates in the universities, were on the defensive. Increasingly, during years of economic depression and industrial unrest, they succeeded in gaining the attention of the Republican Party and reaching a nation-wide public through newspapers. But with the advent of war, the Brahmin crusade receded from public attention. The return of prosperity, the excitement of war, and new xenophobic outlets diverted the nation from internal tensions.[43]

In 1899 it became obvious that the League could accomplish "only educational work" for the moment; and the executive committee retired from its official activities, to be quiescent but undaunted until 1901. Prescott Hall, its most ardent spokesman, did not doubt that the tide of sentiment for restriction had only temporarily ebbed.[44]

The aftermath of the Spanish-American War evoked other social protests in New England. Following the lead of Charles W. Eliot and Charles Eliot Norton, most Brahmins had resisted the war as an unwarranted military embroilment in the affairs of the world. War's end confirmed the Mugwumps' worst fears when the United States proceeded to annex the Philippine Islands. The majority of Americans sanctioned this demonstration of manifest destiny, but unofficial warfare against the Filipinos in order to "civilize" them was too shocking. An anti-expansionist surge swept all groups, irrespective of political, economic, or religious affiliations; this anti-imperialist protest found leadership in Boston. Many restrictionists—Robert DeC. Ward, Joseph Lee, Robert Treat Paine, Jr., Samuel McCall, Davis R. Dewey, James R. Dunbar, and John Murray Forbes, wrote letters attacking American imperialism.[45] New Englanders who, since the Civil War, had denounced the influence of finance upon the federal government and had opposed Northern exploitation of the South on the same grounds, again denied the sacrifice of democratic principles to the spoils of economic gain.

The anti-expansionists claimed that the United States' role of conqueror in the Philippines contradicted the political principles upon which the democracy was founded. Turning to his inherited beliefs, Charles Francis Adams, Jr. stated in Jeffersonian phrases, "all men" were "created equal before the law as before the Lord; and that, whether European, American, Asiatic or African, were endowed with an inalienable right to life, liberty and the pursuit of happiness." On the other hand, the imperialists argued that the Filipino was "by inheritance servile, treacherous, possessed of low cunning, and entirely devoid of the sturdy manhood of the Anglo-Saxon." Lodge, again a political enemy, pointed out that the Asiatics were not fit for democratic self-government, because one could "not change race tendencies in a moment." Hailing the republican institutions developed by his own English-speaking people, Lodge excluded the Filipinos from those to whom "the free consent of the governed" should apply. When the anti-imperialists expressed their unwillingness to admit thousands of Asiatics to Anglo-Saxon America, Lodge answered baldly that the Filipinos were not being annexed to the United States, had never sought to emigrate here in the past, and furthermore were not welcome.[46] Significantly, both in his advocacy of immigration restriction and in his avowal of imperialism Lodge spoke in the racist accents of the future.

Few New England restrictionists understood that the idea of equal political and social opportunity for different peoples and groups might be at stake in the immigration policy as it was in the question of imperialism. The sociologist, William Graham Sumner of Yale University, was unique in correlating the problems. Anti-imperialist and anti-restrictionist, Sumner knew that the "disposition to decide offhand that some people are not fit for liberty and self-government . . . gives relative truth to the doctrine that all men are equal." Yet Americans "elevated it into an absolute doctrine as part of the theory of our social and political fabric" although "it . . . stood in glaring contradiction to the facts about Indians and negroes, and to our legislation about Chinamen. In its absolute form it must, of course, apply to Kanakas, Malays, Tagals, and Chinese just as much as to Yankees, Germans and Irish."[47] Restriction and imperialism alike marked the increasing reluctance to accept the consequences of the democratic concept of equality when it applied to foreigners at home and abroad.

New England partisans automatically responded to the anti-imperialist appeal to eighteenth-century principles. But the slogans of 1776 had personal validity for few who had been increasingly influenced by the social cleavages in New England since the 1850's. The dearth of propaganda for the anti-expansionist cause (despite the many writers it included) emphasized its unreality. Thomas Bailey Aldrich who had expressed his feelings on immigration with vitriolic eloquence, "wrote no prose or poetry to show that he hated expansion."[48] For New Englanders, anti-imperialism was a last tribute to pre-Civil War ideals, a futile cry against the new political and economic role of the United States. In 1901 and 1902, after successive defeats, it began to disappear.

But the movement for restriction was soundly rooted in the skepticism of the latter-day Brahmins toward contemporary America. In the twentieth century, as others adopted this view, immigration restriction would become a powerful intellectual force, destined to change a basic tradition of the United States.

CHAPTER VII

The League at High Tide

In forming a race of unknown value, there is being sacrificed a race of acknowledged superiority in originality and enterprise.
—Frederick Bushée[1]

The sponsors of the League resumed active operation in 1901, more than ever convinced that their organization was "a body entrusted with the carrying on of agitation" until the eventual success should come. Although in public journals they still claimed that their only purpose was to improve and to regulate immigration, John Fiske acknowledged to a humanitarian critic at home that the limitations of the literacy test were "far from expressing the feeling of the Immigration Restriction League in this matter." The conception of the crusade deepened in the first decade of the twentieth century and its original champions found themselves in strange intellectual positions not always reconcilable with their inherited principles. When the canvas of restrictionist intentions was fully painted, its racial cast eradicated the humanitarian ideal to which Brahmins were still committed in the 1890's.[2]

The League not only maintained the official backing of highly respected public leaders but also gained new supporters throughout the nation. Upon Fiske's resignation of the titular presidency in 1899, the executive committee appointed one of their own generation, John Farwell Moors, a philanthropic investment banker, to be the official head. The core of real workers continued to be Prescott F. Hall and Robert DeC. Ward, seconded by Joseph Lee and Richards M. Bradley. The vice-presidents included Henry Holt of New York, the publisher and good friend of Henry Adams, John Fiske, and Francis A. Walker; Owen Wister of Philadelphia, the popular novelist; Franklin MacVeagh of Chicago, a public-spirited business man, soon active in the National Civic Federation; James B. Reynolds, a lawyer and student of sociology, prominent in the university settlement movement in New York during the 1890's; J. Hampden Robb, a retired banker whose wife was a Bostonian; and Franklin H. Giddings, a sociologist at Columbia University in place of the deceased Richmond Mayo Smith. These men increased the League's national status.[3]

By 1913 the League was better known. In Boston, Henry Lee Higginson, the sponsor of the Boston Symphony Orchestra, and Robert A. Woods, the city's most prominent social worker, added luster. More significant, college presidents and professors in different sections of the country predominated among the vice-presidents on the League's National Committee. These university leaders included: A. Lawrence Lowell, President of Harvard; William DeWitt Hyde, President of Bowdoin College; James T. Young, Director of Wharton School of Finance; Charles F. Thwing, President of Western Reserve; John R. Commons and Edward A. Ross, professors at the University of Wisconsin; Leon C. Marshall, Dean of the University of Chicago; R. E. Blackwell, President of Randolph-Macon; K. G. Matheson, President of Georgia School of Technology; and David Starr Jordan, President of Stanford University.[4]

The use of these names was important in promoting good will for the League but its role in legislative campaigns was now complemented through more professional lobbying. Charles Edgerton, formerly an expert for the United States Industrial Commission, became the League's official representative in Washington, paid to keep abreast of current legislation and to be a middleman between labor unions and congressmen. Edgerton pressed local unions to support the literacy test at the National Convention of American Labor at

New Orleans in 1902. In the same year the League paid Prescott Hall to attend hearings of the House and Senate and in 1905 allocated $500 to him "for overseeing the League's work" generally. James H. Patten became the assistant secretary at a salary of $3,000 a year and, as its main lobbyist for the next twenty-six years, served the League fanatically. With the entrance of Patten, the amateur standing of the League ended.[5]

A pragmatic view of political relationships also altered League policies. The Republican Party platforms in 1896, 1900, and 1902 had more strongly favored a policy of restriction than did those of the Democrats. Although Henry Cabot Lodge had failed to attain the passage of the literacy test in 1902, 1903, and 1904, the Senator had pledged himself anew to "do anything he could to help along the League's efforts." In addition, from 1902 to 1917, he provided the House of Representatives with a rabid lieutenant, his son-in-law Augustus P. Gardner. Less diplomatic than his father-in-law, Gardner denied the restrictionists' usual distinctions regarding aliens and declared that "all immigrants were undesirable, including the English, the Scotch, the Swedes." Although he failed to stop Speaker Joseph Cannon from blocking the literacy test in 1906, the League worked for Gardner's reelection that year. In 1913 Gardner again pressed without success for a more stringent immigration plank in the party platform; and by reciprocal arrangement James H. Patten campaigned for Gardner among the nativist organizations of Massachusetts. These activities on behalf of a Republican politician nullified the earlier non-political base of the League leaders who had started as New England Independents and Democrats.[6]

Another shift from the League's original stands represented a more critical break from inherited Brahmin values, as the League ceased to act in a non-sectarian way. The group which once had opposed anti-Catholic outbursts casually formed an alliance with the Junior Order of Mechanics. This Order, revived from an old Know-Nothing society, feared the economic competition of the foreign-born and the political influence of Catholics. The nativist organization which had favored immigration restriction at the end of the 1880's petitioned Congress in support of the literacy test in

1897. Early in the new century the League developed a quiet entente with the Junior Order. Advised by Prescott Hall in several conferences from 1902 to 1910, the Order founded one immigration restriction league of 1,500 members in Brooklyn, New York, and another of 300 members in Manhattan. By 1909, under the guidance of the Boston restrictionists "entirely," the national committee of the Order guaranteed to spend $5,000 in the cause and to enlist the aid of various auxiliaries like the Daughters of Liberty. Hall occasionally addressed branches of the Order in Cincinnati and in New York, and, with James H. Patten, carried the major responsibility for the League's negotiations with the group.[7]

In its own publications, however, the League never referred to this questionable consorting. Anti-Catholic sentiment was at low ebb at the time the League cultivated relations with ignorant anti-Romanist groups. At home, Brahmin restrictionists never stooped to religious discrimination, but to aid restriction they willingly co-operated with Know-Nothing nativists elsewhere.

The League also departed from the older New England tradition of reform when the restrictionist leaders objected to a proposal intended to mitigate the current urban problems through the planned distribution of immigrants. A project to remove Russian and Polish Jews from New York's East Side to the New England countryside evoked Richards M. Bradley's pamphlet, revealingly entitled *Spreading the Slums*. Constructive programs to utilize the foreign-born in the national economy and to alleviate the areas of congestion would not meet the Brahmins' real complaints and might defeat the League's ultimate goal.[8]

Therefore the plans of railroad magnates and industrialists to relocate immigrants in the New South alarmed the Boston restrictionists. Robert DeC. Ward reminded the educated classes of the South that the importation of such aliens would provide only temporary relief to the economy; soon the natives would face the problems of pauperism and illiteracy which the North was experiencing. Worse still, the South would add "another race problem." Less subtle than Ward, James H. Patten delivered inciting speeches on the preservation of the Anglo-Saxon Teutonist stock. Paraphrasing

Thomas Bailey Aldrich and Francis A. Walker, Patten described
the steerage passengers en route to America:

> The beaten people of beaten races!
> Wretched refuse!

They came,

> . . . to desecrate
> Thy Sabbath and despoil thy rich heritage
> Purchased with so much Anglo-Saxon blood and treasure.

Patten warned that the southeastern Europeans were "kindred or
brownish" races, and they, like the Negro, meant trouble to white
America.[9]

In less than a decade the League had forgotten its condemnation
of religious and racial bias. The Boston group now condoned Know-
Nothingism outside New England and rabble-rousing in the South.
In the same period, the executive committee voted to use the word
"alien" instead of "immigrant" in League publications. With a new
consciousness of the power of propaganda, restrictionists were prepared to camouflage or exploit their antipathies in order to achieve
their single-minded purpose. While Richards M. Bradley undertook
the task of raising occasional sums from sympathetic Brahmins, the
League's mainstay from 1904 was Boston's distinguished civic leader
Joseph Lee whose money came from the banking firm of Lee, Higginson and Company. As a special contribution Lee undertook to
pay Patten's salary year after year. In 1924, the blatant racist Madison Grant extolled the way in which Lee "financed the Immigration
Restriction League throughout the long period of Egyptian night."[10]

At first League leaders tried to obscure the different ethical levels
upon which they operated simultaneously, but soon it became un-
necessary to justify themselves. In 1906 Joseph Lee confessed that
"immigration restriction . . . proceeded partly upon race lines. Some
people, restrictionists and others, hold that such discrimination is
unjust. But is it necessarily so?" Appropriately, at a national conference of social workers dedicated to the uplift of poor immigrants,
he succinctly made race the crux of the issue involved in America's

immigration policy in the twentieth century: did not something de-finable as race make some groups of immigrants and their descend-ants better Americans than others? In the 1900's, Lee and his as-sociates found seemingly scientific affirmation.[11]

When Lee brought the issue into the open, the educated audience whom the League most wanted to reach was also attracted to the same intellectual form of racism. From the time of Lowell, Norton, and the Adamses, through Fiske and Walker, the thinking of old New Englanders had supported the growing belief in Anglo-Saxon superiority; but their personal sentiments were not systematic. At the turn of the century, several academic writers synthesized the earlier diffuse Teutonist thought into a pseudo-scientific ideology of race. These writers were influenced by the League's opinions; in turn, Brahmin restrictionists were reinforced by the scholars' formal presentations.

While League leaders had been students at Harvard in the 1880's, others studying or teaching elsewhere had also pondered the na-tion's growing economic and social problems. Many, starting as economists, resented a system which left workers at the mercy of employers. These scholars, some of whom had studied German gov-ernmental reform, became proponents of a welfare state. Considering the United States' free immigration policy a possible threat to the standard of living of American laborers, the "new" economists had responded positively to Walker's thesis for restriction. Significantly, they accepted not only Walker's economic arguments but also his "racial" condemnation of the existing immigration. From the 1890's to the 1920's social scientists—especially Edward Bemis, Thomas N. Carver, John R. Commons, Davis R. Dewey, Richard Ely, Franklin Giddings, Jeremiah Jenks, William Z. Ripley, Edward A. Ross, and Richmond Mayo Smith—either directly or indirectly gave aid, coun-sel, or moral support to the work of the Immigration Restriction League.

For many generations, most of the social scientists continued to be native-born. Those who were Midwestern or Western undoubtedly brought regional associations and emotions to their consideration of immigration. But among them were many New Englanders and others attached to the area by past or present associations. In 1909, while a professor at Cornell University, Michigan-born Jeremiah Jenks, who had received his Ph.D. from the University of Halle in Germany, stated the "race feeling" of his colleagues. "Most of us," he declared, were "proud . . . of being Anglo-Saxons" and believed that anyone who came "from Great Britain or anybody who was born in New England must be particularly good." Whether bred on the Teutonist theory at home or abroad, young economists, often believing that New England represented the best of American life, became actively interested in the Brahmins' organized campaign for restriction. The very real interaction between the professional social scientists and the Brahmin amateurs proved consequential in the practical world of public opinion which both groups wanted to reach. However much they differed in other beliefs, the economists shared the restrictionists' use of race ideology and aided its development.[12]

Often leaving their sphere of economics to analyze the society of their times, as social scientists, the economists amplified the racial categories which Teutonist historians had earlier described. As emigrants poured in, the professors of economics, sociology, and government directed their attention toward these Europeans. The nation was a unique laboratory for the study of ethnic qualities; never had the superiority of the old stock appeared more evident.

In the 1890's, there was awareness of the scientific limitations of racial studies. Richmond Mayo Smith noted that there was no proof of the physical differences between different peoples. In 1901, Edward A. Ross, though exulting in the image of his countrymen as "the product of the last, most Westerly decanting of the Germanic race," advised his colleagues to guard against their common fallacy —"race . . . the watchword of the vulgar."[13]

At first, with conscious scientific reticence, the social scientists explored the meaning of race. Mayo Smith evolved "a sociological conception." A strong unity of spirit kept "the members of the same organization together," and was "able to absorb strange blood without losing its character," so that certain groups like the Germanic, the Slavonic, and the Celtic peoples had emerged with different institutions, customs, and standards of living. Rationalizing the common sense of ethnic traits, Mayo Smith, through his loose definition of "race," gave elasticity to academic speculations.[14]

Curiosity about ethnic groups led to the scientific study of their Old World origins in William Z. Ripley's *The Races of Europe*. Ripley, who had grown up near Boston, graduated from the Massachusetts Institute of Technology in 1890, and received his Ph.D. at Columbia University in 1893. Based on massive researches of European anthropologists, the book eliminated some of the current misinterpretations in racial studies. Ripley demolished the unscientific use of the term "Aryan race," which European scholars had employed indiscriminately since 1861. To those who used it solely as a philological term, he demonstrated the impossibility of locating the "original centre of Aryan linguistic dispersion," and condemned the "most mischievous commingling of physical anthropology and linguistics."[15]

More pertinent, he denied the correlation of all social, political, and economic ills to racial causes and effects; as a scientist he belittled the restrictionists' accusation that southern Europeans had a racial tendency to huddle together in American cities. In addition, Ripley demonstrated that physical stature and language were poor tests of racial classification.[16]

But although restrained in his judgments, Ripley added to the race concept. While sensing that social and physical environment altered ethnic factors through a complex, dynamic process, he sought to isolate racial phenomena. With the cephalic index as his guide, he elaborated three European types of the Caucasian race—the Teutonic, the Alpine, and the Mediterranean. Ripley did not "assume that these races of ours ever . . . existed in absolute purity or isolation from one another," but he could not help believing in the classifications. The scientist might never discover a "single individual corresponding to our racial type in every detail," still, in his mind's eye, "the perfect type" was "always possible." Although "racial upbuilding and demolition . . . proceeded side by side," physical characteristics were "so persistent" that it was only "natural" to interpret "every possible phase of social life" in racial terms.[17]

Ripley's text was susceptible to xenophobic misuse. Poultney Bigelow, an expatriate New England writer who admired *The Races of
Europe,* suggested to Ripley that they form an English-speaking
society with such worthy individuals as Charles Francis Adams, Jr.,
A. Lawrence Lowell, and Albert Bushnell Hart, "Men Who Speak
Our Language in the fullest sense—that excludes German-Jews and
white-washed Americans generally." As the standard text for social
scientists until World War I, Ripley's study was ambivalent in its
premises and merely descriptive of "races" in its content; yet inevitably, it aided those who pressed the validity of ethnic criteria for
American citizenship.[18]

For all his scholarly balance, Ripley became increasingly vulnerable to the misgivings of many of his professional colleagues. As a
member of the Harvard economics department from 1903, he concentrated his research on railroads, but his personal interest in immigration increased. As an adviser to the Immigration Restriction
League, in 1909, he preferred to advocate restriction on economic
grounds, because he still deemed the data on racial intermixture
"unreliable." But just as emotionally involved as other Yankee social scientists and the League leaders, Ripley asked whether the
Anglo-Saxon element would long survive the stupendous volume
of immigrants in the twentieth century.[19]

This generation of social scientists agreed with Barrett Wendell
that "the imperial democracy" of the United States was "a tremend-
ous fact" in the world at large, but they too experienced "the racial
agony" of "being strangled by invading aliens." The declining
Yankee birth rate weighed heavily on the intellectuals. The newcomers arriving from "the political sinks of Europe" even included
"large numbers of Greeks, Armenians, and Syrians," Ripley noted
in 1908. Would "the near destiny of the Anglo-Saxon" be "race
suicide?" asked Ross. The perplexed observers debated whether
there would be any recognizable American nationality at all in the
future.[20]

At one extreme, a League vice-president from 1900 to 1903, Franklin Giddings, upheld Fiske's Teutonist view that America could

absorb any kind of European.* With less assurance Hart, the Harvard historian, and Carroll Wright, the director of the Massachusetts Bureau of Statistics of Labor, also clung to the notion that their country could transform "the most unpromising foreign-born citizen." These observers still hoped that "English, Teutonic, Celtic, Latin and even Slavic elements might blend in a people stronger and . . . yet more impressionable than any which has yet enjoyed a historic career." And if they did not, Ripley echoed Wendell, perhaps, when the old stock was physically "inundated by the engulfing flood," the ideals of the older civilization might still "illuminate" the way. At the gloomy extreme, however, the League's Joseph Lee envisaged a medieval empire of autonomous groups in which the newer stocks would live side by side with the old American remnant without fusing into a single nationality.[21]

On middle ground stood Richmond Mayo Smith who assessed the new nation as still in the making. Before his death by suicide he was working on a scientific theory of the mixture of races through the analysis of statistics; thereby he expected to learn both the effect of America's foreign-born upon her institutions and the impact of the environment upon the latecomers to the country.

Younger men continued this analysis of the potential caliber of the American people. As active partners in the League during the 1900's and 1910's, John R. Commons, Edward A. Ross, and Thomas Nixon Carver added to the ideology for restriction to which Francis A. Walker, Richmond Mayo Smith, and William Z. Ripley had contributed in the 1880's and 1890's.[22]

John R. Commons was typical of these younger social scientists in his undisciplined use of ethnic criteria. Born in Indiana in 1862, of native stock originating in Vermont on his mother's side and in South Carolina on his father's, Commons described the background of his childhood as a mixture of "Hoosierism, Republicanism, Presby-

---

* Giddings resigned from his vice-presidency of the IRL in 1903; although he favored restriction in general, he disapproved of the literacy test. He believed that "thousands of our immigrants who are illiterate not because of any lack of intelligence, but because of the circumstances in which they have been reared, are likely to be among the sturdiest elements of our future people." Giddings to Hall, January 22, 1903, Immigration Restriction League Papers.

terianism, and Spencerism." A young man in the 1880's, he joined a Henry George club, aided his mother in an anti-saloon drive, and graduated from Oberlin College. Already an inveterate militant reformer, he became a member of Ely's seminar at Johns Hopkins in 1888 and made his first acquaintance with immigrants through charity work at Baltimore. Leaving Johns Hopkins, he taught in several colleges until he became the director of the Bureau of Research in New York City in 1899. There Commons studied immigration closely to determine its effects upon unionism and by 1902 was eager to attack the national policy. In support of the Boston League's bill, Commons appeared at Congressional hearings in 1902, 1903, 1905, 1909, 1911, and 1913 and advised the League's executive committee.[23]

Commons had approached the study of immigration with the goals of organized labor in mind, but he did not confine his arguments for restriction to economics. As a reformer, in good Jeffersonian tradition he sought for each member of the community an equal opportunity to develop his abilities. But democracy became a disguised oligarchy, he observed, unless all classes and races had equal ability as citizens. In orthodox Teutonist fashion, he demonstrated that the American theory of government was the product of "the so-called Anglo-Saxon" race and hence the dilemma of reformers was how to make its institutions and ideals work for "a congeries of races."[24]

Using Ripley's classifications, in *Races and Immigrants in America* Commons contrasted the colonial elements of the American population with the bulk of the present peasant emigrants from Catholic Europe. Although "all the races of the temperate zones" were potentially eligible for "the highest American civilization," the prospect made the author uncomfortable. He remembered Walker's theory of the birth rate and reiterated that "immigration and the competition of inferior races" would destroy the old Yankee stock. The most terrible threat to democracy lay in the extinction of the Teutonic race which could have been transported from the German woods two thousand years ago and in one generation covered "the progress of twenty generations."[25]

Characteristic of his academic group, Commons confessed to less faith than his predecessors in "the educational value of democracy." Sharing the disillusion of the old Bostonians, this Midwestern intellectual judged the forty years of Negro freedom a failure. Similarly, he disapproved of the motley mass of immigrants in Northern cities; they were further witness to the "fearful collapse" of the democratic experiment. The product of an agricultural society, he was so repelled by urban industrial conditions that he could not see past city bosses and class struggles into the lives of immigrants. Like a native New Englander, Commons reported that the foreign-born lacked "the intelligence, manliness, and public spirit" of his forefathers; like the transplanted Southerner, Nathaniel S. Shaler, Commons denied that the immigrants could overcome the obvious handicaps of "heredity and race" even in the American environment. Ignoring solid scholarly criticism of Prescott Hall's openly biased *Immigration and Its Effect Upon the United States,* he regarded the work as the most important contribution to the subject.[26]

Another economist, Edward A. Ross, claimed even more strongly that immigration was "so much more than an economic matter." Born in Illinois in 1866, Ross grew up in Iowa and graduated from Coe College where, as an undergraduate, he resented the immigrants' use of America as a dumping-ground. After a year of graduate work in Germany and a Johns Hopkins Ph.D. in 1891, Ross, because of his radical support of the welfare state, was forced to teach successively at the universities of Indiana, Cornell, Stanford, and Nebraska before settling at the University of Wisconsin.[27]

Like Walker and Mayo Smith, Ross believed that frontier life had nurtured the solid virtues of the native stock. With the disappearance of open land, "a certain decay of character" would inevitably occur. "The fiber of the pioneering breed" could never be in the veins of the "new" immigrant groups. Now few of them could filter "through the industrial mesentery to the remote farming regions" of the West. Superimposed upon this view, the Teutonic myth so fascinated him that (as he confessed forty years later), he was unable to repress "an unconscious prejudice in favor of the Nordic race and Anglo-Saxon civilization so-called." The immigrants from eastern Europe were "the beaten members of beaten breeds." Ten years later his full-length study of ethnic groups, *The Old World in the New*, widely influenced restrictionist sentiment. But, as an old man, Ross admitted the vulnerability of his generation in making "race" the key to social interpretations.[28]

The same scholars were concerned with the economics of immigration. The American standard of living and, beyond it, the physical problems of overpopulation in the entire world led some of them to dream of a society in which births as well as migrations would be controlled. One exponent of a planned community, Thomas Nixon Carver, favored restriction on these grounds; yet even he did not entirely refrain from the ethnic generalizations of his contemporaries. Like Ripley, he was not immune to the racial notions of his era.[29]

Born on a farm in Iowa, Carver traced his ancestry back to a Russian soldier who settled in North Carolina at the end of the Revolutionary War. Despite a lack of formal education, he was accepted at Johns Hopkins in 1891 and thereafter joined the rising economists at Cornell University. Six years of teaching at Oberlin ended with an invitation to Harvard, where he remained. There his sociology course emphasized "national consciousness" as the foundation of the social order, in which divisive tendencies—such as different groups—were undesirable. In an analysis of educational and hereditary factors which determined the quality of race, Carver tried to preserve a neutral tone but could not help revealing that "hereditary characteristics seemed more important." To his credit, he cautioned against the intellectual fashion of defining races as "superior and inferior" according to the standards of one's own civilization.[30]

Nevertheless he was susceptible to "the natural antipathy" dividing America's ethnic groups. Earlier, in 1893, repeating the conclusions of Walker and Mayo Smith, Carver had noted that native workingmen were degraded by association with recent immigrants, whose "habits of life" were "utterly at variance with American standards of decency." Ten years later at Harvard, he described "the injurious effect" upon the Corn Belt created by the foreign-born; these "peasant-minded" aliens were interested, "aside from the instinct of acquisition," solely in "hunger, thirst and sex." And although Carver often emphasized the economic justifications of restriction, his academic approach to the American economy was so insular that he regarded the consideration of other peoples, either on the economic or the social level, as merely sentimental. While he never made his position entirely clear on the racist logic of the restriction movement, once he went so far as to define "the real question" as "whether we are to continue to have an American commonwealth in spirit as well as form, or whether we are to have a south European state." In 1903, Carver became an adviser to the Immigration Restriction League; in 1910, he joined the intimate circle of the executive committee and was still active in the 1930's.[31]

For all these social scientists, whatever their rational emphasis, immigration became a matter of the survival of the Anglo-Saxon stock. Ripley and Carver found economic defense of restriction more scientific, yet both were caught in the web of racist thinking and its corollaries. And, on an emotional level, although consciously rejecting their Puritanic upbringing, these native intellectuals still felt that cities and their dwellers were peculiarly susceptible to evil. Nostalgic for an agricultural way of life, Commons, Ross, Carver, and others agreed that farmers made the best Americans; the identification of social ills with urban living was as natural to the sociologists as to the sponsors of the Immigration Restriction League. The non-Teutonic aliens, born too late for the rural frontiers, were, in their judgment, hopelessly inferior to the Yankees.

These professors, as much as Brahmins, questioned the extension of democratic principles and faced a dilemma as reformers. Should "the doctrine of inborn rights apply only to the men of Teutonic race?" Hart noted that "the principle that the joys of freedom rightfully belong to a chosen race is like the old-fashioned doctrine of election, very comfortable to the elect. On the other hand . . . certain races have struck out for themselves a high degree of individual liberty, combined with efficient government; and they ought not to lose that birthright by admitting to their communion those who cannot appreciate it." Ironically, those who wanted to equalize social and economic opportunities for their countrymen, applied the ideal of equality only to a people "tolerably homogeneous," who had political education "as in the rural districts and smaller cities of the Northern States." Thus, intellectual reformers limited their confidence in the still growing, plastic American nationality. The ability to conform then became the Anglo-Saxon yardstick by which newcomers were to be judged.[32]

While the social scientists lectured and wrote disturbing books on the racial composition of the American people, New England Brahmins tried to resolve the local social problems which urbanism continued to impose and which immigration continued to increase. Since the 1880's young Bostonians, like other educated citizens, had responded to calls from pulpits and classrooms to help the underprivileged industrial masses in college settlements, charity organizations, and trade union centers. Freshly schooled in the generalizations of the social scientists, the pioneer practitioners of these developing forms of social service were in varying contact with the foreign-born. Consciously and unconsciously the crystallization of racial thought influenced Brahmins and other Yankees who contributed materially or worked directly with the poor. An intimate though not inevitable connection between the aims of social service and the cause of restriction often emerged.

Especially in Boston, philanthropy easily fused with restriction becauses proper New Englanders administered and controlled most communal projects. Men like Joseph Lee, John Farwell Moors, Robert Treat Paine, Jr., and others whose pocketbooks provided for the social needs of the city, were either active in the Immigration Restriction League or at least sympathetic toward it. Although proud of their ancestral tradition of benevolence, latter-day Brahmins were removed from it; not only did they disapprove of the self-righteous *noblesse oblige* of their elders, but they lacked the older generations' strong certainty that the poor could be transformed. A new conception of charity strengthened their sense of burden and intensified their conflict of ideals.

Coinciding with the "new" immigration from southeastern Europe, American philanthropy had developed efficient methods of coordinating the activities of the various charitable agencies in the large cities. England had confronted similar problems of industrialization a little earlier and Americans now adopted English solutions and ideas. The basic faith was the need to be "scientific" in assisting the underprivileged. Material aid and comfort became secondary as social workers helped the poor to help themselves. On the positive side, the new "science" aimed to encourage human independence and to prevent through legislation the conditions which made for urban poverty and corruption. It also hoped to end the practice of smug, personal donations. Negatively, the same principle, however effective in improving methods of social service, limited the role of the helpers to one of detachment. Reliance upon scientific handling of dependents brought about "a certain heartlessness of manner" and general distrust of "the human impulse," leading social workers observed.[33]

Furthermore, this new charities movement reinforced the Brahmin attitudes toward immigration. They now assumed that the social problems of their forbears had been of a different character. According to Joseph Lee, under the factory system of the 1840's, education was the only "charity" needed by the workers, all Yankee girls. By contrast, the present needy were "the squalid imported population." Mrs. James T. Fields, widow of the Boston publisher, was "repelled by the sad issue of our careless hospitality" to "the children of pauperized Europe." Adopting English fears of a chronic poor class, Brahmins ignored the facts of American social and economic mobility: the volume of immigration became an argument aimed at the ultimate rejection of impoverished aliens. A young social worker, who learned her art as a visitor for the Boston Associated Charities, reflected in 1899 the belief of the directors and administrators that the "immigration laws . . . allowed many to come to America for whom there is no place, and charity has kept them alive here," thus "forcing down the standard of living among our poor, and complicating the problem incalculably at every turn." Thus it was easy to claim that unrestricted immigration counteracted the strenuous human efforts involved in the natives' educational and charitable works.[34]

Joseph Lee's thoughts and interests illustrated how the concept of scientific charity reacted upon other Brahmin assumptions, further clouding understanding of the "new" immigrants. Lee, related to Cabots, Jacksons, and Higginsons, was the son of Henry Lee the banker. The father was an aristocrat, famous for his impeccable clothes and frank in his distaste for immigrants. The son, styling himself a democrat, disclaimed all "false ideals of caste," and disapproved of ostentatious dress and expenditure. Nevertheless, he once defined the greatest contribution of the English as "the ideal of the gentleman," and while seeking to expand the horizons of the poor, was as conscious of his past as a Henry Adams, and just as true to the image of an aristocratic father.[35]

Born in 1862, Joseph Lee grew up in the small country town of Brookline, Massachusetts, and knew all the delights of dancing, coasting, sailing, fishing, skating, and picnicking. As an adult, these memories connoted more than physical exercise: they became symbolic of the solidarity of the society into which he had been born and of the superiority of a rural way of life for children. On the day that Lee saw two boys arrested for coasting on Beacon Hill, he decided to remedy the fact, for lads must play, he insisted. Cities had destroyed their birthright, and Lee began a pioneer experiment in the 1890's to restore recreation to the underprivileged children of Boston. Later known as the Father of American Playgrounds, this son of the Puritans conceptualized the idea of play. It meant more than mere enjoyment; as in other contexts, concern for the future quality of the race underlay his theories of recreation.[36]

Like Henry and Brooks Adams, Lee was nostalgic for a preindustrial life where man hunted, fished, and fought; he felt anxiety lest Americans become effete with the disappearance of soldierly virtues. Lee not only had the keen desire to provide children with ample space for their physical activities, but wanted to ensure the preservation of man's natural instincts.[37]

Recreation would not only test the physical strength of the population, but, equally important, would release the imagination now stultified by scientific efficiency. He believed that only England's playing fields still fashioned citizens of heroic character comparable to the ancient Greeks, Romans, and Hebrews or the Renaissance Italians. By contrast, in America, literature and other creative arts were dead; the vulgar yachts and art collections of the newly rich represented "our homesick groping" after lost values. Lee sought a remedy for the maladjustment between human nature and the industrial system through a gospel of play.[38]

By self-definition "a social worker," he devoted himself to the "Athens of America" with magnificent energy and enthusiasm. Whether as a leader in the Good Government Association and the Public School Association or as the founder of the Massachusetts Civic League, he was foremost in the battle to eliminate slums and delinquency, to combat corrupt politics, and to improve the physical and mental health of Boston school children. He was consistently on the side of a better world.[39]

But although Lee helped the offspring of the foreign-born unstintingly, privately he was incapable of believing in them. They were part of the curse which industrialization had placed upon the land of his ancestors. He declared that the old New England culture had represented the real American genius, before it was "distracted in its ideals by the great immigration."[40]

Convinced that Teutonist racial theory was scientifically true, Lee could not imagine the survival of a democracy controlled by the descendants of the newcomers. The foreigners were members of the debased Latin and Slavic races. These, "oppressed in other lands," were downtrodden, he suspected, simply because they lacked the capacity to create good social institutions for themselves.[41]

Both the Puritan sense of the public good and the recent concept of social service governed his program for these aliens. "The idea is not that we, the rich, out of our great goodness and kindness of heart, should help you the poor, but that we . . . insist on being proud . . . of the sort of citizen we produce; for the honor of the family we cannot have rags and drunkenness." He could justify beneficence to the foreign-born on the playgrounds and in the schools but not the sentimental humanitarianism of older reformers. Therefore, the democratic obligation to welcome and elevate them for their own and for the world's sake, which had once pricked New England consciences, disappeared in the abstract rationalizations of a typical restrictionist in the 1900's.[42]

Joseph Lee was the archetype of the socially conscious philanthropist: he planned and worked for the well-being of the immigrants but he was not reconciled to their future in the Boston of his ancestors. Granting "certain fundamentals of human nature," he expected to understand the aliens simply by correct reasoning and was amazed that this "human rubbish" produced a "number of physically, mentally and morally efficient citizens." He forced himself to meet the challenge: "Our courage has risen, and our humanity has expanded, to feel that these new-comers are Americans, and that, whether they are or not, they must be. And we are going to make them so."[43]

Brahmin leadership in local enterprises aided the progress of the Immigration Restriction League through the related channels of social welfare. In 1901, the Boston Associated Charities led the way by endorsing a set of resolutions in favor of the League's policies and influenced charity organizations in other cities to follow suit. In 1904, a school of charity was founded by Brahmin leaders for students of Harvard and Simmons colleges. Jeffrey Brackett, its first director, was a scholarly New Englander, of an old Quincy family; a member of the class of 1883 at Harvard, along with Joseph Lee and John Farwell Moors, he had taken his Ph.D. at Johns Hopkins, where Amos G. Warner synthesized the current Anglo-American philosophy of charity. Both Brackett, as an experienced worker in the Baltimore Charities, and his associate director Zilpha Smith, the first general secretary of the Associated Charities in Boston, transmitted the concepts of modern philanthropy to the young ladies of the Back Bay, the first students of the institution which later became the Simmons School of Social Work. To various classes Robert DeC. Ward lectured on the values of immigration restriction, in 1905, 1908, 1911, and 1912.[44]

While most of the army of social workers did not continuously look to ultimates as did the rich leaders of New England reform, Robert A. Woods, the most distinguished professional social worker in Boston, became Joseph Lee's collaborator in the League's cause. Walking on the Common between their very different homes, each learned the other's view of the diverse people who were becoming American. Woods became the main interpreter of the South End to the Brahmins who footed the bills of his project. As the philosopher of the settlement movement, Woods (like Lee in the charities) evolved complex justifications for restriction, arising out of his personal experiences and the social beliefs of his generation.[45]

Woods was born in Pittsburgh, of a middle-class, Scotch Irish, Presbyterian family, rigid in its theological view and puritanical in social behavior. At Amherst College, class of 1885, he learned that the educated man must help "the people" work out America's labor problems. Then, training for the ministry at Andover Seminary, New England's stronghold of Congregationalism, he concentrated upon this world rather than the next in his studies of the national economy.[46]

In 1890, he departed for England to live at Toynbee Hall, the first settlement of university students in the London slums. Immersed in the tenets of Canon Barnett, Charles Booth, Octavia Hill, and others, Woods was exhilarated. English life represented the advance of civilization: of all the countries in the world, she alone held "for the next following generations the manifest destiny." His own America was one of "the other nations of Great Britain," which should learn "from the mother country" how to solve the even "more difficult problems" of the New World.[47]

At heart he was a little envious of the English people: they were "of the vigorous Anglo-Saxon race, without contaminating mixture." It was easy to identify with the London poor, except for the East End Jews. And, like English intellectuals, Woods was attracted to the problem of status for skilled workmen. Through trade unionism he hoped they would regain the place they had had in the Middle Ages, "when the artisans were poets and artists also." In contrast, at home in the United States, he faced the job of Americanizing immigrants "with their unspeakable degraded standard of life." Unconsciously his respect for the homogeneity of English society and his sympathy for the "better classes" of the workers remained the criteria by which he judged the behavior of ethnic groups in America.[48]

In 1892, Woods moved to Boston and founded the most famous of several social settlements in the city, first named Andover House but soon known as South End House. There he and other students lived in residence, hoping in this way to bring "some wholly new illumination into the life of the common people." In the next few years Woods became the partner and coordinator of Brahmins in philanthropic and municipal reform. Theorizing upon the value of the settlement, of democracy, and of immigration, he both influenced and reflected the Brahmin spirit.[49]

As an outsider, Woods surveyed Boston with different perspective. He believed that the isolation of the Brahmins as "a separated aristocracy" had already debilitated the economic and social development of the city. "The bright young Jew" was condemned "somewhat as in the Middle Ages, to certain narrow lines of trade" and "enterprising young Irish-Americans" had "little recourse aside from the ever open path into corrupt politics." Moreover, the increasing tendency of "the better classes" to reject their civic responsibility left political control to the immigrants and reinforced the social rupture in the community. Originally, Woods regarded the settlement house as an "outpost" where all Americans, irrespective of class, sect, and race, would discover what they owed to each other.[50]

Social reciprocity was Woods's goal, but he limited it both in theory and practice. From the outset, he opposed placing settlements in the worst sections, because there social workers did not reach "the better grades of working people." Admittedly the relation between settlement residents and slum dwellers was, at best, artificial. Yet he also objected to planting whole families in working-class quarters; there was no hope of democratizing the family unit. However, for the individual resident worker there was a constructive experience, almost a religious revelation, which the settlement life could offer. Enriching the point of view of educated American youth was Woods's major concern, as he studied different immigrant groups and sought to "appreciate the distinctive genius of each type." In reverse, how the objects of his planning felt, Woods never understood.[51]

Ultimately, like his Brahmin supporters, Woods had inward misgivings about the power of the settlement: perhaps it could not relate the mass of heterogeneous citizens "to the original American element in the population." By 1905, he compromised his ideal to harmonize with reality: the settlements were, in essence, "bits of neutral territory where the descendants of the Puritans may meet the chosen leaders among the immigrants from Italy, Russia, and the Levant." As the meeting ground for selected representatives of different groups, the settlement provided a restricted intercourse among the city's diverse inhabitants and the goal of social reciprocity became unreal.[52]

This middleman between old and new Bostonians became increasingly attuned to Brahmin anxieties. Although Woods wanted to aid the recent citizens, he saw them as general types. Earlier he had expected the diversity of the community to be only a temporary phase, but looking back in 1922, he concluded that "effort toward assimilation" had been "continuously overwhelmed by the incoming flood." Sharing the racial criteria of the sociologists, Woods found it difficult to reconcile the existence of different ethnic groups with the formation of a distinctive nationality, and staunchly advocated restriction, not just as a measure vital to the protection of "the better grade of working people." Having found the English poor more congenial, this social worker was impressed with Walker's notion that the price of immigration was the sacrifice of the superior Anglo-Saxon people in America. By 1911, Woods became important in the executive committee of the Immigration Restriction League.[53]

Perhaps inevitably, intellectual notions of race had stimulated native prejudice, but some participants in Boston's social movements, like the Rev. George Hodges, Vida Scudder, and Dr. Richard Cabot, insisted that racial judgments were blinders obstructing the responses to the newcomers.

Dean George Hodges of the Episcopal Theological School, was the president of South End House from 1895 to 1919. A Midwesterner by birth though descended from a New England family, he treasured his friendships and associations in the community. Becoming a friend and adviser to Brahmin society, Hodges struggled to avoid the pitfalls of class and ethnic superiority. Sharing the *de haut en bas* attitude of the old New Englander to the very new, he acknowledged the sins of his group, and, with neophyte social workers, prayed that they resist "the temptations" of their occupation; namely, stressing "theories rather than conditions," substituting "books for life." To an audience at Denison House in 1894, he pointed out that different kinds of people rendered different services to society and that none should claim special superiority to the rest. The intellectual and social narrowness of the Yankee upper class created only the fallacies of "class" judgments and xenophobias, and Hodges looked to the settlements for enlightenment and liberation.[54]

Vida D. Scudder described how Brahmin self-containment handicapped "vital intercourse with those most alien and remote." Niece of Horace V. Scudder (the *Atlantic's* editor early in the 1890's), she recorded in a semi-autobiographical novel, *A Listener in Babel,* her early experiences as a resident settlement worker. She had learned economics under John B. Clark at Smith College and read Ruskin for a year at Oxford. Resolved to escape Back Bay's "prison of class," leaving her home on Beacon Street, she became a resident of Denison House in the Italian district of Boston. The novel reviewed the bewildered reactions which almost paralyzed her impulse to live among the poor. Revolted by the slums, which gave "breathless nights . . . squalor . . . the confinement of the city," the heroine Hilda* missed the safe Brahmin haven "where ideals soothed but never stung, where high standards were a private luxury of one's own mind, where the tragic was fine material for literature, and grief only added pathos to the appeal of beauty." Another character, Miss Saltonstall, observed the offspring of "these degraded races that seek our shores," and found it grimly ludicrous to hear little Roman Catholics and Jews sing "Land of the Pilgrims' Pride." Would these small

---

* Hilda, the novel's heroine, expresses the author's viewpoint.

aliens supersede the Americans as "the governing race" in the United States? she inquired.[55]

In spite of themselves, New England philanthropists were bondsmen to the prejudices of their society and of their professions. Dr. Richard Cabot, a distinguished pioneer in social service and mentor to many of the city's immigrant doctors, examined his reactions to a foreign-born patient at the Massachusetts General Hospital:

I . . . look out of my eyes and see, *not* Abraham Cohen, but *a Jew;* not the sharp, clear outlines of this unique sufferer, but the vague, misty composite photograph of all the hundreds of Jews who in the past ten years have shuffled up . . . with bent back and deprecating eyes . . . I see a Jew,—a nervous, complaining, whimpering Jew,—with his beard upon his chest and the inevitable dirty black frock-coat flapping about his knees. I do not see *this* man at all. I merge him in the hazy background of the average Jew.

Assuming that the patient was like so many who had preceded him, Cabot suddenly realized that this Jew had a "muscular . . . prehensile hand. . . That shocks me awake, at last. This is not merely '*a Jew*': this is a new kind of Jew. Why his eyes are further apart than I ever saw before in a Hebrew, and they don't avoid mine, but look straight at me with a long, deep look that somehow reminds me of the child in Raphael's Sistine Madonna. They are blue eyes, thundercloud blue and very steady." Through self-analysis of his prejudice, Dr. Cabot revealed the force of the current stereotypes of the foreign-born, and struggled to individualize immigrants apart from "their generic type, the racial background from which they emerged."[56]

Racial classifications standardized the analysis of America's latest suppliants. Conditioned by the studies of social and political scientists, charity workers regarded ethnic differences among the foreign-born as crucial. During the 1900's the concept of race grew stronger until, finally, physical scientists in England and America gave it new destructive meaning through the science of eugenics.

The biological significance of heredity had been implicit in Darwin's doctrine of selection, and in 1865 Francis Galton had demonstrated "the plasticity of the physical forms of animals under the breeder's selection." Thereafter he presented the hypothesis that heredity determined equally the mental and physical characteristics of human beings. At first, in England, Galton's work stimulated only biological research. But, by 1900, a younger colleague, Karl Pearson, likened the nation to an organism struggling to survive and dependent for success upon the best elements in the state. By then, the ethical ideal of eugenics, ages ago discovered by Plato, had already assumed importance in the twentieth-century United States.[57]

In its unique concentration of nationalities, the notion of eugenics was appealing. New England Brahmins, who enjoyed Dr. Holmes's maxim that it took four or five generations to make a gentleman, regarded themselves as living testimony to Galton's thesis. Even opponents of evolution, like Louis Agassiz, emphasized the importance of heredity. During the 1880's, New Englanders discussed ways to prevent the "physical degeneracy" of the Yankees. One citizen then contemplated an Institute of Heredity to educate Bostonians "on the subject of improving our race by the laws of physiology."[58] Moreover, when reformers debated whether the poorest and the most ignorant of the foreign-born could respond to America's free gifts of education and opportunity, the relationship between heredity and environment reached the essence of the problem.

The sordid aspects of an industrialized society prepared American reformers to respect the ideal of eugenics. In Edward Bellamy's Yankee Utopia the constructive program for the nation involved "race purification." Robert Dugdale's *The Jukes* and Oscar McCulloch's *Tribe of Ishmael,* dramatized the influences of heredity upon criminality and degeneracy. Thereafter, other investigations, reported at the National Conference of Charities and Correction and at the American Prison Association, emphasized the factor of inheritance among delinquents, criminals, paupers, and alcoholics. To be sure, reformers and social workers viewed Galton's thesis with mixed feelings. If characteristics were transmitted from parent to child, then efforts to improve the social environment through education and legislation were futile. Since biologists did not agree among themselves, some sociologists cautioned restraint in utilizing the concept of heredity. Despite these reservations, Amos G. Warner, the author of the representative text on scientific charity, showed where the balance of the intellectual scales lay: "while charity may not cease to shield the children of misfortune, it must, to an ever increasing extent reckon with the laws of heredity, and do what it can to check the spreading curse of race deterioration." Hereditary interpretations of human frailities were magnetic and became a constant in the values of social uplifters.[59]

At the turn of the century, many scientists in America were ready to make a stand for an organized eugenics movement. Its most eminent backer was David Starr Jordan, the biologist and president of Stanford University. As a Cornell undergraduate, he had formed a life-long friendship with its president, Andrew D. White, and like him proudly asserted his English Puritan ancestry and New England background. As a scientist, he was certain that all men followed the race type of their parents undeviatingly. There was "no natural or necessary tendency downward or upward" for "nature repeated what she found." An Anglo-Saxon by blood would always be "Anglo-Saxon in quality." Concluding that degeneration came from interbreeding with an inferior stock, he encouraged the study of hereditary ethnic determinants for the express purpose of improving the quality of the American people. In 1906, he headed the new Eugenics Section of the American Breeders Association founded by plant and animal geneticists a few years earlier. The Boston restrictionists, Hall and Ward, soon became the chairman and secretary of an Immigration Committee of this Eugenics group. Increasingly, Jordan's desire to keep the United States the home of the oppressed conflicted with his skepticism about the innate capacities of various immigrant groups. With reservations, he supported the work of the Boston Immigration Restriction League and by 1913 was a member of its National Committee.[60]

But although Jordan and other biologists favored legislation to ensure the ethnic selection of America's future citizens, their approach was primarily scientific. Despite their interest in restriction as a possible means to their end, there was no unanimity among them as to the best method of selecting immigrants, and their opinions varied considerably from those of the restrictionists. On the other hand, to the League, these scientists represented another potential pressure group quite different from that of labor unions. Significantly, the activities of the eugenicists converged with those of the restrictionists and, in the end, left a permanent effect on the anti-immigration movement.

At the start, however, New England restrictionists were generally more extreme than the eugenicists. Alexander Graham Bell, for instance, had, as result of his studies of the deaf, become fascinated with the correlations between animal and human reproduction. He proposed that the American Breeders Association make an ethnical survey to determine which groups were undesirable for the evolution of the American nationality. But, although Bell supported the principle of restriction and publicly gave his blessing to the Boston League, he himself was an emigrant from Scotland, and he continued to think that many of the foreign-born were desirable.[61]

Bell's idea became the life project of Charles B. Davenport. A Connecticut Yankee with a Harvard A.B. in 1889 and Ph.D. in 1892, Davenport became the Director of the Biological Laboratory of the Brooklyn Institute of Arts and Sciences. In 1910, he set up a Eugenics Record Office, where he used the histories of family pedigrees in order to determine hereditary factors in mental deficiency. He shared Brahmin admiration for the original Puritan stock, but believed that the best descendants of this group had migrated west, leaving behind a legacy of decadence. For a while he refused to condemn any "race . . . *per se*" as "dangerous." By 1911, however, the biological side of immigration seemed more urgent, and Davenport suggested that the admission of aliens should depend upon the quality of the germ-plasm of their ethnic group. Even then, he would welcome annually 200,000 Europeans of "good blood," whose family histories were checked authoritatively. In the abstract, assuming the economic aspect of immigration would take care of itself, he inclined to accept workers (qualified by his standards) and to keep America as a home for the oppressed.[62]

Critical of Davenport's opinions, Robert DeC. Ward wrote him that "we ought to pull together, whether we are wholly agreed or not. I have no intention to disagree with you in any public statements. If we don't all pull together in the same direction, we can do nothing." This policy of solidarity with individuals and groups, who sympathized with some *part* of the League's work, evident in other alliances already, was eminently prudent in attracting the attention of physical scientists and doctors.[63]

To the medical profession League leaders stressed the "vast inheritance of insanity, imbecility and feeble-mindedness" which the United States was garnering in the "desire to be kind to a few aliens today." Stimulating the interest of the Massachusetts Medical Society and of Harvard Medical School graduates, Prescott F. Hall persuaded many doctors to endorse more stringent inspection of immigrants.[64]

Yet medical inspection was only a wedge in the League's drive against the national immigration policy in the 1910's. Literal, severe exclusions, based on twenty-one classifications, already debarred from admission mentally, morally, physically, and economically undesirable immigrants; but the appetite of restrictionists was now insatiable. In essence, they wished to exclude all aliens who seemed "mentally inferior or unstable." The newcomers were so hopelessly beneath the older stocks that "for one immigrant whose defects . . . put him in the classes excluded by law" there were "hundreds, if not thousands . . . below the average of our people . . . as George William Curtis put it . . . 'watering the nation's life blood.' "[65]

In the same years, moreover, Hall and Ward suggested that the passage of the literacy test would have the direct eugenic result of relieving the congestion of the cities, so conducive to mental and physical deterioration. Not all physicians responded to this facile argument; many, like Dr. Alexander Forbes, wanted to ensure the exclusion of defectives and delinquents, but thought some illiterates "might progress wonderfully under the benefits of American civilization."[66]

The genetic principle seemed reasonable when restrictionists urged it to ensure the admission of sound and healthy immigrants. The psychiatrist, Dr. Thomas W. Salmon, who served in the immigration offices at Ellis Island, was avid to prevent an influx of the mentally unfit and interested in any broad measure which would "reduce pro rata the number of insane." Hall publicized this view, but, in 1913, Salmon added that the literacy test or any other "arbitrary" measure against immigration, had no validity, if adopted *solely* as the means of reducing insanity and mental deficiency in the American population. Although, as director of Special Studies for the National Committee for Mental Hygiene, Salmon stressed the burden of the insane and desired more thorough medical control at ports of entry, yet he did not favor an arbitrary cessation of immigration.[67]

On practical ground, Hall and Ward found the medical sphere of influence increasingly useful. They propagandized through the committee of the National Association of Mental Hygiene, the Boards of Charities, and the Commission of the Alien Insane in the various states, along with the committees of the American Genetic Association and the American Breeders Association. With growing concern, in 1914 these and kindred organizations like the Immigration Committee of the American Medico-Psychological Association sent resolutions to Henry Cabot Lodge in the Senate and to John L. Burnett in the House for the greater enforcement of the present laws to exclude the insane and mentally defective immigrants. Now representative physicans demanded the extension of the present classification to bar aliens not only of recognized insanity but those of "psychopathic constitutional inferiority."[68]

Still more than a strategic weapon in the League's campaigns, eugenics was the scientific answer for racists. So impressive was the idea, that Hall wanted to change the organization's name to the Eugenic Immigration League. The propagation of man had become a mere matter of breeding, comparable to that of plants and cattle; weirdly it coincided with the New England ideal, voiced by Henry Adams: could the United States create a higher variety of the human species? Most important, the theory of eugenics became linked with Walker's thesis for restriction. With ever widening interest in the native birth rate, educated Americans ignored alternative explanations and favored the notion that the lowly foreign-born were scaring Yankees out of raising large families. Immigration was a question "as to what kind of babies shall be born" here. Anglo-Saxon-minded scientists agreed that "a race of acknowledged superiority in originality and enterprise" was "being sacrificed." Whatever the future people might be, Ward stated, New Englanders were "satisfied with the characteristics, mental and physical, of the old American stock." Hall asked rhetorically, "Will any one say that the races that have supplanted the old Nordic stock in New England are any better, or as good, as the descendants of that stock would have been if their birth rate had not been lowered?" For the world's good and for America's, the inferior peoples should be segregated from the superior, just as scientists isolated bacteria to limit their influence. From the Brahmin view, the eugenics of immigration had as its primary goal the preservation of the remaining Teutonic strains, "the finest in the world" in recent centuries.[69]

The League, in existence since 1894, had, by 1912, forgotten its nineteenth-century humanitarian antecedents. Superseding Mayo Smith's vague sociological definition of race, eugenics provided the final argument for immigration restriction: the immigrants from southeastern Europe had hereditary passions which were unalterable, regardless of public schools and economic opportunities in the United States. Believing that no nation could produce worthy men without "a certain homogeneity of environment," Prescott F. Hall worked for "the advent of the superman" in America. Birth control, sterilization, and regulation of marriage—all for the preservation of pure races—were the ultimate goals; meanwhile, restriction of immigration could be the first step toward creating this superior race. Eugenics transformed the ambiguous xenophobia of Brahmin restrictionists into a formidable racist ideology. What it would mean to prejudices in the United States in a few years depended on the use made of the sociological and biological data which now scientifically framed the ethnic stereotypes of the foreign-born in America.[70]

CHAPTER VIII

Testing the Races: Stereotypes of the Foreign-Born

Up to the present time we have attempted to sift the immigrants as they come in through Ellis Island, on an individualistic basis ... What are the racial characteristics, if any, by which we might venture to exclude or give preference to certain classes of immigrants? ... That is one of the problems ... to discover some test to show whether some may be better fitted for American citizenship than others ... —Jeremiah W. Jenks[1]

In the fifteen years between the Spanish-American War and the First World War, sociologists and social workers formulated an array of ethnic stereotypes as they viewed the aliens of the community. Long standing images of the various American groups already existed. The Irishman, the German, the Scandinavian, the Italian, and the Jew were, like the Yankee, recognizable according to physical appearance, outward costume, and visible habits. The stock Irishman, German, Jew, and Yankee were common in vaudeville, legitimate theater, and cartoons. These stereotypes, often derived from literary associations of the past, were comic in tone; even when related to real life, they lacked ulterior purpose of malice or insult.[2] But, from 1890 to 1914, the racial ideology of the restrictionists built upon the older stereotypes, which New Englanders had shared, and imparted new meaning to them.

From the turn of the century, the abstract philosophers of "race" and "friendly visitors" of the poor tabulated data on the behavior of the foreign-born in hospitals, prisons, settlements, and slums. Committed to ethnic criteria of superiority and inferiority, social scientists used their data to measure the caliber of whole immigrant groups. On the assumption that human beings were endowed with hereditary characteristics, the qualities of each ethnic group became fixed and rigid. From these assessments, presumably scientific, new stereotypes of the foreign-born emerged. Unlike the earlier, the later images were not neutral: they were permanent judgments upon the ability and the character. And since the restrictionists desired a practical basis of deciding which groups were fit for Americanization, the distinctions between "old" and "new" immigrants entered the final evaluations of each ethnic group strategically.

By 1890, the Irish, in contrast to the more recent arrivals, occupied a peculiar niche in the thoughts of the old New England society; out of the conflict between Yankees and Irishmen an image of intimate, painful proportions had been generated. The lowly peasant from the Emerald Isle was ignorant, shiftless, credulous, impulsive, mechanically inept, and boastful of the Old Country. The inclination toward drinking and related crimes, elsewhere emphasized with humor, induced gloomy deprecations in New England. On the other hand, the controversy over Irish girls as domestics, still prevalent in the 1870's, had ended, and Bridget as cook and nursemaid was the acceptable mainstay of the Brahmin household. Of course the Hibernians as "legislators, mayors. . . Democrats and Catholics" still evoked the disagreeable connotation of rabble-followers and city bosses. The general view was bitter: "the Irishman fails to fit into the complex of our civilization, apparently for the reason that his talents are too little interwoven with the capacities which go to make up the modern successful man."[3]

But this forty-year-old attitude was disappearing into the realm of private, unspoken prejudice. Lodge's pronouncement of the close kinship between the English-speaking natives and the Celtic immigrants was often repeated and modified the existent harsh evaluation. Especially social workers, desiring municipal reform, faced the practical necessity of dealing with the Hibernian City Fathers and stressed the virtues of the Irish who had now progressed toward social and economic success. Social workers emphasized the improved standard of living of some Celts: "their remarkable race trait of adaptability" explained the recent levels of achievement among the "more intelligent and prosperous" of the Boston group.[4] Characterized by considerable delicacy and restraint, a new pattern of interpreting the Irish American replaced the former frank contempt.

Stressing the attractive features of the older stereotype, observers manipulated still further Teutonist theory and historical fact to produce an appealing image. The good-natured, fun-loving, imaginative Irishman of stage and cartoon predominated. Joseph Lee lauded the Celt's social temperament—his response to athletic programs and "gang tendency." By the same token, sociologist after sociologist now attributed Irish political leadership to gregariousness and warmheartedness. Ironically, John R. Commons, who was particularly exercised by the phenomenon of city bosses, described the Irish boss rather glowingly "as the survival of the fittest. . . The Irishman has above all races the mixture of ingenuity, firmness, human sympathy, comradeship, and daring that makes him the amalgamator of races." If there was to be a racial intermixture among the various ethnic divisions of the foreign-born, the gregarious Celt seemed a hopeful leader. Irish preëminence in labor unions was another example of ability to associate with and organize others. Eloquence, personal loyalty, "a generous good nature, and aggressive fighting qualities" made the Celts the natural leaders of the American labor movement. (William Z. Ripley was therefore sorely puzzled by their reticence in the English trade unions of the same period.)[5] On the whole, the new stereotype gave grudging admiration to the Irishman's success in the forum. Ripley looked to "Irish, or Irish-American womanhood . . . to be a potent physical mediator between the other peoples of the earth" because of her "superior adaptability and comradeship. . . her democratic ways and lack of spirit of caste."[6]

Moreover, in this new pattern of social recognition various liabilities traditionally associated with Irishmen now received more elastic, compensatory interpretations. Paradoxically, Irish hatred of England, which had evoked conflict with older Bostonians in the 1880's, appeared constructive in that it solidified loyalty to the adopted country. Moreover, social workers and sociologists made light of the old problem of Irish drinking with its concomitant crimes. Although quarrelsome when drunk, the jolly Celt did not fight to kill, and was always "first and last chivalrous." He was an attractive weakling when he did get into trouble: according to E. A. Ross's image, "the Celtic offender is a feckless fellow, enemy of himself more than of any one else. It is usually not cupidity nor brutality nor lust that lodges him in prison, but conviviality and weak control of impulses."[7]

The fact that a segment of Boston's Irish continued to be poor, prodigal, and unambitious bothered social workers. According to some, the Celts were peculiarly sensitive to environment; others blamed Irish irresponsibility, a race trait which often proved the more dominant force than that of American education. Troubled by the high death rate, a lack of seriousness, and evidences of degeneracy among the Irish, observers balanced their opinions of the strengths and frailities of New England's oldest immigrant group. Their presumed degeneracy derived from "a low stage of social development rather than from the possession of anti-social characteristics"; and, on the positive side, their solidarity was a desirable trait, supplementing the "native optimism." Finally, with diplomatic tact, Frederick Bushée, a Harvard Ph.D. in 1903, resident of South End House, concluded, "their assimilative qualities must be superior to their individual qualities."[8]

But the euphemistic rationalizations did not emerge solely as compromises to firmly entrenched Irish politicians. With the arrival of southern European groups, stranger in appearance than the Irish, these English-speaking aliens were less disturbing; and, irrespective of private sentiments, they had a place in American society. Those who opposed a free immigration policy, had made an emotional transference to more vulnerable objects of distaste, the "new" ethnic groups seeking admission to the United States.

The same social circumstances which were modifying the Irish stereotype affected the New Englanders' impression of the German immigrants. There were elements of paradox in the Yankee attitudes: the undesirable traits of the German became less conspicious when the need to confirm his general desirability became manifest.

Few Germans had emigrated to New England and there had been little contact between these and upper-class Bostonians. On the other hand, ever since George Ticknor and Edward Everett had gone to study in Germany in 1815, the country of Goethe, Herder, Schleiermacher, and Ranke had been a symbol of intellectuality and scholarship to the cultured Brahmins. So Longfellow and Lowell had drunk deep of German literature, Emerson of its philosophical idealism, while Bancroft and the great train of historians thereafter paid a debt to Teutonist principles and methods of research. Louisa May Alcott's Professor Bhaer in *Little Women* (published in 1868) depicted the German as a warm, music-loving, intellectual, conversant in philosophical trends with the New England transcendentalist father.[9]

But after the 1848 generation of liberals ceased to come, the emigrants were usually from the less educated classes. Unshared by them, the German intellectual tradition remained a separate sphere of associations for the descendants of the old New England culture. After the Civil War there was little occasion to identify the German emigrant with the lofty intellectual figures of the nation he was rejecting.[10]

The New England image of the German American closely resembled the caricature prevalent in the rest of the United States. The popular verse of Charles Follen Adams, appearing from 1878 to 1910, pictured the fat jolly Dutchman: an ignorant, good-natured, "stolid" citizen, who guzzled beer most intemperately. Adams was a Yankee dry goods dealer who became acquainted with German immigrants as soldiers during the Civil War. In hundreds of poems the lovable, though droll, Strauss family "moistened thousands of eyes—these old ones of mine among the rest," Oliver Wendell Holmes recalled. Although Adams presented the German as a man of common sense, sentimental in familial relations, still the hero reflected the unattractive elements of the stereotype, "a Deutscher blain and rude":

> Mine cracious! mine cracious! shust look here und see
> A Deutscher so habby as habby can pe!
> Der beoples all dink dot no prains I haf got;
> Vas grazy mit trinking, or someding like dot.[11]

On the whole, the Yankee view of the German was unconsciously patronizing.

Toward the end of the nineteenth century, certain factors kept alive the old distinctions between Yankee and German American, that is, between Anglo-Saxon and Teuton. Although the negative features in the portrait of the German were softening, still the growing Anglophilism placed Yankee affections on the side of England in the current rivalry between English and German imperialisms. As English historians had made clear in the 1880's, the superiority of the Anglo-Saxon was a foregone conclusion by the test of assimilation. "Whether in Britain or in America, the German . . . becomes English; the Englishman never becomes German," Edward Freeman had declared.[12]

Emphasis on the Anglo-Saxon character of the American people reinforced the patronizing stereotype of the German-born group. While not exactly a drunkard, the German was too loyal to his beer. His phlegmatic temperament made him less efficient than the native worker. Even worse, the German was servile to his superiors and brutal to his inferiors especially when they were women. By the same token, he was too emotional and impulsive to administer justice with the sobriety and practicality of the Anglo-Saxon. Finally, in contrast to the old *émigrés* of 1848, the present German American was too concerned with the material advantages of life in the United States.[13] These subtly antagonistic judgments suggest that the long indoctrination in Teutonist thought, so intimately connected with the aspirations of the English-speaking people on both sides of the Atlantic, induced an adulation of the Anglo-Saxon to which his cousin, the German Teuton, was not quite entitled.

A distinguished German professor of psychology at Harvard College, Hugo Münsterberg, was greatly offended by the humiliation which Anglophilism was inflicting on his kin in the United

States. Münsterberg resented that the German, with his Christmas tree, his music, and his breweries, was socially a second-class citizen in this English-speaking world. But although Teutonist theory encouraged the notion that the German American was less capable than the Yankee of English forbears, the stereotype of mediocrity operated in his favor in comparison with later immigrants.[14]

In the last years of the nineteenth century, two new factors further complicated the attitude of New England intellectuals, and increasingly modified the image of the German American in sociological literature. First, as the German migration steadily declined, earlier objections seemed less momentous to those faced with "new" immigrant groups. The dominant element in the stereotype then became the respectability of the German immigrant: hard-working, primarily an agriculturist, healthy, fecund (until recently), proverbially neat, "thrifty and industrious." Moreover, fears of German loyalty to the Old Country through the continuance of customs and language (which had troubled Richmond Mayo Smith), were dismissed. Similarly, German drinking, long a source of disapproval, appeared as a habit of moderation. By 1913, E. A. Ross observed that the German, in comparison with other ethnic groups, was "mediocre" in his vices. Freer from intemperance than other groups, and neither high nor low in his rate of criminality, the German was "very close to . . . the native American" in "criminal bent." And, misleadingly, an analyst of the foreign-born in Boston, where the German group was numerically small, pointed out that fewer Germans applied for poor relief than any other stock, and concluded that they were "the best type of immigrant which has settled in Boston." Thus the virtues of the German group became a static commodity; he was an ethnic type to be taken for granted.[15]

A second force in modifying the old negative view of the German developed from the restrictionist agitation in the 1890's. Henry Cabot Lodge had, in his famous speech on the Senate floor in 1896, scrupulously described the German as a welcome representative of the Teutonic race, fit for American citizenship. Lodge's protestations heralded a new attitude toward the German American. Devotees of the Teutonist thesis, which was privately oriented toward an

English-speaking universe in America, had to swallow the prejudices of the last fifty years. After all, the Teuton was a blood relative of the Anglo-Saxon. For the purpose of restriction, at least, the German was a desirable immigrant, assimilating readily into American society. Thus rural-minded sociologists emphasized the German pursuit of agriculture as a guarantee that this group could absorb the social idealism handed down from the older frontier way of life.[16]

On a smaller scale, the gyrations of the Scandinavian stereotype also mirrored the shifting adaptations of Teutonist theory. Even less did the New Englander know the Scandinavian immigrants. There had been in Cambridge and Boston circles of the 1870's and 1880's historical and literary interest in proving that Norsemen had landed in New England. Although there was some presumed character identification between the adventurous Viking and the early Yankee, it did not extend to contemporary emigrants from Norway, Sweden, and Denmark. But, despite the remoteness of the Scandinavian group, by the end of the 1880's, the Swede, Norwegian, and Dane were objectionable. With a low standard of living, they had upon arrival farmed the soil where native Americans had failed, even as the Irish had survived in the cities. Resistance to the Scandinavians had colored Mayo Smith's judgment; he blamed them along with the other "old" immigrant groups for the degradation of American civilization.[17]

By the 1890's, a more expedient opinion of the Scandinavians had emerged; their status as citizens matched their classification as a branch of the great Teutonic race. Largely agricultural, they now received approval (like the Germans) for their "attachment to the soil." Hall, who gave the Scandinavians slight notice in his study, repeated the standard belief of their desirability: they presented no problems of pauperism or major criminality and assimilated readily, with political instinct on "the side of good government."[18]

Nevertheless the Norseman, the Swede, and the Dane intruded so little upon New England life that little of an intimate nature appeared in the stereotype. There was Hall's shaded opinion that the Swede was superior to the Norwegian and Thomas Nixon Carver's revulsion with the "peasant-minded" newcomers to the Corn Belt.

But, for a detailed image of the Scandinavian, the New Englander would turn to Edward A. Ross's analysis. He found the Scandinavian group too reserved—"ice water runs in their veins"—and they tended toward melancholy and insanity. Moreover, to judge by the children's progress in American schools, the Scandinavian was a plodder, by no means the "flower" of the peoples in the country of his origin. Considered comparatively, the Dane was the most courteous and polished, pleasure-loving, yet moderate in vice; the Swede the most melancholy; and the Norwegian the most primitive, taciturn, aggressive, and nationalistic. In spite of this unflattering view there were compensations. The Scandinavian's "slow reaction" gave him "the right psychology for self-government"; although he lacked qualities of leadership, he provided "an excellent, cool-blooded, self-controlled citizenship for the support of representative government."[19] On the whole, Ross's judgment included, the common opinion of the Scandinavian was now one of superficial approval.

Another "old" immigrant group, whose fate was more closely connected with that of New England, was the French Canadian. Already known as victims of religious persecution in Longfellow's *Evangeline,* many began to cross the border to escape rural impoverishment in the 1870's. Simultaneously, Longfellow's romantic image of the Norman peasant, in picturesque traditional costume, disappeared in the historical works of Francis Parkman. The Brahmin historian admired only the *voyageur coureur de bois* or soldier, who had been subject to the impress of the frontier. But in the "ignorant, light-hearted" farmer, the medieval heritage was more important than the environment of the New World; he was merely an ancient peasant, "born to obey" for whom "the institutions of New England" were "utterly inapplicable." In the racial idiom, as a Celt, the French Canadian was quick, emotional, and generally inferior to the Anglo-Saxon.[20]

Moreover, as the *habitant* had left his native farm for the Yankee textile mill, the stereotype of the French Canadian as a factory worker became even more deprecatory. He, like the Irishman, was a squalid blight on the New England landscape, with a low standard of living and a lack of skilled training. Migrating seasonally without seeking American citizenship, the French Canadian remained under the power of the priest and avoided the public schools for his children. He contributed substantially to the problems of illiteracy and lowered "distinctly the general intelligence and civilization" of the native community. It was common in the 1870's and 1880's to denounce the group as a rootless and permanently alien proletariat, the "Chinese of the Eastern States." At first, suspicion of the second major newcomer to New England colored the Yankee reactions to the French Canadian: in short, he was "shifty, unmechanical and unreliable."[21]

A more generous minority view, however, prevailed even in the 1870's. The sight of French Canadians toiling in the brickyards of Cambridge, prompted William Dean Howells to admire the "windy-voiced, good-humored groups," reminiscent of "so many peasant folk . . . always amiably quarreling before the *cabarets*" in France. Sympathetically he described the French Canadian customer—a shrewd "wary" bargainer, comparable to the sharp Yankee storekeeper. Shaler, although staggered and depressed by the French Canadian's power to multiply, preferred him to the Irishman who had "threatened to overwhelm us for so long," maintaining that the Canadian was "a true French peasant, his speech a little changed but nothing more; in size, manner, habits and propensities, he is wonderfully near to his origin." In New England the group was "a frugal, industrious, even hard-working people, somewhat given to drink and rather immoral, but with none of that shiftlessness which belongs to the Irishman of the same grade."[22] Thus the transatlantic origins of the French Canadian also suggested the pleasant attributes of old France.

By 1900 the peak of the migration was over, and soon negative assumptions about the French Canadian lessened. While Hall, Commons, and Ripley still protested against the border "bird of passage," the French Canadian had established himself permanently in many industrial centers. And although his settlement had engendered some of the local parochial school conflicts of the 1880's and 1890's, this Catholic group inspired little animosity. More impressed with the

French Canadian's function in the native textile mills and with his support of the Republican Party, Lodge presented the group in a congenial light. The Senator, who boasted of his own Norman blood, remarked, "the French-Canadians racially present nothing new. Among the English-speaking people . . . there was always a large infusion of French blood, and the French-Canadians, Americans for many generations . . . have proved to be a valuable and promising element in our population." Carroll Wright, the industrial expert of statistics, repudiated his former skeptical attitude. The second- or third-generation descendant had become a "live American," despite French characteristics in every respect, especially in religion and language. Ripley too admitted that, when the French Canadian became thoroughly Americanized, he joined the trade unions satisfactorily.[23] Content with the usefulness of this group industrially and somewhat remote from it communally, the old New Englander did not contribute many personal impressions to the French Canadian stereotype.

But other sources also contributed to the inconsistency of the stereotype. Although there was still some difference of opinion as to whether the French Canadian made a good American, his acceptance as a citizen had begun. The image of his ignorance and ineptness had disappeared: the French Canadian was industrious, frugal, and "quick to learn . . . an admirable mechanic." The impression of shrewdness, however, gained negative overtones; he was inclined to "deception, trickery, and petty larceny." To others, "docility" seemed the major trait: French Canadian conservatism was an ethnic passivity, inherited in his Canadian home, that bit of Catholic "medieval France" never subject to the French Revolution. Along with this lethargic image, a more appealing one focused on his Celtic temperament: he was gay, prolific, polite, quick tempered and quarrelsome after drinking, good looking, well-dressed, and Anglicized. In educated circles, the poems of an Anglo-Canadian, Dr. William Henry Drummond, portrayed the *habitant*. Bateese Trudeau, who changed his name to John B. Waterhole, after working a season in the United States, was typical:

He's dressim on de première classe, an' got new suit of clothes
Wit' long mustache dat's stickim out, de 'noder side hees nose
Fine gol' watch chain—nice portmanteau—an' long, long overcoat
Wit' beaver hat—dat's Yankee style—an' red tie on hees t'roat.[24]

After the turn of the century New Englanders displayed little interest in the French Canadian. The resultant stereotype was neutral compared with the manifold intense reactions to the Irishman, the Italian, or the Jew. By then, the French Canadian was an acceptable part of industrialized society, and a source of friction and antagonism more to other immigrant groups than to the native New Englanders.

By 1900, Yankee stereotypes of the old immigrant groups had become more sympathetic; but those of new immigrant groups, whom restrictionists wished to exclude, steadily deteriorated. So, the presence of the Italian evoked worse reactions. Since the 1870's, there had been a small colony of Italians in Boston; at first memories of Rome and Florence had colored the view of these first arrivals. Walking through Boston, Howells delighted in the Vesuvian, the Tuscan, the Lucchese, the Genoese, and even the Neopolitan: they were "wily and amiable folk," about whom he could not help casting the romance, the beauty, the charm of Italy itself. The politeness of a Vesuvian widow was a race trait, conjuring up "a lordly mansion standing on the Chiaja, or the Via Novissima, or the Canalazzo."[25]

When the large-scale migration of peasants from southern Italy and Sicily swelled from a trickle in the 1890's to a great wave in the 1900's, affection for the Italy of art and music prompted many Yankees to organize and support in New York a Society for the Protection of Italian Immigrants; appropriately Eliot Norton, son of Charles Eliot Norton, became its first president. New Englanders regretted that the Italian had become "the unthinking wielder of pick and shovel" for industrial America, and wished he could still express himself "racially" through arts and crafts work.[26] By the new century the old admiration for Italy precipitated disapproval of those who had renounced that country to emigrate to the United States.

Henry James on a visit to America in 1907 after an absence of twenty-five years, reflected these changed sentiments as acutely as Howells in 1872 had delineated the earlier romantic attachment to Italians. For James, seeking to recapture "the New England homogeneous" of the past, the Italian proved as distressingly ubiquitous as the Irishman had to Henry Adams; on the top of Beacon Hill and near the House of the Seven Gables in Salem, the presence of Italians was "remorseless." For another expatriate, Poultney Bigelow, visiting in Connecticut, the Italian became the symbol of all the recent immigrants who spoke no English and blotted the native landscape. The attractive peasant, once he shed his Old World "manners" and began "the evolution of the oncoming citizen" in the United States, lost "that element of agreeable address . . . which has, from far back, so enhanced for the stranger the interest and pleasure of a visit" to Italy. Instead of the gracious social exchanges which, abroad, rested upon a static relation of classes, there was, in the United States, a complete lack of communication between the Italian ditchdigger and the upperclass American, though political equals. The Yankees took an aristocratic delight in the Italian in his own country; but, when he could not be identified with the land of his ancestors, he seemed, like all the other strangers in early twentieth-century America, "crude" and "gross."[27]

The Italian was not only divorced from the glamorous aura of his origins, but, in the thought of New England restrictionists, the main emigrant, the *southern* Italian was ideologically undesirable. Earlier, Howells had distinguished between the northern and southern Italian: the first had an appealing "lightness of temper," while the second was a "half-civilized stock" although it produced "real artists and men of genius." In 1891, the lynching of the imprisoned members of the Mafia in New Orleans prompted Henry Cabot Lodge to dwell on the different classes of the Italian; thereafter he excepted from his harsher criticism the northerners who had Germanic blood and belonged to "a people of Western civilization." In the future, this "Teutonic" Italian, with his higher standard of living and capacity for skilled work, was a racial entity, not to be confused with his southern relative.[28]

Boston social service also reflected this differentiation. At Denison

House, Vida D. Scudder ignored settlement work with "the poorer people, mostly of the peasant class" from Italy in favor of a small group of educated Italians. Providing lectures, concerts, and picnics, Miss Scudder organized a Circolo Italo-Americano to relate these "courteous, vehement people" to the life of cultured America. Unfortunately from her view, the group was less devoted to Dante than to Mazzini, Carducci, and Sorel: anticlerical, rationalistic, restive, and ambitious, the middle-class Italian was "mentally alert, capable of enthusiasm for an abstract ideal . . . bewilderingly swift in transition to cynicism and irony." To her disappointment, this "intellectual proletariat" in the city slums found the process of Americanization vulgar and degrading. Despite her professed admiration, the social worker had some misgivings about the educated urbane Italian and wished devoutly to move him, like his southern kin, out of the cities.[29]

Unlike her benevolent, puzzled conception of the Italian intellectual, there was the hostile portrait of the young Italian working his way through Harvard College. In the novel *Philosophy 4,* the popular writer, Owen Wister, ridiculed and vilified the strivings of Oscar Maironi whose parents had come over in steerage. The "paleskinned" alien had heavy black curls, "shiny little eyes . . . furtive and antagonistic," spoke with a "suave and slightly alien accent," and wore the same dark, unattractive clothes summer and winter. He needed money badly and thus "calculation was his second nature." Implicit in the image of Oscar Maironi was the odious contrast he presented to his bona fide Harvard classmates. Rich, carefree "Bertie and Billy," with their "colonial names," had pleasant faces and wore clean white trousers and soft shirts of pink and blue. "Wholesome young creatures," who loved to play, they neglected their studies to set off by horse to the countryside and indulged regularly in fine meals. How different they were from the "patient, Oriental" Oscar Maironi with his deeper, sinister passions. "There were sly times when he took what he had saved by his cheap meals and room and went to Boston with it, and for a few hours thoroughly ceased being ascetic." There were no redeeming qualities in Oscar Maironi, who did not respect education for its own sake. Yet, basically, this portrait lacked the ethnic traits primarily associated with the Italian. Maironi might have been any southern European or Slavic or Jewish intruder in Harvard Yard: the main point of the characterization was his difference from the progeny of English colonial stock.[30] The intellectual Americanized Italian was as indiscriminately offensive to the Anglophile novelist as any immigrant laborer.

The southern Italian worker bore the brunt of criticism. The slur, "birds of passage," registered the earliest complaint against him; for, in the beginning of the period, he, like the French Canadian of the 1870's, had migrated seasonally. The accusation lost its validity when Italians settled with their families and became citizens of the United States in the 1900's. Similarly, early restrictionists complained that the southern Italian was too conservative, addicted to the "faith" and "the tools" of his forefathers.[31]

As social workers came to know him better, the decision was modified: the southern Italian was admittedly industrious and thrifty, although he lacked self-reliance. Now his "sociability, gayety, love of nature, all-round human feeling" was approved, but did not counteract the fear of Yankee authorities lest he degenerate in the second generation through beer and whisky drinking. Moreover, the notion grew that the southern Italian, with his ancient stiletto and his newly adopted revolver, had an innate, spontaneous capacity for violence, which might at any moment culminate a quarrel or feud with murder. Perhaps the Black Hand image led a Boston settlement house resident to label the Italian a people "physically strong but intellectually untrained; perhaps no worse morally than ourselves, yet who offend and shock us because their vices are of a different nature from our own." In general, the opinion prevailed that the poor, hotheaded, southern Italian was neither the best nor the worst immigrant and might later prove to be "a valuable factor" in American civilization. For the moment, he was "tractable . . . and imitative . . . with great capacities for good and evil."[32]

Very much in the minority, a few Yankees insisted on seeing more favorable aspects: the Italian exhibited diverse provincial variations in customs, dress, food, and dialects, and adapted well to the pursuits of agriculture and politics in America. "Far from being a scum of Italy's paupers and criminals," he was "the very flower of her peasantry." Thus a picture of a temperate, law-abiding, familial citizen, tilling the soil with success, existed along with the image of the Italian "with his ready knife."[33]

But, by the eve of World War I, as the restrictionist antipathy deepened, the unfavorable stereotype was ascendant. Climaxing the quiet propaganda of the Immigration Restriction League, in 1912, Prescott Hall stated in the *North American Review* that the southern Italian was undesirable because he was by race partly Negroid. Ross predicted that "the Italian dusk" would "quench . . . the Celto-Teutonic flush . . . in the cheek of the native American" and destroy the physical beauty of the Yankee stock. Summarizing the sociological data, he voted against the unstable, passionate, and vindictive immigrant from southern Italy and Sicily; not all of "the race-stuff in poverty-crushed immigrants" was good material for a democracy.[34]

Among the "new" immigrants, the Russian Jew provoked interest, comment, and judgment. Strictly speaking, the Jews were not a new group, and a very complex tradition entered into the contemporary view of the humble *émigrés* from Russian pogroms. The oldest part of that tradition was intellectual: first, the admiration for the ancient Hebrew as the fountainhead of Christianity, inherited from the seventeenth-century Puritans; second, guilt and sympathy for the persecuted Jew, stimulated by the philosophy of humanitarianism in the nineteenth century. But, as the result of the German Jewish migration to the United States from the 1840's, there was also an aesthetic image of the Jew, quite divorced from his lofty heritage. With his hooked nose and rank German accent, he was usually a seller of old clothes, ridiculed for his abstinence from eating pork; but at the same time, his Oriental passions and even his money-making ability impressed the Yankees. As the "new" immigration began, the Jew was an intriguing subject of discussion in Brahmin circles, but there had still been no personal intimacy or direct conflict in any way comparable to the living tension with the Irishman.[35]

When, in the 1880's, the Jew made his appearance in proper society abroad, the protests of James Russell Lowell or Henry Adams were characteristic of a new reaction. Paralleling the resistance of English intellectuals (like Goldwin Smith, Thomas Carlyle, and Edward A. Freeman) to the role of a few prominent Jews in the exploits of the British Empire, confused Brahmins sometimes reflected their own insecurity in the dread image of the Jewish international banker.[36] Premature in the chronology of prejudice for most educated Americans, the resentment of the Anglophile Brahmin minority toward the rich Jew, extended to the poor Jewish immigrant. In this transference, the "scientific" interpretations of reformers and of sociologists gave a new meaning to the strength of the ancient Hebrew and transformed the harmless image of the immigrant Jew into a questionable stereotype.

In the early 1890's, despite the humanitarian protests of most Americans, the New England restrictionists had been antagonistic toward the Jewish group escaping Czarist Russia. The support of the English social reformer, Arnold White, was influential. White, formerly opposed to England's admission of indigent German Jews, had shifted his attack to the Russian Jews: with their "hereditary ignorance of, and muscular incapacity for, the more elementary conditions of success in a new country," these refugees represented the worst "degradation of the racial type." He warned Americans that London had become a way station where thousands of Jews, physically deficient as well as financially insolvent, were being put into shape for the examination at Ellis Island. Robert DeC. Ward and Frederick Bushée agreed that the United States was only encouraging the despotic practices of European countries by receiving their worst classes. Andrew D. White, American Minister to Russia, thought the admission of Polish Jews should be regulated. With no particular dislike, Henry Cabot Lodge doubted that the country could make good Americans out of Russian Jews or Italians. William Z. Ripley noted that his country, like Germany, had a real problem, for "this great Polish swamp of miserable human beings, terrific in its proportions, threatens to drain itself off into our country as well, unless we restrict its ingress."[37] As yet, these uncharitable descriptions of the Russian or Polish Jew involved no more special discrimination than similar denunciations of the southern Italian.

It became commonplace to regard the Russian Jew with skepticism and clichés from *Races of Europe* received wide currency. With scholarly prudence, Ripley had denied the existence of a Jewish "race" and even tried to dispel the impression that there was a "Jewish nose." The ethnic individuality associated with the Jews was "of their own making from one generation to the next, rather than a product of an unprecedented purity of physical descent." Nonetheless, in the faces of Jews was the stamp of "a people." Ripley generalized about their characteristics in such a way that sociologists and social workers knew in advance that the Jew had extraordinary longevity despite his outward appearance of physical degeneracy. Rarely drunk but very prone to mental diseases, he lived by brain rather than by brawn: moreover, he had an inherent dislike for manual and oudoor labor; and it was "an unalterable characteristic of this peculiar people" to congregate in cities. Despite personal variations, these categories formed the basic concept of the Jew among American intellectuals in the early part of the twentieth century.[38]

In the minds of looser "racists," Ripley provided a jumping-off point for unattractive corollaries. For local social workers his text facilitated an uncongenial image of the Jew in contradistinction to that of the Irishman. Bushée, Lee, Ward, and Hall were affronted by the Jew's serious-mindedness. Lee deplored the lack of "gang tendency," of Jewish youth and remarked that athletics had less appeal than among the Irish. "A Jew boy who has been at school morning and afternoon and worked hard at selling newspapers before and after school hours, would rather spend his evening in wrestling over algebraical problems than give his time to frivolous pursuits that make no contribution to his power of achievement." Developing this chain of associations, Ross claimed that "if the Hebrews are a race, certainly one of their traits is *intellectuality*." So the Jew had a special gift for the abstractions of mathematics and chess-playing. But, negatively, this meant that he had no feeling for concrete details, nor could he be a good craftsman, tiller of the soil, or lover of pets.[39]

Jewish seriousness connoted not only a solemn dedication to work but a lack of kindness. Some found Jewish "morality" without "generosity," polaric to Irish "generosity" and "warm-heartedness." Bushée generalized severely that "the great objection to . . . the Jews is that they are not Christian, and by this I mean that they do not recognize the principle of the brotherhood of man."[40]

By the same token, the Jew had "inherited a wonderful amount of moral strength." Still, some critics complained that "the present Hebrew immigration" had resulted in the "moral degradation" of family life and political activities. It was believed that Jewish crime and prostitution was increasing as the second generation lost the older religious moorings. Ross described "the egoistic, conscienceless Jew as a menace." Others considered his low rate of mortality, criminality, and pauperism an index to the Jew's resistance to social and physical degeneration. The compliment was sometimes dubious as it implied a fixity of purpose and an imperviousness to environment, even worse still, a detachment from the American scene. Bushée explained "the Jewish feeling of superiority to other peoples": although the Jew was politically easy to assimilate, he would not amalgamate socially with other Americans because of his desire to preserve, even more than his religion, his "racial purity." He also sympathized with the Czar's protection of his people from the grasping Russian Jew who was synonymous with the medieval moneylender. More lightly, Robert A. Woods discussed "the Jewish passion for the unearned increment" as a factor in real estate operations.[41]

Consistent with the Russian Jew's self-imposed, unfriendly isolation, he was too individualistic. Defenders of organized labor feared that the "race instinct" of the Hebrew would weaken the development of permanent unions. Commons believed that, even as a trade unionist, the Jew's concept of organization was that of a tradesman rather than a workman. The stereotype of this "city folk" always at home in business and industry, did not fit the Yankee sociologists' conscious preference for an agricultural population as the base of a healthy democracy. In the manner of Henry and Brooks Adams, Ross asked, "To this roaming, hunting, exploring, adventurous breed what greater contrast is there than the denizens of the Ghetto?" The Jew, physically undersized and emotionally uncontrolled, was incapable of outdoor manual labor—the exact opposite of the Yankee's tough, stoic pioneer breed. Or, reduced to Lee's Teutonist formula, the combination of Slav and Jew could hardly contribute to the success of the American nation in the way the Teutonic elements of the colonial stocks already had.[42]

Restrictionist propaganda continuously extended the hostile image of the Jew, but many qualifications perplexed the New Englanders' evaluations. The older pattern of admiration for the Jew persisted. For those who retained the social assumptions of the pre-Civil War community the Hebraic roots of Christianity still nurtured respect for the descendants of the people of the Old Testament. Edward Everett Hale believed that the life of the spirit (as the conception of an unseen God) was Semitic, whereas the life of the body (as the love of nature or of beauty) was Aryan. Charles W. Eliot thought of the Jewish race as "the source of all the highest conceptions of God, man, and nature."[43]

Turning to the present, Edward A. Atkinson noted that most Jews were poor, although there was a "dominant minority of highest intellectual power" distinguished in politics, banking, music, and literature. Hale, becoming acquainted with the "much-dreaded Russian Jew," marked him "a model emigrant." A social worker of South End House observed their lack of meanness in buying tickets to a banquet of a neighborhood association at which they could eat only the ice cream. Another observer was surprised at their willingness "to work with their hands" in "hope of going back to the soil, to the old patriarchal state, to land-ownership so long denied."[44] But, in a more complicated way, friendly critics like Shaler and Wendell, reacted to the old and new elements of the stereotype and blended interest with antipathy.

Shaler became Dean of the Lawrence Scientific School of Harvard University in 1891 and, as an administrator during the next ten years, he had direct contact with many Jewish students. Aware of the injustice of assuming that "all who fall within each category are alike," Shaler strove to override his own doctrinaire concepts. Predisposed to admire the Jew, he was profoundly moved by the struggle for advancement of the poor Boston group. He accepted their invitations to social entertainments, spoke at the annual dinner of a local Purim Association, and helped many of their boys at Harvard. When, at the turn of the century, he discovered signs of anti-Semitism in the college, unknown in the 1870's, he was genuinely distressed.[45]

In the interests of communal harmony Shaler interviewed his own friends to ascertain how "people of the Aryan race" felt "in their contact with Israelites." Shaler's social set admitted a "certain definite repulsion" when "brought into what should be neighborly relations with Jews." This exchange of opinion confirmed his own experience with Jewish students. "These youths usually respond much more swiftly to my greeting than those of my own race." But he condoned this quickness, so different from "our slow Aryan way," as an index to Jewish racial capacity. Like the Aryan, the Jew represented a superior race; unadaptable to environmental influences, he was unreconciled to Aryan domination. But, although a "high species of genus homo" in his organic endurance and in his intellectual and moral achievements, the Hebrew was "somewhat archaic . . . for the life of the genus in its present stage." On the other hand, the Aryan manifested his "government-shaping ability, together with the capacity for research into nature and into the mechanic arts." This interpretation of the Jew gave the older benevolent image negative overtones.[46]

Significantly, Shaler was still a man of the nineteenth century. He sought to supplant the "brutal" attitude of prejudice with the "ideal of the neighbor." Despite his own xenophobic reactions, he proposed a union between Aryans and Semites in the United States in order to create "a safe common element of population." Only by the extermination of the Jews through intermarriage would America benefit from Semitic capacity; and at the same time the obliteration of this racial type would solve the problem of prejudice.[47]

Barrett Wendell also retained an abiding interest in the poor Jewish student, so completely outside the sphere of the Harvard gentleman. As mentor and friend to young Horace Kallen and gracious patron to Mary Antin, Wendell followed the pattern of *noblesse oblige,* already demonstrated by Brahmin support of Bernard Berenson in the 1890's. In addition, Wendell sought to stimulate a revival of classical Hebrew culture and to ignore the Judaic social and religious code of the Russian immigrants. Attracted to the Jew as the transmitter of his ancient culture, Wendell unconsciously slurred the actual immigrant stock in America. Accustomed to honoring the past and current Jacob Wendell scholars of the college at a dinner in his home each year, Wendell once remarked that if "an Ethiopian or a Hebrew" should ever win this ancestral scholarship, the custom of the dinners would have to be permanently abandoned. Nevertheless Wendell, who liked to say with Henry Adams that his "race" was as "oppressed" as ever the Jewish one had been, could imagine the unknown, distant day when the children of a Mary Antin might be "American in the sense" in which Wendell was. "America, for all its faults and its vulgarities" had wrought that "kind of miracle." For Wendell, the Jew represented a social inferior; yet the image remained of a mystifying, exotic people of capacity. In general, the stereotype of the Jew as expressed by men of the older generation—like Shaler, Wendell, Eliot, or McCall—was sympathetic rather than hostile.[48]

But, by 1912, signposts of the anti-Semitic future were being erected. The eugenicist, Dr. Charles B. Davenport, summarized the negative view. Russian and southern European Jews "with their intense individualism and ideals of gain at the cost of any interest," represented "the opposite extreme from the . . . English and the . . . Scandinavian immigration with their ideals of community life in the open country, advancement by the sweat of the brow, and the uprearing of families in the fear of God and the love of country."[49] By inference, the nature of the Jew, fixed by biological heredity, was not suitable to the American way of life.

Hall showed how a frustrated restrictionist made the Jew an object of hatred. Jews he had known at college, and after graduating from Harvard Law School, he had formed a partnership with a lawyer named Adler. Although the young crusading restrictionist had viewed with horror the immigrant Russian Jew, as late as 1906, he had disassociated the German Jew from the physical and moral degeneration of his southeastern European kin. But, at the time Hall dissolved his law partnership in 1907, he knew that German Jews like Lucius Littauer, Oscar Straus, Jacob Schiff, and Cyrus Sulz-berger actively opposed the literacy test. Although other Americans —of German, Italian, Polish, Irish, Armenian, and Syrian back-ground—had also by 1912 protested against the legislation, Hall and other rabid partisans insisted that "the Jewish race" was waging a "systematic campaign in newspapers and magazines" against restric-tion. When Taft vetoed the literacy bill in 1913, Hall exploded "to Hell with Jews, Jesuits and Steamships."[50]

By then, he and his close associates veered to a noxious anti-Semitism through their devotion to eugenics. The works of Houston Stewart Chamberlain, Joseph Arthur de Gobineau, and Dr. Alfred P. Schultz gave a genetic meaning to the survival of the long-suffer-ing Jew. Sustained by these anti-Semites, Hall attributed the Jew's energy and mental alertness to race purity, and rebuked Louis Brandeis for not agreeing that "the Jews of all people" should understand the importance of the "eugenic selection of immigrants." Hall demanded an American people similarly unsullied by half-breeds; and while still professing to esteem Jewish genius, he damned the existence of the American Jew.[51]

Ross approved "the race line" against Jews in private schools, hotels, and clubs because "this cruel prejudice" had grown out of "contemporary experience" with "vulgar upstart parvenus."[52] The ideas of Teutonist-minded reformers had transformed the older stereotype. When an individual Jew tried to reach outside the ghetto for social or intellectual status, the principle of assimilation no longer applied. The stereotype had become malignant, justifying restricted intercourse between Yankee and Jew.

But in the America of the 1900's, the Jew was not an exclusive ob-ject of deprecation and social ostracism. H. G. Wells reported, after a visit to the United States in 1905, that at times he "could have im-agined there were no immigrants at all. All the time, except for one distinctive evening," he talked "to English-speaking men, now and then to the Irishman, now and then, but less frequently to the Americanized German. In the clubs there are no immigrants. There are not even Jews, as there are in London clubs. One goes about the wide streets of Boston, one meets all sorts of Boston people, one visits the State-House; it's all the authentic English-speaking Amer-ica."[53]

Prejudice against the country's latecomers had become habitual. As Yankees gathered facts about each ethnic group, every experi-ence with an individual Italian, Slav, Pole, Armenian, Greek, or any other outsider, became a generality. A Boston social worker, usually "just and fair," felt that the Syrians "could not make good." Although stereotypes fluctuated in emphasis, involving hu-man inconsistencies, the total impression gained credence. So, the Italian murdered, the Irishman drank, or the Jew bargained; one group was gayest, another most political, another most intellec-tual. Each group not only varied in its predominant virtues and vices but, more important, as it was different in major or minor ways, so it was the more alien and inferior to the Anglo-Saxon. In the development of a living xenophobia, outsiders were "figures merely. 'They ain't *folks,* they're nothin' but a parcel of images.'"[54] These images transmuted by the "scientific" values with which the restrictionists endowed them, became ethically impersonal. Now, the goal of assimilation with its Teutonist criteria of racial homo-geneity had a limited circumference and negated the democratic ideal of the nation.

CHAPTER IX

The Minority with Faith

I should like to be saved from loss of faith in democracy as I grow old and foolish. I should be very sorry to wind up as the three Adamses did. I shall not, unless I lose my mind.

—Charles W. Eliot[1]

If a Yankee philosophy of "race" had steadily matured since the 1890's, it was not altogether for lack of opposition to the "scientific" doctrine of Anglo-Saxonism. Unheeded, a distinguished minority still understood the older meaning of immigration. Not all college presidents, not all social workers, not all families necessarily agreed that the American people was deteriorating ethnically. Charles W. Eliot, Emily G. Balch, and William James did not fear the strangers who were peopling the nation. With faith in the ideal of democracy as great New Englanders had expressed it in the 1840's and 1850's, a few leaders in business enterprise, social reform, and philosophical speculation ignored the current racial doubts.

Edward A. Atkinson was typical of the spokesmen of free immigration, for whom the economic and the social assets of the immigrant were inseparable. A self-made man, he was born in Brookline, Massachusetts, of a modest family; his personal success in New England textiles gave him confidence in the laissez-faire functioning of private industry. He was also concerned with Southern economic problems, the promotion of the Boston Manufacturers Insurance Company, and the extension of free trade. A thoroughgoing Mugwump, this businessman sought a broad comprehension of economic factors and in the same way valued the material benefits of immigration to American society as a whole.

Atkinson attributed the enormous demand for domestic manufactured goods in part to the influx of immigrants, who were consumers as well as producers. He insisted that the standard of living of the native workingman had steadily advanced since 1865. And even contract labor had a useful function: the foreigners were imported only when they were needed and filled the gap left by those who had advanced to better jobs. Beyond the horizon of factories, Atkinson analyzed the impact of the western frontier and concluded that there was still "no lack of land" in America. Unoccupied areas of Texas, large parts of the South and abandoned farms in New England awaited intelligent, energetic owners, comparable to the original pioneers. How, he asked, could economists predict the lack of land within a given period of time, since no one knew "the productive capacity of an acre?"[2] Characteristic of older generations, Atkinson had an irrepressible zest for capitalistic expansion and could not comprehend the attitude of academicians and intellectuals toward the economy, still less their suspicions of the immigrant workers.

Atkinson, who had espoused abolition in his youth and maintained faith in the freed Negro, watched the progress of immigrant groups with optimism. The distinction between "old" and "new" emigrants contradicted his experience. He recalled, "without any reflection upon one race as compared with another," that no more "hopeless class could have been dealt with than the poorest class of Irish . . . of 1846."[3] Surely, Boston had nothing to fear from the thrift and ambition of Jews or Italians, who had arrived in the last ten years.

At the turn of the century, Atkinson viewed the foreign-born with the premises of the old New England civilization. His confidence sprang partly from his stubborn loyalty to the economy of his lifetime. Business was an adventure in which immigrants played an essential part. Moreover, Atkinson was a Unitarian, still influenced by William Ellery Channing, for whom education was the infallible means of improving any human material. Whatever the goal—abolition, Negro education, free trade, anti-monopoly, anti-imperialism—or free immigration, an America in which any individual was free to develop, was attainable. One's judgment upon the problem of immigration varied only with one's trust in a free government. For Atkinson, it was "almost pusillanimous to refuse a refuge to the oppressed and to the industrious, for fear that the institutions of this country may suffer."[4]

But even some Yankees who were more critical of American business practices found the economic and social goods of immigration indivisible, as the attitudes of Edward Everett Hale, Thomas Wentworth Higginson, and John Graham Brooks revealed.

Hale and Higginson, descendants of well-known families of the favored stock, had both started their careers as Unitarian ministers before the Civil War. Becoming immersed in the literary and reform movements of the time, these reformers felt keenly the increasing disparity between rich and poor in an industrialized community. In the later era, they endorsed Bellamy's intellectual socialism. But although they favored a government-directed cooperative society, they respected the function of immigrants in the economy. In the 1850's, Hale had observed that the Brahmin level of culture, symbolized in the Boston Athenaeum, existed because of immigrants who built railroads and canals. In the 1890's, Hale again noted that migration "has enriched us without our care." Higginson dismissed the standard of living argument; with a backward glance at the appalling aspect of the early emigrants to Boston, he asked, "Does anyone now complain that Irish families stint themselves in food and clothing, or that Irish cooks and chambermaids do not ask and obtain as high wages as anybody else?" Remembering with delight that "the ancestors of most of our present patricians were plebians," this Brahmin gentleman welcomed more poor immigrants.[5] The gradual rise of all able-bodied and able-minded people was the social reality these older New Englanders had known, and they continued to relate it to general economic prosperity.

Of a later generation, leaving the Unitarian pulpit to study the relations between capital and labor in the 1890's, Brooks became a staunch supporter of the trade unions. Nevertheless, he held that immigrants, if not used as scabs, would provide additional strength to labor organizations. In general, they had increased the standard of living, and were functional as migratory workmen, going back and forth to Europe. In the present development of the United States, its eight thousand industries had a greater capacity to absorb newcomers than ever before. Altruistically, Brooks rejoiced in the meaning of America, both for those who went back and spread its influences and for those who stayed. This defender of labor did not doubt that the New World which "millions . . . found . . . and still find . . . the land of opportunity," could still provide economic and social mobility.[6]

But even more than the materialistic rise of the world's masses in the United States, immigration aroused the old-fashioned humanitarian instinct of these New Englanders. Hale never forgot "the curious wave of feeling," that idealizing of man which knew no limits in Boston of the 1840's. He had then acknowledged the Brahmins' debt to the Irish laborers, "fugitives from a grinding slavery, . . . fugitives, indeed, who come in obedience to an unchanging law of human movement." Later he identified all ethnic groups as brothers, equal in the sight of God. Others like Alice Stone Blackwell, W. L. Garrison, Edwin Mead, Charles Dole, James Jackson Storrow, and Samuel J. Barrows never doubted that America should remain the asylum for the downtrodden of the world. To the great annoyance of Prescott F. Hall, immigration restriction was, in the opinion of Charles W. Eliot, both ungenerous and ungrateful.[7]

These heirs to New England tradition disputed restrictionist claims that the presence of the foreign-born had created the evils of urban congestion, insanity, and crime. Brooks ridiculed the notion that the mere numbers of aliens arriving each year had produced the contemporary social ills. Hale declared that the basic shock to American society came not from immigration but from urbanization. Critical of organized Christianity for its habitual "indifference" to the needs of the foreign-born, he conceived the Church in a new role—as a neighborhood center befriending lonely and confused immigrants. When in the 1890's it was commonly assumed that the urban masses were immoral, Eliot recognized how "easy" it was "for people whose forefathers came to this western world one or more generations ago to believe that the people who have just come are the source of all municipal woes." Atkinson believed the solution to social problems arising out of slum conditions lay in plans "to break up the concentration of the factory system." The anti-restrictionists separated "abuses from uses" of immigrants in the urbanized society of America.[8]

Early in the 1890's, some Brahmins protested against the literacy test. In Emersonian language, Hale countered that "what we want is men who have been trained to use hand and eye and brain. Many a man who can read has not had such training." Higginson pointed out that an illiterate Puritan matriarch had founded a prominent Boston family and that a President of the United States had not learned to read until manhood. The standard of literacy for admission discredited physical brawn and energy as the base of a vigorous nation. Those who respected the cost of migration to the immigrants, welcomed the "bone and sinew" of the Old World, saying, in effect, let them learn to read in their new home.[9]

These New Englanders accepted the economic value of immigrants and acknowledged an ethical obligation to receive Europe's poor and oppressed. But even the most enlightened citizens occasionally felt pangs of nostalgia and uncertainty. Traveling in San Diego in 1891, Hale found he was "more in the midst of Americans" than he had "been for forty years." To the members of the Cambridge Historical Society Eliot confided his anxiety while the city filled up with "many races," and "the Puritans no longer control Cambridge."[10] It would have been unnatural if men devoted to their own traditions had not felt some resistance to the changes in their society. More significant, however, Eliot, Hale, and other opponents of ethnic antagonisms worked out in their minds and in their feelings more than a passive reconciliation to the future, and even affirmed its unknown character.

The non-restrictionists were skeptical of doctrinaire Teutonist assumptions of race. Higginson, who repudiated the cult of Anglo-Saxonism in the old antislavery days, maintained that no "one race" monopolized "all the virtues." Eliot ridiculed those who boasted of

English descent, forgetting that they were descended from "a veritable ethnological conglomerate very like that . . . now forming . . . in the United States." William James, the Harvard philosopher, expressed no formal view on race or immigration, but had only disgust for the psychology of the Anglo-Saxons. Reflecting upon Kipling's verse, he wished "the Anglo-Saxon race would drop its sniveling cant." Then "it would have a good deal less of a 'burden' to carry. We're the most loathsomely canting crew that God ever made."[11]

His colleague Josiah Royce, who had taken his Ph.D. at Johns Hopkins in 1878, made a point of detaching himself from formalized "racist" fallacies. A Californian, son of English immigrants, Royce knew painfully well the conflict between old and new. But even while he sought the Absolute in religion and philosophy, he rejected existing ethnic classifications as not "sufficient guides to an interpretation of the whole inner contrast of the characters and of the mental processes of men," and noted that the typical racial theorist used "his science to support most of his personal prejudices." Royce wondered "whether a science which mainly devotes itself to proving that we ourselves are the salt of the earth, is after all so exact as it aims to be."[12] Although not closely acquainted with the "new" immigrants, he found the Teutonic dogma intellectually vulnerable.

Charles W. Eliot's energetic stand for the principles of free immigration was especially striking, because the president of Harvard was no simple, sentimental democrat. A traditionalist, proud of his personal descent from solid Boston Lymans and Eliots, he upheld values shaped by generations. For him, the old Puritan ministers and lawyers, often handing on their professions from one generation to the next, were still the gentry of New England: good families, such as had appeared "for one hundred years or more, on the catalogues of Harvard and Yale colleges . . . families in which comfort, education, and good character have been transmitted, if riches and high places have not." The lowered birth rate of Harvard graduates troubled Eliot as much as the restrictionists, but he did not blame the immigrants. Although he urged Yankee procreation, he believed that the American way of life could produce new "good" families. The combination of individual freedom and social mobility, facilitated by political suffrage, permitted "the capable to rise through all grades of society, even within a single generation."[13] Since America was a dynamic expanding society, a Slavic peasant family might eventually produce the social and intellectual counterpart of an old New Englander. Unlike his restrictionist associates, Eliot regarded the immigrant as an integral part of the unique American civilization still in the making.

Nevertheless Eliot was a realistic snob about the nature of American democracy. He affected none of the inhibitions of Norton or Fiske or Walker toward the existing class divisions which presumably immigration had solidified. Neither political democracy nor economic fluidity implied the goal of social equality; differences in human beings tended to create groups based on "common tastes and common occupations." Mechanics, clerks, tradesmen whom he admired or persons whom he met at the polls or in charitable work, were Eliot's political equals in Massachusetts but he saw no reason to meet them "in society." Moreover, it was good that men's differences in skills and abilities inevitably produced differences in conditions, even in the accumulation of property. The best community should develop "every man's peculiar skill, faculty or aptitude . . . to the highest possible degree."[14]

Eliot's faith in the infinite variety of mankind, almost outmoded at the end of the nineteenth century "sprang naturally from the soil of progressive thinking in and about Boston" during the first half of the century. Whether in religion, education, economics, or in immigration, insistence upon limitless individuality within "the essential unity of a democratic community" was the firm basis of his thinking and acting.[15]

He liked to call himself "emphatically a birthright Unitarian." And he lived up to that birthright in placing freedom of thought first in the construction of a great university. Since uniformity had no place in the democratic ideal, he offered "equality of treatment for all religions" within Harvard Yard. Here was a singular opportunity to gather together young men of different communions and teach them a respect for each other's creeds. Eliot was proud to establish religious services in which preachers of different denominations took part. And, even as the college should inculcate toleration for every individual's religion, so the primary and secondary schools should foster respect for the labors of the individuals of the many races all over the world.[16] Not too early in life could one start to stress the obligation of each generation to all mankind both in the past and in the present.

Eliot was always willing to accept the full consequences of an immigration policy which brought all types of Europeans to America. As a young man, he had believed they were capable of "complete assimilation"; in maturity, he urged their preservation as races in the United States. He had become a consistent opponent of uniformity wherever he found it; he eliminated assimilation as a desired end, thus cutting through the most sacred ideal of New England restrictionists. To their cry that the foreign-born no longer amalgamated with the old native descendants, Eliot replied that there had been little social and physical blending of the older immigrant stocks in the first half of the nineteenth century. What was more, he denied the theoretical value of the melting pot. Amalgamation was "not only extraordinarily slow, but of doubtful issue." It was enough that "the different races already in this country live beside each other, and all produce in time good citizens of the Republic." Whoever accepted the principles of freedom, justice, and government as the servant of the people had by "acceptance of the common American ideals" become sufficiently assimilated.[17] Diversity of races was fitting in a society which made freedom of thought an essential goal.

But since his principles rather than his emotions governed Eliot's attitude toward immigration, he never considered the psychological barriers which prevented understanding among the different kinds of Americans. William James, another spiritual descendant of Emerson, although much less consciously social-minded, recognized the basic lack of communication between people alien to each other's way of life. On a journey through the mountains of North Carolina, he was startled by his own revulsion at the "unmitigated squalor" of the hillbillies' existence. But he corrected himself with the realization that he was "blind to the peculiar ideality of their conditions as they certainly would also have been to the ideality of mine, had they had a peep at my strange indoor academic ways of life at Cambridge." Since it was impossible to understand completely the myriad values of others, "no one should presume to judge" or to interfere with the peculiar ways of different people in an "off-hand" way. Like an answer to the scientifically documented stereotypes of the foreign-born, James reduced the significance of being different to petty proportions. "In God's eyes the difference of social position, of intellect, of culture, of cleanliness, of dress, which different men exhibit . . . must be so small as practically quite to vanish." With a "feeling of reverence and awe," he enjoyed not only the vitality of the peasant women of Vienna but equally that of the Italian and Hungarian laborers in the Boston subway. And in the belief that each individual was put on earth to struggle upward through peculiar difficulties, James expected at least the intellectuals, mindful of man's "ancestral blindness" toward his fellowman, to try to live "by sympathies and admirations, not by dislikes and disdains."[18]

As James explored the personal relationships of individuals and added to Eliot's principle of toleration a drive of warm curiosity toward the infinite variations of mankind, so John Graham Brooks, an admirer of James's open universe, made a third link in relation to immigration itself. Condemning the ignorance and prejudice which set race against race, Brooks looked to "the free and friendly movement" of peoples to produce tolerant relationships in America for all the world to learn the lesson of harmony among different races.[19]

This spirit of "live and let live" prevailed in the concrete attitudes of the non-restrictionists toward Catholics and Jews. Despite the intellectual chasm between the adherents of the Roman Church and the Unitarians of the Channing tradition, Higginson, an admirer of Catholicism, read local parochial newspapers with respect. In old age, Higginson singled out Hoar's repudiation of the American Protective Association as the most important act of the Senator's political career.[20]

Visiting Rome as a young man, Eliot had hated Catholicism like "poison." Later, during the parochial school conflict of the 1880's and 1890's, without condemning denominational education, he had contended that all groups should avoid sectarian schools and colleges. He felt a broad education would enhance the importance of Catholics in the community. In his prime, he got along well with the Catholic clergy. Like James, he was an "enemy of all that the Catholic Church *inwardly* stands for," but for him as for James "the concrete Catholics, including the common priests . . . are an entirely different matter. Their wish to educate their own, and to do what proselytizing they can, is natural enough; so is their wish to get state money. 'Destroying American institutions' is a widely different matter . . . I should like to hear one specification laid down of an 'institution' which they are now threatening."[21]

In 1911, Eliot refused to consider anti-Catholic motivations for immigration policy. To restrict immigration because it was more Catholic than Protestant "would be the public confession of lack of faith in the efficacy of religious toleration and the independence of church and state as bulwarks of political freedom." Eliot expected that American environment would in the long run modify the Roman Church more than the Church would affect the character of the country.

With more personal involvement these New Englanders pondered the question of social relations with Jews. The Dreyfus Case became, for William James, not only a symbol of French corruption but also a challenge for American intellectuals to "work to keep our precious birthright of individualism. . . One must do *something* to work off the effect of the Dreyfus sentence." Expressing more than moral indignation when he received from a New England hotel (which he had previously enjoyed) a circular stating that "applications from Hebrews cannot be considered," he answered: "I propose to return the boycott." James admired without reservation his Jewish friends. He described one of his sons as a "wonderfully beautiful Jewish-looking" child.[23]

The idea of homogeneity which obsessed restrictionists and assimilationist leaders of new Americans did not interest James. But in the notebooks of John Graham Brooks the Yankee conception of the Jewish problem was articulated: "How much of his Jewishness do we want him to give up and how much difference and variety do we want?" For Eliot, who agreed with eugenicists that each race should preserve "through many generations its own bodily and mental advantages and historical characteristics," there was no doubt that the Jew should keep his individuality and his survival was proof of "the value of racial purity." Harvard's president, who had a "long and intimate friendship" with Jacob Schiff, the Jewish financier, was almost unique among philo-Semites in advocating the eternal separateness of the Jew.[24]

There was no unanimity among these New Englanders as to the means of overcoming anti-Semitism. But those who respected the religion of the Jew and accepted him as one among many in the United States, did not blink at the growth of anti-Semitic discrimination.

More revealing than his acquiescence on the subject of the Jew was Eliot's repudiation of other inferences of eugenics. For the believer in man's perfectibility, the premises and analogies which seemed legitimate to the modern scientist of heredity denied the humanitarian tenets of the 1840's and 1850's. Upon reading Ward's *The Crisis in Our Immigration Policy,* Eliot advised his climatology professor that one neither could nor should improve human beings by methods which were suitable for horses, dogs, and cattle, for "the processes of animal breeding are wholly and forever inapplicable to human breeding." In essence, eugenics had reduced man whether American or immigrant to animal, devoid of moral consciousness. To Eliot, the descendant of Puritans and the disciple of Channing and Emerson, the upward struggle of man's soul and his responsibility for his brother were realities which superseded the abstract justifications of scientific heredity.[25]

Eliot did not deny the importance of protecting the public health from the effects of pauperism, criminality, feeble-mindedness, and insanity. He preferred legislation and administration to "prevent *all* the insane from breeding—natives and aliens alike." "The vice of natives as well as aliens" was "poisoning" the American caliber. To

Ward's complaint about the admission of undesirable aliens who were theoretically excluded by law, Eliot replied, "We know that in the present state of medical knowledge and of the means of diagnosis it is impossible for any process of inspection to detect all the persons liable to insanity within one year or five years or even all those actually insane. The same is true of border cases of feeble-mindedness." To Ward's objection that the existing laws were also unenforceable because of the difficulty of coping with "sentiment" or "humanity," he answered again with humanitarian emphasis: "Who would have it otherwise? This is *good* human nature." In cases involving the separation of families, Harvard's president preferred to ignore the rigid letter of the law. "Any other policy" was "inhuman" and a departure from "the parable of the Good Samaritan." Eliot characterized the restrictionist resistance to the "never-ending burden of care" of the mentally defective as a "mean motive." The anti-immigrationists had mistaken the negative aspects of immigration for basic influences and had lost sight of the "true doctrine": it was impossible to select by legislation the best specimens of each race applying for American citizenship, and equally it was impossible "to exclude all undesirable immigrants without excluding a great number of very desirable immigrants."[26]

Yet no New Englander cared more for the quality and the character of the American people than Eliot. With the same motivation as kindred and professional opponents he denied that alien stocks were watering the nation's lifeblood. Instead of blaming immigration for the decline of the native stock, he suggested that "the American race" was "dying out because of its own shortcomings—not because of alien admissions."[27] He never doubted that the principle of free immigration was one of America's major contributions to the civilization of a free world.

Acting upon this faith, Eliot became the most impressive foe of the Immigration Restriction League. He wrote to the president of the Society for Italian Immigration that "the more Italian immigrants that come to the United States the better. . . The only way that I can help you is to state these opinions wherever and whenever I can appropriately do so. That help I propose to give steadily." In

1906, as a member of the Immigration Department of the National Civic Federation, he worked with opponents of restriction. As a supporter of the National Liberal Immigration League in 1911, he was the mouthpiece for the most active opposition to Boston restrictionists.[28]

And, on the eve of World War I, when others faltered, Eliot saw no cause to invalidate the ideal of a lifetime. He never ceased to believe that the United States could use more laborers. Not wealthy himself, he held that in a diversified free society there should be economic inequalities; and that America needed rich capitalists as well as professors and workers in modest circumstances. Immigration suited his faith in the industrial economy of the nation. "Not a single argument for further restriction of immigration" satisfied his Brahmin conscience, and he asked, "Is this generation to be frightened out of this noble policy by any industrial, racial, political or religious bogies?"[29]

Another New Englander, Emily Balch, assented to the implications of this question. Her experience with the challenges she faced convinced her of the immigrants' value to American life. Of an old Boston family, Emily Greene Balch grew up in Jamaica Plain, Massachusetts among "people like ourselves . . . in straitened circumstances," but where "there never was any lack of money for medical care or education." This way of life turned out a very proper, well-bred young lady attending Miss Katherine Ireland's School in Louisburg Square and the select Brookline dancing parties. A member of Bryn Mawr's first graduating class in 1889, she became a student of Franklin Giddings. Newly aware of contemporary social problems, Emily Balch turned from romantic dreams of novel-writing to the more pressing study of economics.[30]

After further study in Paris with Émile Levasseur and a stint of practical social service under Charles Birtwell in Cambridge, Massachusetts, she joined the staff of Denison House in 1892. When she left social work to teach at Wellesley College in 1896, her classes on labor legislation, immigration, and socialism interested young women in social service. Imparting a sense of obligation untainted by *noblesse oblige,* Emily Balch felt that all of her contemporaries were "charity scholars—beneficiaries of those who have worked before us. That we are not dirty, cruel, stupid, cave dwellers is due to the efforts of others."[31]

With humility, she interpreted the much maligned Slavic immigrant. In 1905, she spent several months in Austria and Hungary to observe the source of this "emigration on the spot" before visiting the Slavic settlements in the United States. Probing deeply into the life of the peasants who migrated from southeastern Europe, her book *Our Slavic Fellow Citizens* refuted many restrictionist assumptions. The old Francis Walker argument—that the steamship companies had artificially created the "new" immigration—was a mere "rhetorical commonplace"; modern transportation had only greased the wheels of the vast movement of peoples caused by fundamental economic changes. In explaining the operation of the real forces which were still uprooting the peasants from their stable, ordered way of life, Miss Balch also made short shrift of the frequent cry that the emigrants were the pauper scum of Europe.[32]

Analyzing the impact of migration upon the participants, she corrected nativist criticism of the strange nationalities. She described the process by which the Slovak or Pole who came to the United States gained a stronger ethnic consciousness than he had ever had in his little rural village, and how, upon meeting others from the land of departure, he developed new nationalistic passions, which native and foreign-born leaders alike exploited. Still more, she recognized that these emotions had become ephemeral in the second-generation members of the group. "Pan-Slavic feelings" died out, as the sons of immigrants found nearer goals more meaningful.[33] For the children of the aliens, the real focus of life lay in how to pass the barriers which lay between native Americans and foreigners, between those who were inside and those who were just outside, unable to reach the fruits of the promised land. And Emily Balch inferred that natives who feared aliens' loyalty to their former countries, simply did not know nor understand America's foreign-born.

Discovering that immigrants came to the United States "at once so ready and able to learn of Americans," she became more interested in finding means for the foreign-born to partake of what was best in the national experience than in bemoaning their weaknesses. Like Eliot, she knew that "ignorance and dirtiness" could be cured; she too cast aside as unworthy of consideration the contemporary fears of disease, crime, pauperism, and illiteracy.[34]

Miss Balch debunked "the bugbear of racial intermixture." Skeptical of ethnic generalizations, she stated that there were no such individuals as Teutons, Slavs, or Celts. With characteristic Unitarian faith in environment, she concluded that group types were not fixed by heredity. Instead they were "quite as much products of social development and imitation, determined by historical causes economic and other, as they are the expression of innate qualities."[35]

One dilemma in evaluating the effects of immigration had to be faced: how to surmount the exploitation of the immigrant labor market. Although an ardent supporter of trade unions and in the foreguard of those who battled against sweatshops, she had not limited her interest to the skilled laborer. Instead of attacking the immigrant masses for lowering the standard of living of older American, trained workers, Emily Balch blamed the public for tolerating low wages in cases where "only foreigners" were involved. With a sense of guilt for their brutal and demoralizing treatment, she repeated what one Slav leader had told her: *My people do not live in America, they live underneath America. America* goes on over their heads. America does not begin till a man is a workingman, till he is earning two dollars a day. A laborer can not afford to be an American." Still, even under the worst conditions, as in the New England cotton mills, she had faith that the immigrant masses would rise; that they were alive was "the main thing" of promise.[36]

Emily Balch did not ignore the restrictionist claim that the ease of acquiring immigrant labor did, in fact, facilitate inferior working conditions and a low scale of wages. However, she favored Paul Kellogg's solution of a minimum wage for immigrants hired by corporate employers for a given period of time. Thus, "an obligatory standard" would ensure both the American worker and the ignorant newcomer of a decent living and remove the only possible grounds for immigration restriction.[37]

Unlike most Brahmins, she did not grieve over the fate of her

New England, but dwelt on the suffering which emigration inflicted upon the foreign-born. Observing that peasant groups came from places where they had been a part of a culture—"a set of values, customs, manners and taboos which interlocked into an organic whole"—she described the immediate break-down of this culture in the course of settlement in American industrial centers. The loss to the foreign-born was all the more destructive, for, in contact with the poorest aspects of life in the United States, they gained so little. She would have liked to slow down the process of Americanization for the immigrant in order to salvage much that he had brought with him.

But, although sensitive to the emptiness which so often followed the great adventure of coming to America, Emily Balch anticipated a better future. Like Higginson, she reflected more lightly that, as "an omelet" was never "made without breaking eggs," after the first shattering of old ways the foreign-born would make adjustments to the new life.[38] In time, they too would participate in the building of a new culture. Differing from the other intellectual sympathizers with the recent immigrants, she was able to identify herself with the feelings of a foreign-born group to such an extent that she no longer interpreted them with Anglo-Saxon criteria. With less reliance upon the Yankee cultural past than Eliot, Royce, Hale, or Higginson, Emily Balch conceived of an unknown civilization which all kinds of Americans would produce.

These men, like most old New Englanders, assumed that the ideals of the United States had already been molded permanently. Although Eliot welcomed any European who accepted American concepts and, at the same time, countenanced "an affectionate regard for the old country from which the original immigrant into America took his resolute departure," beyond this, he never considered any reciprocal activity by which the newcomer might contribute to Yankee civilization. Surprisingly, Hale as an old man urged the youth of the country to "have their being in one nation," with special recognition of "Anglo-Saxon . . . passion for freedom and its devotion to law. . . Keltic and Latin . . . quickness of perception . . . subtleties of thought . . . tenderness," and "affection."[39]

Listing the stereotypes of diverse citizens, Hale implied that each group could add something to English-speaking America. Yet what kind of amalgamation, if any, and what kind of culture would result, Hale did not suggest.

The cultural problem which weighed upon all New Englanders was how to preserve the older American values in a changing society. Royce, a New Englander by adoption, articulated the limitations of Yankee vision. Like Charles Eliot Norton, he was repelled by the uniformity of American culture, and yet found in the continuous migrations of foreigners only the element of instability which created *"the self-estranged spirit of our nation."* For all his intellectual resistance to ethnic prejudices, he was temperamentally fearful of the immigrant groups in the United States and resigned to their presence only as an existing condition of American life. Despite his philosophical devotion to individual wholes, Royce differed from other individualists, in regarding homogeneity as "the basis of healthy national life." He favored the continuance of the various national types and of distinct races in separate countries throughout the world, and reconciled the desirability of ethnic wholes with his philosophy of individuality by advocating variety among individual nations.[40]

In the United States, however, the cultural problem of diverse ethnic groups was more complex. In Royce's terms it became how to keep alive "the central principle of the moral life in a population . . . constantly being altered by new arrivals and unsettled by great social changes." His solution was to stimulate "loyalty" in individual citizens, that is, devotion to any cause in local relations, and, if possible, to encourage national unity. With a broad tolerance for all loyalties provided that they did not interfere with one another (even that of an immigrant group to the nationalist cause of a former country), Royce expected diverse loyalties to operate simultaneously.[41]

But, in a vital application of loyalty, he hoped to preserve in any local American community, "a true consciousness of its own unity." For example, in New England, pride in ideals and customs would keep intact a great heritage and the nation would profit from the individuality of the milieu. Royce did not explore the potential collisions or conflicts which provincial loyalties, if isolated, might project among old and new Americans within a single community.[42] Basically, he did not face all the social operations of his loyalty principle. Nor did Royce any more than Eliot focus upon the consequences of parallel ethnic cultures in relation to the ultimate character of American civilization.

Among the apostles of individuality only Emily Balch accepted the unpredictable role of immigrants in the future culture without preconceiving a desired result. While Eliot and Royce had not adopted the commonplace restrictionist view that a beneficent assimilation under Anglo-Saxon tutelage was the only social and cultural goal, even they did not imagine a dynamic civilization uncontrolled by the Yankee heritage. In contrast, Miss Balch thought her fellow citizens might hold too closely to their own "particular Garibaldi story." Rejoicing in the knowledge that America was an idea, universal in its appeal and its inclusiveness, she believed that "liberty achieved by democratic action" was absolutely fitting for "Catholic and Jew, Italian and Pole, Slovak and Yankee and Chinaman." And it followed that each should participate in the fullest outpouring of life, "each freely irradiating each." Without "too narrowly an American stamp" on the new civilization, she envisaged "these conglomerate elements finding unity not by making themselves like us but by building up themselves and us alike into a greater and wiser culture."[43]

Few had Emily Balch's vision, which transcended the limits of her own time and place. But for all these representatives of New England the idea of immigration solidified the obligation to maintain a free society, in which individuality rather than conformity or assimilation must be a first precept. More significant, an Eliot, James, or Balch, however influential in other spheres, could not stem the tide of restriction. As New Englanders shrank from the presence of immigrants in each successive decade, the older symbolic view of immigration vanished, until the exponents of an open, diverse world seemed strange and almost incomprehensible. As Thomas Wentworth Higginson had predicted, restriction, like the ancient wall of China, came to isolate America.[44] So, in the early decades of the twentieth century the late voices of the great New England tradition went unheard, and for a long time to come the racial basis of restriction would be the natural way of thinking.

CHAPTER X

The Consequences

There was once the supreme chance of breeding here the finest race and nation in the whole history of mankind . . . The English Puritans thought that "God had sifted the whole nation that he might send choice grain into the wilderness," and this sifting gave us the sturdy, liberty-loving, New England stock of our early history. If God had only continued to sift the nations for our benefit, or if our fathers had exercised only reasonable caution . . . we might have had here only the choicest blood and the highest types of culture of all lands, we might have replaced the slow and wasteful methods of natural selection by intelligent selection and thus have enormously advanced and hastened human evolution. That chance has gone forever.   —Edward Grant Conklin[1]

By 1912, those who believed in free immigration were an unheard minority in the old New England community. As the ethnic stereotypes hostile to the "new" immigrant groups became fixed, the long-awaited achievement was almost within the grasp of the Immigration Restriction League. Others would take up the burden in the next few years and share the responsibility for the ultimate legislative success of restriction. But the League left a permanent impact both upon the nation and upon New England society.

For almost two decades the League had preached against the European newcomers in university classrooms, in settlement houses, at meetings of businessmen and of union laborers, and at Congressional hearings, and in thousands of newspapers. The League had coordinated the interests and sympathies of individual sociologists, eugenicists, trade union leaders, and other partisans of restriction. And although Brahmins complained even in 1912 and 1913 that the American people were still indifferent, many intellectuals, once resistant, now heeded the alarms of restrictionists.[2]

In 1911, the recommendations of Theodore Roosevelt's Immigration Commission marked the advance of the League's cause. Roosevelt, Harvard class of 1880, whose first wife had been a Lee of Boston, became an intimate friend of Henry Cabot Lodge early in their political careers, and seemed a natural ally to Brahmin restrictionists. When, in 1896, Cabot delivered his classic speech on immigration to the Senate, Theodore, then New York's police commissioner, marked it "A-1." That same week he approved "heartily" the proposed literacy test in a letter to Prescott Hall. But, despite these expressions of accord, Roosevelt retreated from helping the League directly.[3]

During Roosevelt's Presidency the League missed no opportunities to impress upon him the validity of the educational test. In 1904, Lodge presented him with Robert DeCourcy Ward's current article in the *Charities* magazine. In 1905, Roosevelt incorporated Ward's recommendations in the President's annual message to Congress. Its final form echoed the League's emphasis on immigration "of the right sort," and, at Ward's suggestion, extended the list of undesirable aliens to "the physically unfit, defective or degenerate." Roosevelt qualified his attitude toward the relocation of immigrants in the South in Ward's very words: "distribution" was merely "a palliative, not a cure." But, despite Ward's pressure, there was no mention of the literacy bill. While Roosevelt gave the League some assurances of his sympathy, publicly he did not spell out its entire policy of restriction.[4]

The Boston group continued to pursue their inside track to the White House. Lodge was not their only asset. One of the League's vice-presidents, James B. Reynolds, was a "confidential adviser of the President on immigration matters." When appointed "to investigate conditions" in Ellis Island in 1906, he took the League's James Patten as an assistant. Together they examined labor conditions in the South, and, at the League's request, furnished data to show that the Ellis Island Immigration Service was being "demoralized" by appointees of Oscar Straus, the Secretary of Commerce and Labor. Despite the combined efforts of Reynolds, Patten, and Hall, however, both Lodge and Roosevelt remained impervious to allegations against Straus.[5]

In 1907, Roosevelt appointed a Commission of senators, representatives, and economic experts to survey the immigration problem in all its economic and social aspects. The board of investigators included Senators Dillingham, Lodge, and Latimer, Representatives Howell, Bennett, and Burnett, and three industrial experts, Charles P. Neill, Jeremiah W. Jenks, and William R. Wheeler.[6] The League determined to see that these men gave a report favoring restriction.

By January 1908, the Commission was under the close surveillance of the League. Senator Latimer employed Patten to canvass the needs and desires of the South. When Latimer died, Hall wrote to Lodge for a careful appointment of "some one to fill Sen. Latimer's place." Thoroughly agitated, the League kept Patten in Washington "to hammer at the Commission." Although Patten was sure by March 1909 that the majority of the Commission favored the educational test, the Boston leaders were not over-confident. Next they planned "to work on Senator Lodge" and "to help defeat Congressman Bennett."[7]

As the work of the Commission drew to a close, restrictionists used all their political and social connections in the final drive. The attempts first to influence and then to discredit Congressman Bennett were futile. The plans to enlist the support of the American Federation of Labor, the Immigration Restriction League of Arizona, the Junior Order and other patriotic societies were more successful. In addition, Harvard's president, A. Lawrence Lowell, inquired of his Senator friend about getting a "good" report, and Lodge answered affirmatively. Prescott Hall appealed to Congressman Gardner, and Professor Carver to Professor Jenks. Joseph Lee interviewed all the members of the Commission and guaranteed to get Major Henry Lee Higginson, Curtis Guild, Arthur Lyman, and other prominent Bostonians to write to Lodge. On November 10, 1910, a much desired conference between Senator Lodge, John Farwell Moors, and Prescott Hall took place. On December 15, 1910, the League recorded the triumphant finale: the Commission had not only answered in favor of restriction to the Congress of the United States; still better, the Report had specified the "illiteracy test" as the means of halting immigration.[8] Thus, Theodore Roosevelt had indirectly advanced the League's cause through the Commission which he established.

The Commission experts classified all immigrant groups by race and then passed judgment upon America's foreign-born. No greater tendency to criminality or pauperism among the newcomers was uncovered; in general, the process of Americanization was succeeding. Nevertheless the majority of the commissioners commended further restriction because of *"economic, moral,* and *social* considerations."[9] By approving the literacy test, the Commission confirmed the League's intellectual position. The educational device would favor the earlier immigrant groups and exclude largely the latecomers from southeastern Europe.

The superiority of older-stock Americans was implied throughout the Report. The main theoretician and coordinator had been the economist Jeremiah W. Jenks who was highly regarded by Roosevelt. Jenks was one of the scholars who had accepted Francis Walker's challenge at the start of the 1890's; at Cornell and then at New York University, he had expounded and sympathized with the New England pulse of the movement. But Jenks denied that there was any intent of racial discrimination in the Report. He saw nothing invidious about its "Dictionary of Races," which applied Teutonist race assumptions to the ethnic stereotypes of Americans.[10]

With far greater discrimination than Prescott Hall appreciated, the Commission presented the current theory of race. The moral difference between the "old" and "new" immigration emerged to the discredit of the late arrivals, as it were, factually: they came to America only to better themselves economically in contrast to their predecessors, who sought political and religious freedom. In effect, the materialistic ambition of the southeastern Europeans proved the academic thesis of their inferiority, and at the same time their financial motivations transferred the question of immigration policy to the sphere of economics. Since the Report held that there was no room in American industry for unskilled labor, patently there was no reason to continue the exploitation of these poor foreigners whose standard of living threatened that of the native workingmen.[11]

Seemingly restrained in its ethnic judgments, the Report really fulfilled the restrictionist tradition initiated by Walker and extended by the Immigration Restriction League and sympathetic sociologists. As a result, intellectuals and reformers associated ethnic and economic liabilities of the latest immigrants so loosely that the one set of impressions inevitably suggested and complemented the other. Many humanitarian observers did not recognize the racial discrimination in the discreet phrases of the Commission. They heeded the economic justifications of restriction and wondered whether the nation could provide a living wage for all its workers.[12]

In this light, turbulence within the labor movement made new converts for restriction. Since the 1880's, native middle- and upper-class Americans had increasingly accepted the organization of skilled workers. By contrast, in the 1900's, the influence of the syndicalist, anarchistic Workers of the World upon the unskilled laboring classes dismayed intellectuals and social workers. After several general strikes, like the one in Lawrence, Massachusetts, the relationship between labor and capital posed a serious problem. The peasant masses of unskilled workers seemed unprepared for organized representation; the native laborers and employers, ignorant of the immigrants' habits and traditions, had dangerously alienated the newcomers from American attitudes. On the other hand, the message of the I.W.W. "obliterated every distinction of race," and the striking underprivileged responded to a philosophy of "no Poles, no Greeks, neither Jew nor Italian here, but only brothers."[13] The Workers of the World offered to the unknown inert throngs of aliens something which the English-speaking society would not.

Bewildered by the Lawrence terror, even an enlightened New Englander like John Graham Brooks asked, "What have we done that a pack of ignorant foreigners should hold us by the throat?" Robert A. Woods feared workers would be grateful to I.W.W. leaders like Bill Haywood and J. J. Ettor. Florence Kelley, an able social worker whose opposition to restriction was well-known, concluded after strikes in Portland, Oregon, that anarchy had "become hereditary from generation to generation among immigrants and their children."[14] Faith in the foreign-born was running out among their greatest admirers. Men and women who had watched a pattern of violence periodically threaten the orderliness of the American labor movement were, more than ever before, vulnerable to the restrictionists' claims.

Economically, to partisans of organized labor, the general strike also revealed that "the interests of Mr. Haywood's 'man in the gutter'" were not the "interests of the 'eight dollar a day man.'" The restrictionist insistence that America could never increase the standard of living of the recent immigrants by peaceable means seemed undeniable. These nationalities would never rise in the United States, because living in "compact and congested . . . masses" solidified their "impossible standards." In 1915, Jeremiah Jenks wrote to senators and congressmen that employers, as in Lawrence, would never improve wages because of the immigrants' low standard of living. He stated that a vote for the literacy test, which would limit the numbers entering, was a vote to end economic suffering for the unskilled masses.[15]

After 1912, many thoughtful citizens saw no hope of developing a civilized relationship between industrialists and laborers under present conditions. Democratic society in the United States could not attain, on the industrial level, either peace between management and labor or cooperation among different unions, while fresh immigrants could be exploited by their own countrymen, native employers, and employees. Defeatist in view of the multiple factors operating against a more equitable way of life for all Americans, reformers admitted a compulsion to "draw a sharp line between kinds of immigrants, actively enforcing our claim to select whom we will henceforth admit."[16]

While the Immigration Restriction League of Boston still led an active life, by the eve of World War I, it had lost its significance as an advance-guard among intellectuals. In the next decade new spokesmen for restriction would converge to shatter America's traditional welcome.

In the interim before the United States entered the war, a fairly late arrival among Brahmin restrictionists popularized the biological side of Yankee racism even more widely. Madison Grant, a lawyer, Yale class of 1889, was prominent in many social clubs. The secretary of the New York Zoological Society, he was an amateur student of race and heredity. Becoming a national vice-president of the League in 1909, Grant thereafter worked in various eugenics committees along with Hall and Ward. In 1914, Grant made a vain attempt to draw Woodrow Wilson to the side of the restrictionists.[17]

Based upon their views, Grant's *The Passing of the Great Race in America* told the story of the Yankee birth rate. "The poorer classes of colonial stock" had refused to compete with the Slovak, the Italian, the Syrian, or the Jew, and the "former masters" in America were now outbreeded. "The weak, the broken, and the mentally crippled of all races" had replaced the idealistic Yankee "soldiers, sailors, adventurers . . . explorers . . . rulers, organizers, and aristocrats." Human society was like a serpent: the head symbolized the Nordic Yankees' advance over the rest of mankind; the tail represented the anti-social forces—the inferior races. For Grant as for Hall, eugenics destroyed the "pathetic and fatuous belief in the efficacy of American institutions and environment to reverse or obliterate immemorial hereditary tendencies" of the "poor helots" who migrated here. Of these, the Polish Jews were the worst. "These immigrants adopt the language of the native American; they wear his clothes; they steal his name; and they are beginning to take his women, but they seldom adopt his religion or understand his ideals." More openly than Hall, Grant denied the possibilities of progress in a society which permitted universal suffrage. On the contrary, only an aristocracy of the wisest and the best could serve mankind. He echoed the rationale spread by the League and his slurring tone reflected the dawn of a new period.[18]

Only in recent years had restrictionists publicized their race prejudice. In the dim past of 1895, the young League had denied any intent to discriminate; in 1906 Shaler, had even sought to improve

relations between different groups. Almost unconsciously, the condemnation of prejudice, a link with the pre-Civil War past, ceased.
Later, restrictionists justified prejudice. Jeremiah Jenks inquired
whether assimilationists could really favor intermarriage with more
recent stocks of Americans. And Edward A. Ross, unresigned to the
lowered Yankee birth rate, argued that no people could survive
without respect for ancestry and race. Prescott Hall believed in prejudice as a "conserving force." Madison Grant gave it eugenic validity. "Race feeling," might seem like "prejudice" to "those . . .
cramped by it," but it was really "a natural antipathy" which func-
tioned to "maintain purity of type" in a people.[19] Thus, the instinctive love of kin which had molded the superiority of a Charles
Francis Adams, Jr. and a Henry Cabot Lodge had become elevated
into a scientific value, a moral force for evil as well as good.

The extreme restrictionists had become more strident as the tide
of restriction swept in other intellectuals and reformers. In 1917,
the United States Senate and House passed the literacy bill over
Wilson's second veto. Even in the hour of triumph, Hall's rejoicing
had reservations:

The work of the League, instead of being finished, has, however,
really only begun. The effects of the new law must be carefully studied,
and any loopholes which are discovered must be stopped. Furthermore,
it is probable that primary schools will be presently established in many
parts of Europe . . . so that the reading test, while improving the quality
of immigration, is likely to diminish in value as a means of restriction
as time goes on.[20]

The advocates of restriction were still dissatisfied.

The next step, a more definitive ethnic exclusion of Europeans,
was already in the making. As war shook the nation's stability, the
old restrictionist suspicion of divided national loyalties among the
foreign-born—hyphenism—reëmerged. In the 1890's, Mayo Smith
had questioned the loyalty of immigrants from Ireland and Germany. After 1914, the shadow of hyphenism again fell upon citizens
of Irish and German descent, mocking the recent assurances of a
sociologist that their "inherited sentiments" and "principles of mind"

were similar to those of the Yankees. With war's end, hyphenism lent itself to the nativists. Anxieties induced by members of old immigrant groups were transferred: complaints against "German-Americans" and "Irish-Americans" lessened; those against "Italian-Americans or Jewish-Americans" increased.[21]

Still more than the negative responses of small segments among the foreign-born to certain policies of the United States, the Bolshevik Revolution gave new meaning to the warnings of Yankee racists. After anarchists and socialists in the 1880's and 1890's, and I.W.W. syndicalists in the 1900's, many Americans were terrified of the new communist assault. Even employers, tired of recurring strikes, were ready to give up cheap foreign labor which was now inextricably identified with radicalism. And, as in earlier periods of social crisis, many restrictionists understood that "these alien Socialists, Radicals, I.W.W.'s and Bolshevists served a very useful purpose in rousing Americans to the peril of an increase in their numbers. The danger to the Government, however, is a more or less temporary one."[22]

On the other hand, some intellectuals were in a state of panic: Lothrop Stoddard interpreted the Russian Revolution as the latest stage of rebellion of the depressed races of man against the Nordics of England and America. Of an old New England family, Stoddard had graduated from Harvard College in 1905 and earned a Ph.D. in history by 1914. Studying with many professors who examined the implications of race and heredity for the native political institutions, he was imbued with the New England background of restrictionist thought. At first, he himself concentrated on the international aspects of race relations, upon the world-wide conflict for power among the white, the brown, the yellow, and the red men. Later, in terror of the "Asiatic-Slavic-Semitic" advance through Bolshevism, he viewed America's immigration problem as part of the conspiracy against the Anglo-Saxon.[23]

To Stoddard, the extension of democratic hopes beyond the control of Nordic leaders spelled the end of Western civilization. Emigration of Europeans and Middle Eastern peoples, like the existing Negro habitation of the United States, might some day mean the victory of radical alienism within the Anglo-Saxons' very own citadel. This threat had been foreseen by Walker, Hall, and Ward; he singled out Hall as a great unrecognized patriot of past decades.[24] Extending the use of the restrictionist ideology, in the 1920's Stoddard climaxed the anti-democratic trend of his New England predecessors.

A new argument for restriction came after the war when social scientists produced statistics on the caliber of American soldiers. Psychological tests, designed to measure the "intellectual capacity or inherited ability" of the young men, seemed to prove that 46 per cent of the foreign-born soldiers had a very low grade of intelligence. This supported the basic restrictionist contention that the "new" immigrant groups were, altogether aside from the factor of literacy, simply "inferior-minded." A distinguished scientist pointed out that the low mentality prevailing among most of the foreign-born led them into "pauperism, crime, sex offenses, and dependency." The different forms of crime already associated with each ethnic group in the country were probably fixed by heredity. Deploring the quality of present immigrants, a doctor stated that America would "degenerate to the level of the Slav and Latin Races." Concerned observers asked how democracy could work with such an electorate and assumed, in accordance with biological concepts, that the hazard was permanent. Extreme restriction was essential in order to exclude in advance "that ever-widening circle of . . . descendants, whose blood may be destined to mingle with and deteriorate the best we have."[25] Wartime experiences enhanced the ideal of eugenics, and the biological side of immigration commanded new respect and interest among educated Yankees generally.

But the problem of stemming the ethnic tide did not always involve the elimination of the "inferior-minded" aliens from the country's bloodstream. In 1922, A. Lawrence Lowell, an early supporter of the Restriction League and a national vice-president since 1912, investigated the "race distribution" within Harvard College. Albert Bushnell Hart reported of one government course that 52 per cent of the men were "outside the element" from which the college had "been chiefly recruited for three hundred years." Suggesting a quota for Jews, Lowell applied restrictionist thought to preserve the priority of the Anglo-Saxons in American colleges. Although Harvard's Board of Overseers publicly repudiated the racial discrimination implied in President Lowell's discussion of the "Jewish problem," significantly, some students confirmed his stand. Indifferent to cultural and social criteria of assimilation, representative Harvard men feared that the number of Jews would create an "abnormal unbalancing of races" in their student body. Such youths imitated unquestioningly the adults' hunger for a homogeneous society in which there must be a limit to all ethnic groups other than the "true American."[26] This form of nativism, inconsistent with the prevailing complaints as to the immigrants' lack of innate intelligence, showed how real other biological assumptions of "race" had become.

Finally, in 1921, virtually excluding the "new" southeastern European stocks, the Johnson Act through ethnic quotas gave preference to the old "Teutonic" groups. Still applying only to Europe, the Immigration Act of 1924 fixed the quota of each nation at 2 per cent, based upon the number of its immigrants in the United States in 1890; after 1929 the total number of immigrants was permanently set at 150,000 persons a year and numerical quotas allotted to each national group were based on the 1920 census. The intent was clear: to preserve the Teutonic composition of the American people in its present proportions so that the descendants of the foreign-born would never dominate the Yankees. Although the United States had already lost the opportunity to create "the finest race" in the history of mankind, *the blood of the nation* had been recognized as the first concern of the legislators.[27] The tradition of free immigration had given way to the verdict of science against the world's unknown millions.

Long after the passage of the Exclusion Act, the little Brahmin League continued its vigil. From 1921 to 1929 the group associated with other professional restrictionists, particularly eugenicists. After 1929, it decided to be strictly a New England organization. Chronically obsessed with the Yankee-Nordic control of the United States, they watched lest liberal interpretations of the legislation permit the admission of relatives of immigrants. In 1933 and 1934, those oldtimers who were still alive, fought the "sentimental" impulse to receive refugees from Hitler's Germany. Still applying Walker's principle of population, this small group wanted to cut European quotas even further and to secure similar laws for emigrants from Mexico and Latin America. Joseph Lee told his Harvard classmates in 1933 that when "the birth rate of the chocolate races has been put in low . . . the '83, and generally American brand of citizen may last for quite a while."[28] To the end of their lives the New England restrictionists were never satisfied that they had saved America from ethnic deterioration.

The compulsion to insulate the nation from further change evoked the dread of alienism in other ways, as in the tragic resolution of the Sacco and Vanzetti case. Since 1890, a complex of associations had created two images (not necessarily complementary) of the murderous southern Italian and of the radical foreigner. When the postwar Bolshevik hysteria was added to these older stereotypes, it was simple in 1921 to believe the circumstantial evidence against two Italians, who were aliens, anarchists, and draft-dodgers. Still, the conscience of Massachusetts did not rest easily, and six years later Harvard's Lowell headed a presumably impartial committee to review the case. The conclusion of the committee that there had been no prejudice in the treatment of these foreign-born men in the Bay State courts "did more to make the death of Sacco and Vanzetti acceptable to a doubting world than any decision of judge and jury." Lowell denied the influence of "race feeling" in the trials. Yet the court had refused to believe the testimony of eighteen Italian-born witnesses, and Judge Thayer had claimed that Vanzetti's ideals were "cognate with the crime." Moreover, District Attoney Katzmann had appealed to the Yankee consciousness of the jury, the "Men of Norfolk"; and he profited from the defendants' inept testimony given in broken English. Cumulative prejudice against the foreign-born and Yankee weariness with the burden of immigration helped condemn the two aliens. By 1927, A. Lawrence Lowell was representative of most Brahmins: like the unthinking majority, he went beyond the old hostility to the aliens, and upheld the sanctity of native institutions against the criticisms of those who questioned the Sacco and Vanzetti verdict. In Boston, the pair of Italians had become a symbol of alien-mindedness, an evil to be stamped out of a Yankee society determined to preserve itself and its culture.[29]

The negations of the democratic ideal, by which the Brahmin restrictionists had stood for so long in the company of a few economists and sociologists, now gained fresh supporters. In the 1920's, not only uneducated men became Ku Klux Klanners and anti-Semites, but well-informed people descended to the same level of prejudices through the intellectual brand of racism. Therefore, when restrictive legislation finally became acceptable, Americans, by dint of repetition, were accustomed to the ideology of race. This ideology was woven into the laws which ended the centuries of free migration to America.

Members of old New England society, which since the 1850's had suffered from inner conflict and social disunity, had led the way in establishing the terms of that ideology presumably in the name of the older democratic ideal. By the end of the 1880's, some Brahmins had been ready to renounce the humanitarian idealism of the past when it applied to Negroes, Irishmen, or others even more alien. In 1890 many university reformers, groping for solutions to the problems of an industrialized society, contrasted the earlier nation with its simpler rural economy and its sturdy pioneer settlers to conclude that Young America could more comfortably afford an economic, social, and political way of life based upon democratic principles. And paralleling the Brahmins' often unconscious preference for English mores and standards, social scientists seized upon the criteria of English historians, biologists, and social workers. In the process of solving American problems, the native conception of democratic society became somewhat Anglicized. The country which had received all the European nationalities, as well as the Chinese, Japanese, and Negroes, was offered another, higher image of the American: Anglo-Saxon in coloring, lineaments, and physique; Protestant in religion; masterly in nation-building. The abstract ideal of homogeneity, so lacking in the concrete land of diverse Americans, then dominated the thoughts of most native educated citizens.

The Teutonist idea of assimilation became the second-best alternative, a vague process by which another English race in the United States would slowly evolve. This optimistic view of assimilation, however, had disintegrated because of Walker's interpretation of the declining native birth rate. The real cost of immigration appeared to be the loss of the Yankee stock. Haunted intellectuals feared that assimilation could only subordinate their Teutonic blood to newer elements in the growing community. The threat of extinction affected and confused their estimates of the immigrants' adaptation. It was not enough for the foreign-born to conform to native conduct—ranging from the superficial imitation of American dress or the Anglicization of names to the more profound rejection of Old World sentiments. It was not enough for the "new" immigrant groups to adjust as well as the "old" ones. Since eugenics corroborated the importance of "pure race," the serious advocates of homogeneity insisted more certainly that the American environment could never overcome the innate inferiority of the recent citizens, however much they accepted the democratic principles of government. Ultimately, the concept of assimilation thus became an elusive, negative tool for race-conditioned Americans.

In the 1920's, an isolationist revulsion against Europe and her poor, and a mounting deference to organized labor solidified the final appeal of the restrictionist ideology of race. If the Immigration Act symbolized America's maturation, a defeated quality also permeated this law of exclusion. It demanded an economy in which fewer laborers would be needed and idealized a society in which fewer citizens should be born. Still more, the law's ethnic pattern fulfilled the original desire of old New Englanders who wanted the nation to return to the provincialism of its colonial heritage.

The Second World War destroyed the easy acceptance of racism all over the globe. And in the United States there were the younger generations descended from the foreign-born to illuminate the futility of "scientific" racial judgments which had once seemed credible. In the mid-twentieth century, the democratic birthright, which

Channing, Emerson, and Eliot had accepted and enlarged, contained fuller meaning and applications in the intellectual and social environs of Boston. But, although no longer tenable, the older ideology of race lingered in the immigration laws of the land, a legacy half-forgotten in its actual content and little understood as a betrayal of the continuing faith in the potentialities of America's democratic people.

$\mathcal{A}$ Note on Sources

ABBREVIATIONS USED

A.D.C.	Alfred D. Chandler III, Brookline, Mass.
B.A.	Boston Athenaeum, Boston, Mass.
B.P.L.	Boston Public Library, Boston, Mass.
C.J.G.	Mrs. Clarence J. Gamble, Milton, Mass.
E.G.B.	Emily G. Balch, Wellesley, Mass.
E.T.L.	Episcopal Theological Library, Cambridge, Mass.
H.A.	Harvard University Archives, Cambridge, Mass.
H.D.W.	Henry DeC. Ward, Lincoln, Mass.
H.L.	Houghton Library, Cambridge, Mass.
L.B.	Judge Lawrence G. Brooks, Medford, Mass.
L.L.	Lamont Library, Cambridge, Mass.
M.H.S.	Massachusetts Historical Society, Boston, Mass.
M.L.S.	Margaret Lee Southard, Quincy, Mass.
N.Y.P.L.	New York Public Library, New York, New York.
R.A.	Women's Archives at Radcliffe College, Cambridge, Mass.
S.E.H.	South End House, Boston, Mass.
T.R.L.C.	Theodore Roosevelt Collection, Library of Congress, Washington, D. C.
W.L.	Widener Library, Cambridge, Mass.

This book is an outgrowth of a doctoral thesis, entitled "New England Pride and Prejudice: A Study in the Origins of Immigration Restriction." The thesis is available at the Radcliffe College Library, Cambridge, Massachusetts, to those interested in the extensive documentation of the original study and in its comprehensive bibliography of published and unpublished works.

A study in intellectual history is, by nature, diffuse in its sources. The thought of a group of people is a shifting, dynamic combination of ideas and emotions, formed by the residual heritage of previous generations and the spontaneous reaction of contemporaries to the conditions and experiences of their own lives. In a broad sense, three hundred years of creative literature in old New England supplied material for this book; and the critical interpretations of that literature by generations of scholars also contributed to the conception of this study.

Seven main types of primary material were used: published autobiographies, memoirs and correspondence; historical, literary, and sociological works; periodicals and newspapers; Harvard College data; manuscript collections; public documents and pamphlets; and personal interviews.

I   PUBLISHED AUTOBIOGRAPHIES, MEMOIRS, AND CORRESPONDENCE

Old New Englanders. In the initial stage of research these introspective writings were crucial. Repetitive patterns of thought produced common attitudes among the Brahmins from the 1850's to the 1890's. Since New Englanders loved to reminisce, the fruitful works in this category were numerous. Apart from the books and collections of James Russell Lowell, Charles Eliot Norton, Charles and Henry Adams, cited in the text, Edward Everett Hale's, *A New England Boyhood and Other Bits of Autobiography* (Boston, 1893); *The Letters of John Fiske* (edited by Ethel F. Fisk, New York, 1940); and Henry Cabot Lodge's *Boston* (Cambridge, 1891) were typical of the many personal volumes of the New England group.

The Irish Immigrant Group in Boston. A very different perspective on the attitudes of old New Englanders appeared in William Cardinal O'Connell, *Recollections of Seventy Years* (Boston, 1934); and Katherine E. Conway and Mabel W. Cameron, *Charles Francis Donnelly A Memoir, With an Account of the Hearings on a Bill for the Inspection of Private Schools in Massachusetts in 1888–1889* (New York, 1909).

British Writers. W. R. W. Stephens, *The Life and Letters of Edward A. Freeman* (2 vols., London, 1895); Edward A. Freeman, *Some Impressions of the United States* (London, 1883); *A Selection from Goldwin Smith's Correspondence* (edited by Arnold Haultain, New York, 1913); and *Letters of Cecil Spring-Rice* (edited by Stephen Gwynn, 2 vols., Boston and New York, 1929) exemplified well Old World attitudes which affected the views of Brahmin intellectuals toward America's immigrants.

Yankee Social and Physical Scientists. John R. Commons, *Myself*

(New York, 1934); Edward A. Ross, *Seventy Years of It* (New York, 1936); Nathaniel S. Shaler, *Autobiography* (Boston and New York, 1909); and David Starr Jordan, *The Days of Man* (2 vols., New York, 1922) were among the volumes which helped explain what values were at work in the restrictionist ideology. By the same token, personal records like Jane Addams, *Twenty Years at Hull House* (New York, 1912); and Mary K. Simkhovitch, *Neighborhood, My Story of Greenwich House* (New York, 1938) suggested what values conflicted with the emerging restrictionism in the arena of social service.

II CONTEMPORARY HISTORICAL, LITERARY, AND SOCIOLOGICAL WORKS

Old New Englanders. The standard works—histories, essays, poems, and novels—of Ralph Waldo Emerson, James Russell Lowell, the Adams brothers, Barrett Wendell, Henry Cabot Lodge, John Fiske, and others need not be enumerated. Many of these are cited in the footnotes of the text, and in the original bibliography. They were essential complements to the autobiographical records and private correspondence of the authors, whose inward anxieties and views of the times entered into formal works in varying extent.

Yankee Social and Physical Scientists. Their contributions in economics, sociology, and genetics from the 1890's to the 1920's, which are less well-known, conceptualized the prevailing Brahmin sentiments about the foreign-born and facilitated the growth of restrictionism. A few of the most significant works were Richmond Mayo Smith, *Emigration and Immigration* (New York, 1890); John R. Commons, *Races and Immigrants in America* (New York, 1920); William Z. Ripley, *The Races of Europe* (New York, 1899); and Edward A. Ross, *The Old World in the New* (New York, 1914).

III PERIODICALS AND NEWSPAPERS

General Brahmin Thought. These were essential in formulating the total impression which prominent New Englanders as individuals left about their society from the 1850's to the 1890's. The most rewarding magazine files were those of the *North American Review*, L-CL (1840–1890) and of the *Atlantic Monthly*, I-LXXXXVI (1857–1900). The most important newspaper was the *Boston Daily Advertiser* (1880–1894); there was additional evidence in the *Boston Evening Transcript* and the *Boston Traveler* of the same years. (B.A.)

Immigration. The United States Library of Congress, *A List of Books on Immigration* (With Reference to Periodicals, Compiled under the Direction of Appleton Prentiss Clark Griffin, Washington, 1907), was an excellent starting point and led to academic journals, general magazines for the educated reader, and social service magazines. The main academic journals were *American Academy of Political and Social Science; American Economic Review; American Journal of Sociology; Education; Political Science Quarterly;* and *Quarterly Journal of Economics.* General magazines for the educated reader included among others *Century; Forum; Harper's Weekly; Nation; Outlook; Scribner's Magazine;* and *Yale Review.* Important social service magazines were *Charities* (later *Survey*) and the *Proceedings of the National Conference of Charities and Correction,* I-XXXIII (1874–1906) which clarified the relation between immigration restriction and more direct concerns of social service. The special collections of periodicals on immigration compiled by Robert DeCourcy Ward (W.L.) and by Prescott F. Hall (W.L.) were helpful.

Newspaper reporting on immigration was thoroughly covered in the Scrapbooks of Prescott F. Hall (1894–1920, 11 vols., W.L.) and Robert DeC. Ward (1891–1907, 3 vols., W.L.). These large collections recorded public sentiment for and against immigration all over the United States; the newspapers were not limited to those of Boston. In addition, there was a valuable small collection of newspapers and correspondence, Scrapbooks of the Far Eastern Bureau (January-June, 1915, 4 vols., W.L.).

Other Special Aspects. The files of the *Johns Hopkins University Studies* provided an excellent introduction to Teutonist historical research and thought. On the Catholic School fight of the 1880's and on the Imperialist and anti-Imperialist views of the 1890's, the Boston newspapers were useful; in addition, the following newspaper collections covered these topics: United States Imperialism Newscuttings (3 vols., W.L.), Scrapbook of Charles Eliot Norton on Imperialism (H.L.); Scrapbooks of Winslow Warren, Richard Olney, and Gamaliel Bradford, Sr. (M.H.S.) and Scrapbook of Alfred Chandler (A.D.C.).

IV   HARVARD COLLEGE DATA

The Harvard University Archives was a rich source of information about undergraduates from the 1850's to the 1920's. It produced identifications and dossiers (even courses of study) on the many New Englanders, especially minor figures, in this book. The Archives made available collections of lecture notes taken by students and voluminous manuscripts by and about Harvard graduates and professors. Informative college publications were also accessible: the files of the student newspaper, *The Daily Crimson,* and of the *Harvard College Catalogue;* the *Reports* of the Alumni Classes; *Reports of the President and of the Treasurer of Harvard College;* and *Baccalaureate Sermons, Class-Day Orations and Poems.*

V MANUSCRIPT COLLECTIONS

New Englanders were considerate archivists, and their papers left to libraries or families constitute a remarkable source. Some of these collections are not cited at all in the text, and others very rarely, but all of them gave insights and confirmed impressions of the era and of the community's reactions to it.

There were two indispensable collections pertaining to the New England immigration restriction movement: the Papers of Prescott F. Hall (H.L.) and the Papers of Robert DeCourcy Ward (H.D.W.). The Hall Papers include: correspondence, 1894–1921; Records of the meetings of the Executive Committee of the Immigration Restriction League of Boston (1894–1921, 3 vols.), registering confidential opinions not found elsewhere; Notebook of Contributors to the League, 1910–1919; Membership Lists of the League (n.d., presumably 1900–1920); and miscellaneous published documents. The Ward Papers include: correspondence, 1894–1931; Notebook of Records (1894–1917); published Reports of the Executive Committee of the League; and Records of the meetings of the Executive Committee of the League (1921–1931).

These isolated manuscripts were also of primary significance: Charles Francis Adams, Jr. to Moorfield Storey, July 5 – September 24, 1912 (M.H.S.); Henry Adams, "Class Day Oration" (1858, H.A.); Richards M. Bradley, typewritten copy of manuscript on Immigration Policy, 1934 (C.J.G.); John Farwell Moors to the *Boston Herald,* typewritten letter upon the death of Joseph Lee, July 29, 1937 (M.L.S.); Theodore Parker, Correspondence, Letter Boxes III and IV (M.H.S.); Robert DeCourcy Ward to Theodore Roosevelt, September 30, 1905 (T.R.L.C.); and Barrett Wendell, "Recollections of Harvard 1872–1917" (H.A.).

Ranking next in importance were the collections of the following:

Emily Balch, manuscripts and pamphlets relating only to immigration; John Graham Brooks, including general correspondence, notebooks and annotated volumes from his library (1870–1930, L.B.); Selected Papers from the Official Collection of Charles W. Eliot (H.A., by the kindness of the Harvard Corporation) including correspondence indicating the extent of Eliot's support of the opponents of immigration restriction; Letters and Miscellaneous Notes Relating to President Eliot, collected by Ralph Barton Perry (H.A.), revealing other social attitudes; Albert Bushnell Hart (40 boxes, H.A.) including correspondence, lists of publications, records of students and clippings; Rev. George Hodges, Private Journals and Scrapbooks (1881–1907, 32 vols., E.T.L.); Scrapbook and Correspondence relating to the Massachusetts Society for Promoting Good Citizenship (B.P.L.); William Z. Ripley, including correspondence, autobiographical material, and clippings (6 boxes, H.A.); and Robert A. Woods, including correspondence, pamphlets, and typed manuscripts (S.E.H.).

In addition, the collections of the following men included relevant correspondence with many leading New Englanders: John Jay Chapman (H.L.), Robert Grant (H.L.), Thomas Wentworth Higginson (H.L.), Charles Eliot Norton (H.L.), George Woodberry (L.L.), and Edward A. Atkinson (M.H.S.).

Of less importance were the collections of the following: Henry Baldwin, Library Americana, a miscellany of nativist correspondence and pamphlets which indicated no connections with the New England Brahmin restriction movement (N.Y.P.L.); Papers of Gamaliel Bradford, Sr., Richard Olney, and Warren Winslow (all M.H.S.) were confirming but not distinctive records.

VI   PUBLIC DOCUMENTS AND PAMPHLETS

Voluntary Public Organizations. In addition to the publications of the Immigration Restriction League (1894–1919, W.L.), those of other associations gave a picture of related community interests often shared by the restrictionists. These organizations varied from Anglophile, civic, anti-imperialist, and anti- and pro-suffrage clubs, to New England societies and settlement houses. Of the many associations, the publications of the following were the most useful: Anti-Imperialist League, *Annual Reports* (1899–1919) and Pamphlets (1898–1911, W.L.); Massachusetts Civic League, *Annual Reports* (1900–   , W.L.) and Leaflets (1905–

, W.L.); New England Society in the City of Brooklyn, *Proceedings* (1891–1903, W.L.); New England Society of Pennsylvania, *Annual Festivals* (1885–1889, W.L.); Denison House, *Annual Reports* (1894–1921, W.L.) and South End House, *Annual Reports* (1894–1922, S.E.H.); and Massachusetts Association Opposed to Further Extension of Suffrage, Pamphlets (1899, R.A.).

Government Documents. Official records of the United States were less important than the works of private individuals and groups. But the *Congressional Record,* Fifty-first Congress, Second Session, XII, Part III (Washington, 1891), 2955–2958; Fifty-fourth Congress, Second Session, XXIX, Part I (Washington, 1897), 235–239; Sixty-first Congress, Third Session, XLVI, Part I (Washington, 1911), 9r8; the United States Census Office, *Tenth Census . . . Compendium* (Washington, 1880); *Tenth Census . . . Manufacturers of United States,* II (Washington, 1883); *Eleventh Census . . . Report of the Population of the United States,* Part I and II (Washington, 1895 and 1897); *Twelfth Census . . . Report of the Population of the United States,* Part I and II (Washington, 1901 and 1902); and *Thirteenth Census, Abstract of the Census of Manufacturers* (Washington, 1914), were not only essential background to the development of the restrictionist ideology but also reflected its growth at times. In addition, Massachusetts Bureau of Statistics of Labor, *Reports* (Boston, 1881 and 1904); Massachusetts Labor Bulletin, *Aliens in Industry* (Boston, 1903); *Reports of the U. S. Industrial Commission,* XV and XIX (Washington, 1901–1902, 1903); and the *Reports of the U. S. Immigration Commission* (41 vols., Washington, 1911) were significant reflectors of the social and intellectual attitudes of Yankee economists and sociologists. Likewise, the *Transcript of the Record of the Trial of Nicola Sacco and Bartolemeo Vanzetti in the Courts of Massachusetts and Subsequent Proceedings* (4 vols., New York, 1928) revealed some of the intellectual and social assumptions about ethnic groups embedded in Yankee thinking.

VII   PERSONAL INTERVIEWS.

The book profited from the interest of several people who were related to it in one way or another. There were surviving contemporaries treated in the book: Emily Balch, whose sympathetic understanding of her own society, did not bar frankness; the late John Farwell Moors, who reminisced freely about the early days of the Immigration Restriction

League; the late Robert Treat Paine, who provided a significant anecdote by telephone; the late Vida D. Scudder, who confirmed the insights of her own books; and Eleanor H. Woods, the widow of Robert A. Woods, who collaborated with her husband in the leadership of the settlement movement of Boston.

In addition, Professor Ralph Barton Perry was stimulating in his reminiscences of Harvard at the turn of the century, especially in his discussion of William James. Mark A. DeWolfe Howe, friend and biographer of so many Brahmins, conveyed much of the spirit of their lives. Horace M. Kallen was suggestive in his memories of Barrett Wendell. And distinguished leaders in Boston social service—Katherine G. Hardwick, Eva Whiting White, and Ida Cannon, as well as the Rev. Raymond Caulkins, clarified, in different ways, the spirit of pioneer social work days. Herbert B. Ehrmann gave the benefit of his association with the defense counsel of Sacco and Vanzetti.

Above all, the book grew abundantly from the cooperation of Henry DeCourcy Ward, Judge Lawrence Graham Brooks, Margaret Lee Southard, Elizabeth Hodges, and Sara Bradley Gamble, who were generous in lending papers of their fathers or in granting personal interviews.

The secondary source material of this book fall into three main categories: Biographical Studies; Social and Economic Histories; and Intellectual Histories.

VIII   BIOGRAPHICAL STUDIES

Most of the well-known figures of New England have been treated amply in biographies written by admiring relatives, friends, or acquaintances. In the same category belong the short memoirs which appear in the *Proceedings* of the Massachusetts Historical Society. Although useful in conveying the facts of a man's life, such accounts usually confirmed the subject's own perspective rather than presented a detached historical interpretation. Of the many volumes of this kind, the best for purposes of this study were Henry James's *Charles W. Eliot, President of Harvard University 1869–1909* (2 vols., Boston, 1930) and Horace Scudder's *James Russell Lowell A Biography* (2 vols., Cambridge, 1901).

A slightly different variation on these filiopietistic biographies included primary evidence such as copious letters and excerpts from journals, which greatly enhanced the value of the biography itself. Alexander V. G. Allen's *Life and Letters of Phillips Brooks* (3 vols., New York,

1901); John Spencer Clark's *The Life and Letters of John Fiske* (2 vols., Boston, 1917); and Mark A. De Wolfe Howe's *Barrett Wendell and His Letters* (Boston, 1925); were excellent examples of this fruitful source.

To some extent the *Dictionary of American Biography* added to the accounts presented by contemporaries and younger associates. Thus Jeanette P. Nichol's essay on Francis A. Walker (XIX, 342 ff.) was a necessary complement to James P. Munroe's *A Life of Francis Amasa Walker* (New York, 1923). The contributions to the *Dictionary of American Biography* were uneven in quality; at their best, however, they offered a high degree of excellence, as in Ralph Barton Perry's essay on Charles W. Eliot (VI, 71 ff.).

The biographical studies of recent historians were less helpful. Unfortunately, many New England figures still await the work of modern scholars. One who has attracted considerable attention, however, is Henry Adams. Of the steadily growing critical interpretations, the most useful for the purposes of this study was Ernest Samuel's *The Young Henry Adams* (Cambridge, 1948). This painstaking piece of scholarship analyzes his life up to the time of the writing of the *History of the United States* and qualifies Henry's own account of himself in *The Education* with well-documented discrimination. Another book, William Jordy's *Henry Adams: Scientific Historian* (New Haven, 1952), appeared after my chapter on the Adamses was completed, and Jordy's evaluation of Henry's scientific thought in relation to his personality, harmonizes with the interpretations to be found in Chapter II above.

None of the biographies of Henry Cabot Lodge was entirely satisfactory. Karl Schriftgiesser's *The Gentleman from Massachusetts* (New York, 1944) was an improvement over earlier traditional accounts but proved less illuminating than Lodge's own writings. There was no fresh interpretation in the latest volume, John A. Garraty's *Henry Cabot Lodge A Biography* (New York, 1953) although the author had access to the now restricted Lodge family papers. Claude Fuess's "Carl Schurz, Henry Cabot Lodge and the Campaign of 1884; a study in temperament and philosophy," *New England Quarterly,* V (1932), 453 ff., is an excellent short piece on a limited aspect of Lodge's career.

Finally, Edward McNall Burns's *David Starr Jordan: Prophet of Freedom* (Stanford, California, 1953), an enlightening account of the California educator, of New England origin, proved useful in the context of this book.

IX   SOCIAL AND ECONOMIC HISTORIES

A History of American Life, VI-XI (edited by Arthur Meier Schlesinger and Dixon Ryan Fox, New York, 1927–   ), especially Arthur M.
Schlesinger's *The Rise of the City,* X (New York, 1933), provided background on the economic and social conditions of the period. Oscar
Handlin's *Boston's Immigrants* (Cambridge, 1941) was indispensable
for understanding the social and economic milieu of Boston in the first
half of the nineteenth century. In addition, *The History of the Archdiocese of Boston* (edited by Robert H. Lord *et al.,* 3 vols., New York,
1944), especially vol. III, emphasized relevant material on public relations
between old Bostonians and Irish members of the community. Alvin
Packer Stauffer's Doctoral Thesis, "Anti-Catholicism in American Politics" (Harvard University, 1933, H.A.) delineated the rise of the Irish
in Boston and Massachusetts politics.

X   INTELLECTUAL HISTORIES

Several excellent studies of related aspects of intellectual history were
particularly stimulating: Fred H. Harrington's "The Anti-Imperialist
Movement in the United States, 1898–1900," *Mississippi Valley Historical
Review,* XXII (1935), 211 ff., and "Literary Aspects of American Anti-
Imperialism," *New England Quarterly,* X (1937), 650 ff.; W. Stull Holt,
"Historical Scholarship in the United States, 1876–1901 As Revealed in
the Correspondence of Herbert Baxter Adams," *Johns Hopkins Uni-
versity Studies,* LVI (1938), No. 4, 7 ff., and "The Idea of Scientific
History," *Journal of the History of Ideas,* I (1940), 352 ff.; and Russell
B. Nye, "Lowell and American Speech," *Philological Quarterly,* XVLII
(1939), 249 ff.

Certain full length studies offered necessary groundwork. Richard
Hofstadter's general account, *Social Darwinism in American Thought*
(Philadephia, 1945), and Samuel E. Morison's *The Development of
Harvard University Since the Inauguration of President Eliot 1869–1929*
(Cambridge, 1930), and *Three Centuries of Harvard* (Cambridge, 1937)
were informative and suggestive. Finally, Louis Joughin and Edmund
M. Morgan's *The Legacy of Sacco and Vanzetti* (New York, 1948) gave
a monumental coverage of the social and intellectual aspects of a con-
troversial case.

Other intellectual studies relating directly to the subject of immigration
were valuable. Oscar Handlin's "American Views of the Jew at the

Opening of the Twentieth Century," The American Jewish Historical Society, *Publications,* No. XL, Part IV (1951), 323 ff. gave initial insight on the development of ethnic stereotypes. Ernest Saveth's *American Historians and European Immigrants 1875–1925* (New York, 1948) offered a thorough presentation of the Teutonist ideology of race as it appears in the writings of American historians. John Higham's "Origins of Immigration Restriction, 1882–1897: A Social Analysis," *Mississippi Valley Historical Review,* XXXIX (1952) correctly emphasized the vagueness of anti-immigration sentiment and its general lack of anti-Catholic motivation in the 1890's.

Finally, while this volume was already in the process of publication, two relevant books appeared. John Higham's *Strangers in the Land* (New Brunswick, New Jersey, 1955) gave the first comprehensive survey of public opinion toward immigration restriction on a national scale without analyzing the growth of attitudes within the framework of any specific group. In his penetrating study, *The Age of Reform* (New York, 1955), Richard Hofstadter reëvaluated the heritage of the Progressive movement which brought many reformers to the support of restriction.

Notes

I. NEW ENGLANDERS BETWEEN TWO WORLDS

1. Letter to Mrs. —————, July 4, 1876, *Letters of James Russell Lowell* (edited by Charles Eliot Norton, New York, 1894), II, 173.

2. Oliver Wendell Holmes, *Our Hundred Days In Europe* (Boston and New York, 1887), p. 100.

3. Perry Miller and Thomas Johnson, *The Puritans* (New York, 1938), pp. 10–11, 152, 181–194, 199; see also Robert H. Lord, John E. Sexton, and Edward T. Harrington, *History of the Archdiocese of Boston* (New York, 1944), I, 12, 29–30. Worthington Chauncey Ford "Ezekiel Carré and the French Church in Boston," Massachusetts Historical Society, *Proceedings*, 3d ser., LII (1918–1919), 121–132.

4. Lord, *Archdiocese of Boston*, I, 32. "Verses by Chief Justice Sewall," with remarks by Samuel A. Green, Massachusetts Historical Society, *Proceedings*, 2d ser., II (1885–1886), 41–43; George Foote Moore, "Judah Monis," *ibid.*, 3d ser., LII (1918–1919), 301–302.

5. Lord, *Archdiocese of Boston*, I, 267–325. For the abatement of anti-Catholic feeling during the next few decades, *ibid.*, I, 493, 551, 761–812.

6. John Adams to his wife Abigail, October 29, 1775 and August 3, 1776, *Familiar Letters of John Adams and His Wife Abigail Adams During the Revolution* (edited by Charles Francis Adams, Boston, 1875), pp. 120, 207. Henry Cabot Lodge, *Boston* (London and New York, 1891), p. 205.

7. Holmes, *Our Hundred Days*, p. 100; Edward Everett Hale, *A New England Boyhood and Other Bits of Autobiography* (Boston, 1893), pp. 49–51. See also James Freeman Clarke, *Autobiography* (edited by Edward Everett Hale, Boston, 1899), pp. 1–50.

8. O. W. Holmes, *Elsie Venner* (Boston and New York, 1891), p. 6, which originally appeared in the *Atlantic Monthly* in 1859; Oscar Handlin, *Boston's Immigrants* (Cambridge, 1941), p. 226; Oscar Handlin and Mary Flug Handlin, *Commonwealth A Study of the Role of Government in the American Economy: Massachusetts, 1774–1861* (New York, 1947), pp. 3 ff., 197 ff.

9. Hale, *A New England Boyhood*, p. 241.

10. Ralph Waldo Emerson, "The Transcendentalist," "The Young American," *Works* (New York, 1904), I, 327–395; "Power," *ibid.*, VI, 57; "Life and Letters in New England," *ibid.*, X, 344–345; Theodore Parker, "A Sermon on

Merchants," quoted in *The Transcendentalists* (edited by Perry Miller, Cambridge, 1950), p. 455.

11. E. E. Hale, *Letters on Irish Emigration* (Boston, 1852), pp. 53–54; Henry David Thoreau, *Walden and Other Writings* (New York, 1937), pp. 31, 67. Handlin, *Boston's Immigrants,* pp. 29–58, 128–150.

12. Hale, *Letters on Irish Emigration,* pp. 51–54; E. J. Sears, "Ireland Past and Present," *North American Review,* LXXXVI (1858), 135; A. P. Peabody, "The Financial Crisis," *North American Review,* LXXXVI (1858), 171. Edward Waldo Emerson, *The Early Years of The Saturday Club 1855–1870* (Boston, 1918) treats previous club-making, pp. 1, 4 ff.

13. Theodore Parker to James Orton, February 22, 1855, MSS, Letters IV, No. 281, The Massachusetts Historical Society; Parker, "A Sermon on Merchants" p. 453; R. W. Emerson, quoted in Ralph H. Gabriel, *The Course of American Democratic Thought* (New York, 1940), p. 45.

14. Handlin, *Boston's Immigrants,* pp. 183 ff., 208–213; Theodore Parker to Francis Jackson, August 21, 1859 and to James Orton, February 22, 1855, MSS, Letters, III, No. 69 and IV, Nos. 280–281, Massachusetts Historical Society.

15. James Russell Lowell, "Cambridge Thirty Years Ago," *Prose Works* (Boston and New York, 1890), I, 53.

16. Thomas Wentworth Higginson, *Old Cambridge* (New York, 1899), p. 23, gives an excellent description of the various changes in sentiment which a contemporary New Englander experienced. Lowell, "A Fable for Critics," *Poetical Works* (Boston and New York, 1890), IX, 64.

17. Lowell to C. F. Briggs, December 1848, *Letters of Lowell,* I, 148; Lowell, "Mason and Slidell A Yankee Idyll," *Poetical Works,* II, 250–251; Lowell, "Cambridge Thirty Years Ago," *Prose Works,* I, 43; Lowell, "On a Certain Condescension in Foreigners," *ibid.,* III, 253.

18. Lowell, *The Anti-Slavery Papers of James Russell Lowell* (Boston and New York, 1902), I, 20, 22, 101, 131, 198–199; II, 29.

19. *Ibid.,* I, 19–20; II, 25–26, 85, 110–111.

20. Lowell, "Review of D'Israeli's *Tancred or the New Crusade,*" *North American Review,* LXV (1847), 210, 212–214. See especially, "In simple truth, it seems to have been a provision of nature that divine ideas should have been committed to the Jews as great fortunes come to unthrift[y] heirs, because they were unable to keep possession of them." It was logical that "the idolaters of ceremony and tradition" in Biblical times "should become the venders of old clothes, that the descendants of those who, within earshot of thunders of Sinai, could kneel before the golden calf, should be the moneychangers of Europe." In 1847, Disraeli was also a special subject of antagonism, for, as one of the "Young England" Conservatives, he approached reform issues, such as the Irish land question, in a way incomprehensible to Lowell the reformer.

21. See "The Anglo-Saxon Race," *North American Review,* LXXIII (1851), 34–43, 53 ff. See the aims of the *Atlantic Monthly,* I (1857), on the back cover of the first issue: "In politics, the *Atlantic* will be the organ of no party or

clique, but will honestly endeavor to be the exponent of what its conductors believe to be the American Idea." Lowell to Charles Eliot Norton, August 31, 1858, *Letters of Lowell,* I, 284–285. Henry Cabot Lodge, *Early Memories* (New York, 1913), p. 16.

22. Norton to A. H. Clough, October 16, 1854, *Letters of Charles Eliot Norton* (edited by Sara Norton and M. A. DeWolfe Howe, Boston and New York, 1913), I, 116–117.

23. *Ibid.,* I, 82–83; Norton to George Woodberry, October 11, 1877, and to A. H. Clough, April 4, 1857, *ibid.,* II, 73–74 and I, 166.

24. Norton, *Considerations on Some Recent Social Theories* (Boston, 1853), p. 130. From a conversation with Norton about 1856 quoted in Thomas W. Higginson, "Ruskin and Norton," *Proceedings of the American Academy and the National Institute of Arts and Letters,* I (1910), 23.

25. Norton, *Considerations,* pp. 19, 158.

26. *Ibid.,* p. 21; *Letters of Norton,* I, 26–27; Norton, "Dwellings and Schools for the Poor," *North American Review,* LXXIV (1852), 464–489.

27. Norton, *Notes of Travel and Study in Italy* (Boston, 1859), p. 105; Lowell, "The Cathedral," *Poetical Works,* IV, 47; Rose Hawthorne Lathrop, *Memories of Hawthorne* (Boston, 1897), pp. 369–370, 378.

28. Norton, "Model Lodging Houses in Boston," *Atlantic Monthly,* V (1860), 673; Norton, "Goldwin Smith," *North American Review,* XCIX (1864), 536; Arthur G. Sedgwick to Sara Norton, excerpt, *Letters of Norton,* II, 432–433.

29. Norton to Lowell, July 21, 1861, *Letters of Norton,* I, 237; *ibid.,* I, 221–223.

30. Lowell to Norton, January 1865 and to Leslie Stephen, April 10, 1866, *Letters of Lowell,* I, 343, 360–361; for Norton's anti-English sentiment, see Norton, "Goldwin Smith," *North American Review,* XCIX (1864), 526; see Lowell, "A Great Public Character," and "Abraham Lincoln 1864–1865," *Prose Works,* II, 280 and V, 177–209; see also Norton to Miss Gaskell, October 2, 1865, *Letters of Norton,* I, 285–286.

31. Norton to G. W. Curtis, October 2, 1861, *Letters of Norton,* I, 243; Norton, "America and England," *North American Review,* C (1865), 332, 341–344.

32. Arthur Sedgwick quoted in *Letters of Norton,* II, 434–435; Julius Ward, "The Decay of New England Thought," *North American Review,* CXXXIII (1881), 282.

33. Norton, "Emancipation and the Constitution" (proof of an unpublished pamphlet) (Boston, 1861), pp. 6–10; Norton to Miss Meta Gaskell, August 30, 1862 and October 2, 1865, *Letters of Norton,* I, 256 and 284–288. Lowell, "Reconstruction," "Scotch the Snake or Kill It," and "The Seward-Johnson Reaction," *Prose Works,* V, 217, 225–227, 237, 257–261, 308–312. Lowell to Edmund Quincy, September 1867, *New Letters of James Russell Lowell* (edited by M. A. DeWolfe Howe, New York and London, 1932), p. 123. Lowell, "A Look Before and After," *North American Review,* CVIII (1869), 270–271. Lowell to Mrs. Charles R. Lowell, September 16, 1876, *New Letters,* p. 220;

E. L. Godkin to C. E. Norton, April 13, 1865, *Life and Letters of Edwin Lawrence Godkin* (edited by Rollo Ogden, New York, 1907), II, 47–50.

34. Lowell, "Cambridge Thirty Years Ago," "On a Certain Condescension in Foreigners," "Reconstruction," and "A Great Public Character," *Prose Works,* I, 55, 65, III, 220, V, 237, and II, 290.

35. Norton to Lowell, July 7, 1864, *Letters of Norton,* I, 271.

36. Norton to Lowell, May 26, 1866 and to George W. Curtis, July 14, 1864, *ibid.* pp. 290 and 274.

37. Lowell to Norton, January 11, 1873, *Letters of Lowell,* II, 90; A. A. Lowell, "Memoir of James Russell Lowell," Massachusetts Historical Society, *Proceedings,* 2d ser., XI (1896, 1897), 196. Lowell to Joel Benton, January 19, 1876, *Letters of Lowell,* II, 159.

38. Norton to Miss Gaskell, December 21, 1869, to Ruskin, May 1870, to Miss Gaskell, July 12, 1870, *Letters of Norton,* I, 372, 384, 395.

39. Norton to his Mother, August 9, 1868, to Chauncey Wright, May 1, 1865 and to Lowell, November 24, 1873, *ibid.,* I, 302–305, 328, and II, 21–23.

40. Lowell to Edward Fitzgerald, September 4, 1880, *New Letters,* p. 252. See also *Forum,* XII (1891), 145, quoting a dedicatory verse for the window of an English church. Lowell to Mabel (Mrs. Edward Burnett), August 16, 1886, *New Letters,* pp. 289–290. Raymond Blathwayt, "James Russell Lowell," *Review of Reviews,* IV (1891), 247.

41. Horace E. Scudder, *James Russell Lowell A Biography* (Cambridge, 1901), II, 310–311; Lowell to ———, September 21, 1875, *Letters of Lowell,* II, 148; Hale, *James Russell Lowell and His Friends* (Boston, 1899), p. 275. See Russell B. Nye, "Lowell and American Speech," *Philological Quarterly,* XVIII (1939), 249–256. H. James to Norton, August 26, 1891 quoted in Ferris Greenslet, *The Lowells and Their Seven Worlds* (Boston, 1946), p. 342.

42. Lowell, "New England Two Centuries Ago," *Prose Works,* II, 1–2, 13, 32. On his attachment to the Old Testament, see also Lowell to Leslie Stephen, May 15, 1876, *Letters of Lowell,* II, 168. On his knowledge of Hebrew, see Lowell, "The Study of Modern Languages," *Latest Literary Essays and Addresses* (Boston, 1892), p. 131.

43. Lowell to William Dean Howells, May 2, 1879, *Letters of Lowell,* II, 240–241. Lowell, "A Moosehead Journal," *Prose Works,* I, 26; see also Lowell to James T. Fields, January 1862, *New Letters,* 102 and Lowell to Fields, April 5, 1869, *Letters of Lowell,* II, 22.

44. Lowell to Mabel (Mrs. Edward Burnett), August 18, 1872, November 14, 1872, and to Henry Adams, June 27, 1873, *New Letters,* pp. 160, 172, 199. See also Lowell to the Misses Lawrence, October 1, 1888, Horace E. Scudder, *Lowell,* II, 386.

45. Norton to Edward Lee-Childe, September 24, 1876, when Norton's mother was reading *Daniel Deronda, Letters of Norton,* II, 64.

46. "Lowell's Impressions of Spain," *Century,* LVII (1898), 143; Lowell to H. James, January 26, 1889, *New Letters,* p. 328; Hale, *Lowell and His Friends,* p. 276; see also Lowell to Lady Lyttleton, January 7, 1890, *Letters of Lowell* (Elmwood Edition), III, 263.

47. Lowell to Hughes, February 16, 1875, November 17, 1878, and to Norton, August 12, 1878, *Letters of Lowell*, II, 136, 234, 222. "Lowell's Impressions of Spain," *Century*, LVII (1898), 143. Lowell to H. James, January 26, 1889, *New Letters*, p. 328.

48. "Conversations with Mr. Lowell," *Atlantic Monthly*, LXXIX (1897), 127–130. Leslie Stephen to Norton, August 11, 1892, *Letters of Lowell*, I, 415–416.

49. On Thomas Carlyle's views, see a full report in Norton to Miss E. C. Cleveland, June 7, 1869, *Letters of Norton*, I, 334–335; Lowell, "Democracy," *Prose Works*, VI, 18–19.

50 Lowell to William W. Story, November 10, 1855 and to H. James, May 8, 1879, *New Letters of Lowell*, pp. 72, 242; Lowell, "Harvard Anniversary," *Prose Works*, VI, 172.

51. An excerpt Norton to John Ruskin, September 1879 quoted in Norton's Journal 1868–1873, *Letters of Norton*, II, 91–92. Norton to Chauncey Wright, December 5, 1869, *ibid.*, I, 371–372. Norton to Lowell, November 24, 1873, *Letters of Norton*, II, 21–22.

52. Norton to Lowell, dateless excerpts in *Letters of Norton*, II, 88–90. Norton, "The Intellectual Life of America," *New Princeton Review*, VI (1888), 312–313; "Address," The Cambridge Historical Society, *Publications*, I (1905), 12–14.

53. Norton, "The Lack of Old Homes in America," *Scribner's Magazine*, V (1889), 636–640; Norton to E. L. Godkin, August 2, 1889, *Letters of Norton*, II, 287–288.

54. Lowell, "Note on Motley," *Nation*, XXIV (1877), 337; Lowell, "The Independent in Politics," *Prose Works*, VI, 201; *Letters of Norton*, II, 89–90. See also "Men of Letters and the Hayes Administration," *New England Quarterly*, XV (1942), 110–141.

55. Norton to Chauncey Wright, September 13, 1870, *Letters of Norton*, I, 399; Norton, "The Intellectual Life of America," p. 315; "The Educational Value of the History of Fine Arts," *Educational Review*, IX (1895), 346; see also Norton, "Lectures of Fine Arts 3" compiled by W. E. Weaver (1898). Norton, *Commencement Address Radcliffe College* (1901), Norton Papers.

56. Norton, "The Intellectual Life of America," pp. 319–322.

II. THE DISSOLUTION OF THE DEMOCRATIC IDEAL

1. Henry Adams to Charles Francis Adams, Jr., November 10, 1911, *The Letters of Henry Adams* (edited by Worthington C. Ford, Boston, 1938), II, 575–576. Charles and Henry left their personal records, *An Autobiography* (Boston, 1916), and *The Education of Henry Adams* (Boston, 1918). They form the basis of interpretation in this chapter, to which other sources and studies contributed.

2. Henry to Charles M. Gaskell, September 27, 1894, *Letters of Henry Adams*, II, 55. Brooks Adams, "The Heritage of Henry Adams" *The Degradation of the Democratic Dogma* (New York, 1920), p. 93.

3. H. Adams, *The Education*, p. 34. A fellow classmate claimed that Henry as a student had exhibited the same traits of character as he expressed in the later *Education*, Winslow Warren, "Recollections of Fifty Years," Massachusetts Historical Society, *Proceedings*, 3d ser., LVI (1923), 230.

4. Charles Francis Adams, Jr. to his Father, June 10, 1861, *A Cycle of Adams Letters, 1861–1865* (edited by Worthington C. Ford, Boston, 1920), I, 10-11.

5. C. F. Adams, Jr., *Autobiography*, pp. 137, 163–164; Charles Francis Adams, Jr. to Henry, April 6, 1862, January 23, 1863, to his Mother, May 12, 1861, to his Father, August 10, 1862, *A Cycle of Letters*, I, 237–238, 130–131, 3-4, 174.

6. Henry to Charles, February 14, 1862, *A Cycle of Letters*, I, 112–113; see also the reaction to Henry's despair in Charles to Henry, January —, 1862 and January 23, 1863, *ibid.*, I, 102–103, 237–240.

7. From a series of letters published in the *Boston Courier* in 1860 quoted in Ernest Samuels, *The Young Henry Adams* (Cambridge, 1948), p. 69. Henry to Charles quoted in *ibid.*, p. 78. Henry to Charles, November 21, 1862, *A Cycle of Letters*, I, 196.

8. H. Adams, *The Education*, p. 272. C. F. Adams, Jr., "Railway Problems in 1869," *North American Review*, CX (1870), 147–150; H. Adams, "The Session," *North American Review*, CXI (1870), 62. C. F. Adams, Jr. and H. Adams, *Chapters of Erie and Other Essays* (Boston, 1871), p. 95.

9. C. F. Adams, Jr. and Henry Adams, "The Independents in the Canvass," *North American Review*, CXIII (1876), 435–436, 439, 460; C. F. Adams, Jr., "Individuality in Politics," *Independent Republican Campaign Documents*, No. 2 (New York, 1880).

10. C. F. Adams, Jr., *Autobiography*, pp. 173–175, 187–188, 190, 195.

11. C. F. Adams, Jr., "The Era of Change," *A Chapter of Erie*, pp. 343–344, 353–354.

12. C. F. Adams, Jr., *Autobiography*, p. 202.

13. C. F. Adams, Jr., *Three Episodes* (Boston, 1892), II, 922–932, 946–948, 951–952.

14. *Ibid.*, pp. 949, 951–952, 957–958.

15. *Ibid.*, pp. 972–973.

16. C. F. Adams, Jr., *Autobiography*, pp. 177–178.

17. C. F. Adams, Jr., *Three Episodes*, II, 986, 989–998, 1008–1009.

18. C. F. Adams, Jr., *Autobiography*, pp. 194–195, 202; and C. F. Adams, Jr., *Three Episodes*.

19. C. F. Adams, Jr. *et al.*, *The Genesis of the Massachusetts Town and the Development of Town-Meeting Government* (Cambridge, 1892), pp. 6–8.

20. Charles to Moorfield Storey, August 17, 1912, MS, The Massachusetts Historical Society. C. F. Adams, Jr., *Charles Francis Adams* (Boston, 1900), pp. 1, 3, 104, 214–215.

21. C. F. Adams, Jr., *The Sifted Grain and The Grain Sifters* (Cambridge, 1900), p. 3. Lowell, "Harvard Anniversary," *Prose Works*, VI, 146.

22. C. F. Adams, Jr., *The Sifted Grain*, pp. 3, 14, 22–23, 47–48.

23. C. F. Adams, Jr., *The Solid South and the Afro-American Race Problem* (Boston, 1908), pp. 16–18; *'Tis Sixty Years Since* (New York, 1913), pp. 10–12.

24. C. F. Adams, Jr. to R. M. Bradley, July 28, 1905, Papers of Immigration Restriction League.

25. See John Eliot Alden, "Henry Adams As Editor, A Group of Unpublished Letters to David A. Wells," *New England Quarterly,* XI (1938), 146–152. Henry to Carl Schurz, Feburary 14, 1876, Henry to Henry Cabot Lodge, February 15, 17, 23, 27, and September 4, 1876, *Letters of H. Adams,* I, 273–283, 297–299. H. Adams, *The Education,* p. 317.

26. Henry to Charles M. Gaskell, November 25, 1877, and to Lodge, May 26, 1875, *Letters of H. Adams,* I, 302, 268. Henry to Charles W. Eliot, March 2, 1877, and to Isaac Wayne MacVeagh, July 9, 1881, *Henry Adams and His Friends* (edited by Harold Dean Carter, Boston, 1947), pp. 81, 108.

27. H. Adams, *Democracy* (New York, 1880), pp. 4, 5, 9, 10, 77, 196, 353, 370, 374.

28. H. Adams, *History of the United States During the Administration of Thomas Jefferson* (New York, 1889), I, 184; *History of the United States of America During the Second Administration of James Madison* (New York, 1891), III, 225. Even the final paragraph of the last volume composed in a different mood after his wife's death, did not detract from his hopes for America in "another century of experience," *ibid.,* III, 241–242.

29. See H. Adams' book reviews, *North American Review,* CXIV-CXXI (1872–1875). H. Adams, *Essays in Anglo-Saxon Law,* pp. 3, 6–8; H. Adams, *Historical Essays* (New York, 1891), pp. 1–41 ff. Henry to Henry Osborn Taylor, May 4, 1901, *Letters of H. Adams,* II, 332; Marian H. Adams to Dr. Hooper, January 22, 1882, *Letters of Mrs. Henry Adams, 1865–1883* (edited by Ward Thoron, Boston, 1936), pp. 331–332.

30. See Henry to Francis Parkman, December 21, 1884, *H. Adams and Friends,* pp. 133–134.

31. H. Adams, *The History of the United States,* I, 159–160, 168, 170, 175.

32. Henry Adams quoted in Samuels, *Young Henry Adams,* p. 300. H. Adams, *Esther* (New York, 1938), p. 125. This was originally published in 1884.

33. H. Adams, "Harvard Class Day Oration," MS (1858). H. Adams, *The Education,* p. 345.

34. Henry to Henry Holt, January 6, 1885 and February 9, 1899, *H. Adams and Friends,* pp. 136–137, 456; *The Education,* pp. 327–328, 331, 337, 343–345. Henry to Charles W. Eliot, June 12, 1892 and Henry to Seth Low, March-April 1894, *Letters of H. Adams,* II, 7, 43–45.

35. H. Adams, *The Education,* p. 352. Charles Eliot Norton to James Russell Lowell, January 13, 1856, *Letters of Charles Eliot Norton,* I, 144. Henry to Elizabeth Cameron, September 18, 1899 and Henry to Henry Osborn Taylor, May 4, 1901, *Letters of H. Adams,* II, 240, 332. H. Adams, *Mont-Saint-Michel and Chartres* (Boston, 1933), p. 44; contrast this work with great-grandfather John Adams' "A Dissertation on Canon and Feudal Law," *Works* (edited by

Charles Francis Adams, Sr., Boston, 1851), III, 448–464, and with Henry's own earlier criticism of Norman feudalism as undemocratic, pointed out by Samuels, *Young Henry Adams,* p. 251.

36. M. H. Adams to Dr. Hooper, May 8 and October 23, 1881, *Letters of Mrs. H. Adams,* pp. 287, 292; Henry to Charles M. Gaskell, October 28, 1888, *Letters of H. Adams,* I, 394; Henry to Elizabeth Cameron, January 24, 1910, *ibid.,* II, 531.

37. Richard Cumberland, *The Jew; A Comedy in Five Acts,* in Mrs. Inchbald, *British Theatre* (London, 1832); V. H. Adams, (unsigned) "Reading in College," *Harvard Magazine,* III (1857), 307–317; Henry Hart Milman, *The History of the Jews* (New York, 1855), viii; I, 103; II, 14; III, 246, 339. H. D. Cater, "Henry Adams Reports on a Prussian Gymnasium," *American Historical Review,* LIII (1947), 71–72. H. Adams, *The Education,* p. 79.

38. H. Adams, *Democracy,* pp. 41–42, 44–46, 159, 202.

39. M. H. Adams to Dr. Hooper, June 29, 1879, November 2, 1879 and December 3, 1882, *Letters of Mrs. H. Adams,* pp. 149–150, 197, 404; Lowell to H. Adams, June 27, 1873, *New Letters of James Russell Lowell,* p. 199; Henry to Charles M. Gaskell, October 24, 1879 and November 21, 1879, *Letters of H. Adams,* I, 315–317.

40. Henry to Elizabeth Cameron, June 10, 1888, *Letters of H. Adams,* I, 388–389.

41. Henry to Elizabeth Cameron, September 15, 1893, to Charles M. Gaskell, January 23, 1894, February 14, 1914, *Letters of H. Adams,* II, 33–35, 620; Henry to John Hay, July 28, 1896, to Brooks Adams, October 12, 1899, *H. Adams and Friends,* pp. 376–377, 481–482; H. Adams, *Mont-Saint-Michel and Chartres,* pp. 278, 311–312. By contrast, Henry did not condemn the English entirely. See Henry to Sir Robert Cunliffe, February 17, 1896, *Letters of H. Adams,* II, 98, "You dear simple-minded Britisher and bucolic, I love you, but I don't love your Lombard Street Jews who rule you."

42. See Brooks Adams, "The Heritage of Henry Adams" in Henry Adams' *The Degradation of the Democratic Dogma,* pp. 90–100. For the full use of the terms "imaginative" man and "industrial" man, with the accompanying anti-Semitic inferences, see B. Adams, *The Law of Civilization and Decay* (New York, 1898), pp. 321–325, 365–372, 381–383 and Preface, x. Henry's *Mont-Saint-Michel and Chartres* drew upon the same premises, pp. 99, 173.

43. B. Adams, Introduction to *The Degradation of the Democratic Dogma,* pp. 93, 96; H. Adams, *The Education,* pp. 3, 238. Henry to Brooks Adams, April 12, 1906, *H. Adams and Friends,* p. 583.

44. Henry to Charles Gaskell, February 3, 1892, February 19, 1914; Henry to Elizabeth Cameron, December 10, 1897, January 6, 1898, July 13, 1899, January 28, 1901, August 3, 1901, and to Henry James, September 3, 1909, *Letters of H. Adams,* II, 5, 620, 138, 141, 233, 311, 335, 522.

45. For contemporary American public opinion of the Dreyfus case, see Peter Finlay Dunne, *Mr. Dooley in the Hearts of His Countrymen* (Boston, 1899), pp. 240–285; *Nation,* LXVII (1898), 90–91, 255–256, 480–481; Richard W. Hale, *The Dreyfus Story* (Boston, 1889), particularly pp. 65–68. Henry

to Charles M. Gaskell, August 24, 1896; to John Hay, August 20, 1899; to Elizabeth Cameron, July 27, 1896, January 13, 1898, August 14, 1899, September 5, 12, 18, and 25, 1899, *Letters of H. Adams,* II, 116, 235, 110, 144–145, 238–242.

46. Henry to Elizabeth Cameron, August 14, 1901, *Letters of H. Adams,* II, 338. Contrast Henry's interest in Max Nordau's *Degeneration* (New York, 1895) which analyzed symptoms of anti-Semitism; see Henry to Charles M. Gaskell, June 20, 1895, *Letters of H. Adams,* II, 72. H. Adams, *Mont-Saint-Michel and Chartres,* pp. 99, 121, 173, 278.

III. BRAHMINS AND IRISHMEN IN THE 1880's

1. Editorial, *Boston Evening Transcript,* March 5, 1880.

2. Francis Parkman, *Our Common Schools* (Boston, 1890), pp. 3–4.

3. Nathan Allen, "Divorces in New England," *North American Review,* CXXX (1880), 560–561; "New England Transformation," *Nation,* XLI (1885), 148–149; Davis R. Dewey, "Statistics of Suicide in New England," *Publications of the American Statistical Association,* III (1892), 161, 164. See also Barrett Wendell, unpublished diary, quoted in *Barrett Wendell and His Letters* (edited by Mark A. DeWolfe Howe, Boston, 1924), p. 47. Parkman, "The Failure of Universal Suffrage," *North American Review,* CXXVII (1878), 4.

4. U. S. Bureau of Census, *Tenth Census of the United States: 1880 Manufacturers of United States* (Washington, 1883), II, 950. *Boston Daily Advertiser,* December 7, 1882, July 7 and July 15, 1884.

5. Robert H. Lord *et al., History of the Archdiocese of Boston,* III, 64–65, 67–69.

6. Eleanor Hallowell Abbott, *Being Little in Cambridge* (New York, 1936), pp. 32–34, 36–37, 67.

7. *Ibid.,* pp. 75–76. Henry Adams, *The Education of Henry Adams,* pp. 41–42; Henry Cabot Lodge, *Early Memories,* pp. 19–20; Henry James, *Charles W. Eliot* (Boston, 1930), I, 14–15, 19.

8. Charles Francis Adams, Jr., *Autobiography,* pp. 15–16; Robert Grant, *Fourscore* (Boston, 1934), pp. 30–31. Abbott, *Being Little,* p. 187. Eleanor Woods, *Robert A. Woods* (Boston, 1929), pp. 98–99.

9. Abbott, *Being Little,* pp. 188–189; Phillips Brooks to Arthur Brooks, November 27, 1883, Alexander V. G. Allen, *Life and Letters of Phillips Brooks* (New York, 1901), II, 474; Edwin D. Mead, *The Roman Catholic Church and the Public Schools* (Boston, 1890), p. 53.

10. Katherine E. Conway and Mabel W. Cameron, *Charles Francis Donnelly, A Memoir, With an Account of the Hearings on a Bill for the Inspection of Private Schools in Massachusetts in 1888–1889* (New York, 1909), p. 25.

11. Lord *et al., History of the Archdiocese,* III, 68–69, 70–74.

12. Edward Everett Hale, *The Duty of the Church in the Cities* (Boston,

1878), pp. 12–13; Mrs. C. A. Hopkinson, "The Poor in Cities," *Atlantic Monthly*, XXII (1868), 55.

13. William Cardinal O'Connell, *Recollections of Seventy Years* (Boston, 1934), p. 5.

14. Alvin Packer Stauffer, "Anti-Catholicism in American Politics 1865–1900" (Doctoral thesis, Harvard University, 1933), pp. 97–98; *Boston Daily Advertiser*, November 8, 1882; Leslie G. Ainley, *Boston Mahatma* (Boston, 1949), pp. 135–137.

15. Stauffer, "Anti-Catholicism," pp. 98–99, 250. For the reaction of proper Boston, see *Boston Daily Advertiser*, November 27 and December 10, 1884.

16. *Boston Evening Transcript*, January 14 and February 17, 1880. Lord *et al.*, *History of Archdiocese*, II, 622–623, III, 345–349. See "Parochial Schools in Massachusetts," *Education*, X (1890), 321–322.

17. Lord *et al.*, *History of Archdiocese*, III, 100–136, 144; see also Conway and Cameron, *C. F. Donnelly*, pp. 31 ff.; Stauffer, "Anti-Catholicism," pp. 256–270; *Woman's Voice*, April 11, 1891, p. 2.

18. Rev. C. E. Amaron, "The French-Canadians in the United States," *National Needs and Remedies* (New York, 1890), pp. 239–247; see also, Albert L. Bartlett, "The Transformation of New England," *Forum*, VII (1889), 634–644.

19. Editorial, *Boston Daily Advertiser*, January 3, 1888; Thomas Wentworth Higginson, quoted in Julia Ward Howe, *Reminiscences 1819–1899* (Boston and New York, 1899), p. 285. *Boston Traveler*, March 30, 1880; Lord *et al.*, *History of Archdiocese*, III, 407–415.

20. Joseph Cook, *Socialism* (Boston, 1880), pp. 180 ff.; Report of Julius Ward's Lecture, "What Catholics and Protestants Agree Upon as to the Public Schools?" *Boston Transcript*, January 18, 1880. Cyrus Bartol quoted in Conway and Cameron, *C. F. Donnelly*, pp. 59–60.

21. M. J. Savage, "What Shall the Public Schools Teach?" *Forum*, IV (1888), 470, and Francis E. Abbott, "The Catholic Peril in America," *Fortnightly Review*, XIX (1876), 385–405.

22. Francis A. Walker to the *New Haven Register*, undated, quoted in James P. Munroe, *A Life of Francis Amasa Walker* (New York, 1923), pp. 277, 290. In addition, Walker approved the use of foreign languages as the means of teaching immigrant pupils until they mastered English, Conway and Cameron, *C. F. Donnelly*, p. 58. Mead, *Roman Catholic Church*, pp. 1–7, 14, 38–42, 49, 82.

23. Thomas Wentworth Higginson quoted in Conway and Cameron, *C. F. Donnelly*, pp. 64–66 and Edward Everett Hale quoted in *ibid.*, pp. 61–62. See also Hale, "Formative Influences," *Forum*, X (1890), 64–71.

24. Charles W. Eliot quoted in Conway and Cameron, *C. F. Donnelly*, pp. 34–36. Mead, *Roman Catholic Church*, pp. 49, 52–53, 90.

25. *Boston Daily Advertiser*, January 11 and March 13, 1888. Statement by John Farwell Moors, who recalled the anti-Catholic bias of leaders of the Public School Union Movement, personal interview. Parkman, *Our Common Schools*, p. 4.

26. Francis A. Walker quoted in Munroe, *F. A. Walker*, p. 291.

27. Julius Ward, "The Decay of New England Thought," *North American Review*, CXXXIII (1881), 282; O'Connell, *Recollections*, pp. 27–28; Hale, *Candor in the Pulpit* (Boston, 1879), pp. 6–9. Joseph Cook, *Socialism*, p. 289. "Certain Dangerous Tendencies in American Life," *Atlantic Monthly*, LXII (1878), 397.

28. Hugh O'Brien quoted in Stauffer, "Anti-Catholicism," pp. 102–103.

29. James Russell Lowell, "The Independent in Politics," *Prose Works*, VI, 219. Editorials and Comments in the *Boston Daily Advertiser*, January 11, March 7, March 14, March 16, March 17, May 7, 1888, and June 10, 1889.

30. "People of a New England Factory Village," *Atlantic Monthly*, XLVI (1880), 460–464. Parkman, "The Failure of Universal Suffrage," *North American Review*, CXXVII (1878), 9, 13.

31. Parkman to Pierre Margry, December 15, 1875, "Letters of Francis Parkman to Pierre Margry," *Smith College Studies in History*, VIII (1923), 165; J. Cook, *Labor* (Boston, 1880), p. 5. *Woman Suffrage Unmoral and Inexpedient* (Boston, 1886), which represented the views of Rev. O. B. Frothingham, Prentiss Cummings, W. W. Goodwin, Richard H. Dana, and two Catholics, John Boyle O'Reilly and Rev. J. B. Bodfish. See also, Pamphlet (Boston, 1899), the Standing Committee of the Massachusetts Association Opposed to Further Extension of Suffrage of Women, Women's Archives, Radcliffe College. Margaret Deland, *Golden Yesterdays* (New York, 1940), p. 290. Parkman, *Some of the Reasons Against Woman Suffrage*, undated, p. 6. See also Parkman, "The Woman Question," *North American Review*, CXXIX (1879), 319–320 for his explicit opposition to woman suffrage because it might extend the political power of the Catholics.

32. *Boston Evening Transcript*, January 12 and 17, March 3 and 17, April 20, 1880.

33. William Dean Howells, *Literary Friends and Acquaintance*, pp. 217–219; Lowell to Thomas Hughes, July 18, 1870, February 7, 1871 and to Mabel (Mrs. Edward Burnett), August 25, 1878, *Letters of Lowell*, II, 60, 70–71, and II, 228.

34. Lowell to O. W. Holmes, December 28, 1884, *Letters of Lowell*, II, 293–294. Scudder, *Lowell*, II, 280, quoting Lowell to W. M. Evarts, February 26, 1881.

35. Lowell to Thomas Bailey Aldrich, May 8, 1882, *Letters of Lowell*, II, 268. Lowell quoting his own sonnet to George Smalley, April 17, 1882, Lowell to William J. Hoppin, October 29, 1881 and August 27, 1882, and to Lady Lyttleton, January 4, 1888, *New Letters of James Russell Lowell*, pp. 264–266, 256, 268, 320; see Lowell to Thomas Hughes, March 7, 1891, *Letters of Lowell*, II, 434–435. Lowell quoted in Horace Scudder, *Lowell*, II, 281.

36. A. L. Lowell, "Irish Agitation in America," *Forum*, IV (1887), 401, 405. See Richard H. Dana, "An American View of the Irish Question," *Forum*, XIII (1892), 708–717; Dana reacted against the new attitude and reminded his readers of the justice of the Irish cause despite "the excesses of the Irish agitators." "Politics," *Atlantic Monthly*, XXXI (1873), 125.

37. O. W. Holmes, *Our Hundred Days in Europe,* pp. 310–313. Holmes's prediction was well confirmed in Tom Stevenson, *The Reminiscences of Tom Stevenson* (Boston, 1941), p. 159.

38. Statement by Vida Scudder, personal interview. Woods, *Robert A. Woods,* pp. 98–99. Robert Lincoln O'Brien, "The Last Half Century of Transcript History," The Massachusetts Historical Society, *Proceedings,* 3d ser., LXVII (1941–1944), 507. Statement by Emily G. Balch, which confirmed Miss Scudder's opinion, personal interview.

39. Ralph W. Emerson, July 1866, *The Heart of Emerson's Journals* (edited by Bliss Perry, Boston, 1909), p. 317; "Certain Dangerous Tendencies in American Life," *Atlantic Monthly,* XLII (1878), 385. Lowell to Lady Lyttleton, January 4, 1888, *New Letters,* p. 320; Lowell to Thomas Hughes, March 7, 1891, *Letters of Lowell,* II, 434–435.

40. Lowell, "Democracy," and "The Independent in Politics," *Prose Works,* VI, 10, 12, 25–26, 32, 203, 205. A. L. Lowell, "Irish Agitation in America," pp. 397–398.

IV. THE ANGLO-SAXON COMPLEX

1. John Fiske, *American Political Ideas* (New York, 1885), p. 143.

2. Francis A. Walker, "Immigration and Degradation," *Forum,* XI (1891), 642.

3. "Men of the Sea," *Atlantic Monthly,* III (1859), 51; James Russell Lowell, "Shakespeare Once More," "Chaucer," and "Reconstruction," *Prose Works,* III, 7, 9, 13, 320, and V, 218.

4. L. Sears, "The Study of the Anglo-Saxon," *Fifty-Seventh Annual Meeting of the American Institute of Instruction* (Boston, 1887), p. 76.

5. W. Stull Holt, "The Idea of Scientific History in America," *Journal of the History of Ideas,* I (1940), 352–362.

6. H. C. Lodge, *Early Memories,* pp. 186–187; J. L. Laughlin, "Some Recollections of Henry Adams," *Scribner's Magazine,* LXIX (1921), 576–585; Henry Osborn Taylor, "The Education of Henry Adams," *Atlantic Monthly,* CXXII (1918), 484–491; Lindsay Swift, "A Course in History at Harvard College in the Seventies," The Massachusetts Historical Society, *Proceedings,* 2d ser., LXII (1918–1919), 69–77; Stewart Mitchell, "Henry Adams and His Students," The Massachusetts Historical Society, *Proceedings,* 3d ser., LXVI (1936–1941), 294–310; George Woodberry to Lewis Einstein, January 31, 1919, Woodberry Collection; Charles F. Thwing, *Education and Religion* (New York, 1929), p. 181. For Edward Channing's broader scope, see his discussion in Charles F. Adams, Jr. *et al., The Genesis of the Massachusetts Town and Development of Town-Meeting Government,* pp. 73–76. See also H. Adams to H. O. Taylor, May 4, 1901, *Letters of Henry Adams,* II, 332.

7. Fiske to his Mother, October 28, 1861; to Abby, November 1, and November 2, 1863; to his Mother, May 10, 1867; to Mr. Gilder, February 13, 1889, *The Letters of John Fiske* (edited by Ethel F. Fisk, New York, 1940), pp. 72, 108–109, 162, 558. Samuel E. Morison, *Three Centuries of Harvard*

(Cambridge, 1937), pp. 333, 348. Fiske, Preface to *American Revolution* (Boston, 1891), p. vii. Fiske to his Mother, November 2, 1878, *Letters of Fiske,* p. 374.

8. John S. Clark, *The Life and Letters of John Fiske* (Boston, 1907), II, 49. Fiske to his Mother, March 16, 1869, *Letters of Fiske,* p. 182, in which he referred to a series of articles he planned for the new *Appletons' Journal* to be entitled "Are We Celts or Teutons?" See Fiske, "The Races of the Danube," *Atlantic Monthly,* XXXIX (1877), 401–411; Fiske, *American Political Ideas,* preface, pp. 5–10, 35–36. Fiske, "Who Are the Aryans?" *Atlantic Monthly,* XLVII (1881), 233–234. Fiske to his Mother, July 6, 1877 and October 9, 1879, *Letters of Fiske,* pp. 366, 417.

9. J. M. Vincent, "Herbert B. Adams," *Herbert B. Adams Tributes of Friends* (Baltimore, 1902), p. 10. See W. S. Holt, Introduction to "Historical Scholarship in the United States, 1876–1901," *Johns Hopkins University Studies,* LVI (1938), 11. H. B. Adams to Daniel Coit Gilman, July 3, 1882, Holt, "Historical Scholarship in the United States," p. 55.

10. H. B. Adams, "The Germanic Origin of New England Towns," *J.H.U. Studies* (Baltimore, 1883), I, 5, 8.

11. See Table of Contents, *ibid.,* I–VI (1883–1886).

12. James Schouler, "Tribute to John Fiske," and James F. Rhodes, "Tribute to Herbert B. Adams," The Massachusetts Historical Society, *Proceedings,* 2d ser., XV (1901), 193–200. For Freeman's high regard of Fiske's work, see Freeman to J. A. Doyle, August 19, 1889, and to Hannis Taylor, November 8, 1889, W. R. W. Stephens, *The Life and Letters of Edward A. Freeman* (London, 1895), II, 405, 410; for Freeman's intimate association and approval of Adams' program, see H. B. Adams, "Mr. Freeman's Visit to Baltimore," and Freeman, "An Introduction to American Institutional History," *J.H.U. Studies,* I (1883), 5–39.

13. Freeman, *Lectures to American Audiences* (Philadelphia, 1882), pp. 9–11, 55, 137, 200–201.

14. *Ibid.,* p. 15. Freeman to Miss Edith Thompson, December 4, 1881, W. R. Stephens, *Life and Letters of Freeman,* II, 240. Goldwin Smith to Mrs. Winkworth, November 22, 1887, *A Selection from Goldwin Smith's Correspondence* (edited by Arnold Haultain, New York, 1913), p. 208. James Bryce, *The American Commonwealth* (London, 1888), II, 706.

15. Freeman, *Lectures to American Audiences,* pp. 199, 201. Freeman expressed the hope that every Irishman would kill a Negro and be hanged for it. Freeman to F. H. Dickinson, December 4, 1881, *Life and Letters of Freeman,* II, 242; see also Freeman to Professor Dawkins, October 15, 1881, to Miss Helen Freeman, October 30, 1881, to Rev. Pinder, March 24, 1882, *Life and Letters of Freeman,* II, 234–236, 254; G. Smith, "The Jewish Question," *The Nineteenth Century,* X (1881), 494, 515 and "The Jews A Deferred Rejoinder," *The Nineteenth Century,* XII (1882), 687–709. G. Smith, "Is Universal Suffrage A Failure," *Atlantic Monthly,* XLIII (1879), 79.

16. G. Smith, "Is Universal Suffrage A Failure," pp. 75, 78. Herbert Spencer quoted in *Boston Daily Advertiser,* November 10, 1882. A conversation of

Herbert Spencer with Fiske quoted in Clark, *Life and Letters of Fiske*, II, 248–252.

17. James K. Hosmer, *The Last Leaf* (New York and London, 1912), pp. 2, 19, 173 ff., 179 ff., 216 ff.; Hosmer, *The Story of the Jews* (New York, 1885), pp. 5, 253, 298, 355–356, 366–367.

18. H. B. Adams to Andrew White, November 24, 1883, W. S. Holt, "Historical Scholarship in the United States," *J. H. U. Studies*, pp. 69–70. The experience of a Jewish student at Johns Hopkins in those years corroborates Adams' attitude; see Abraham Flexner, *I Remember* (New York, 1940), pp. 44–65. J. M. Vincent, "A Biographical Sketch," *H. B. Adams Tributes of Friends*, p. 23.

19. Fiske, *American Political Ideas*, pp. 23–24, 26. Fiske to his Mother, June 3, 1862, *Letters of Fiske*, p. 88. Fiske to his wife, May 9, 1874, *The Personal Letters of John Fiske* (Cedar Rapids, 1939), pp. 186–187. See also Francis Parkman, "The Failure of Universal Suffrage," p. 7.

20. Hosmer, "Samuel Adams, The Man of Town-Meeting," *J. H. U. Studies*, II (1884), 15–17. Hosmer to H. B. Adams, February 6, 1888, quoted in W. S. Holt, "Historical Scholarship in the United States," p. 110. Edmund J. James, "Emigration and Immigration," *Cyclopaedia of Political Science* (edited by John J. Lalor, Chicago, 1883), II, 90.

21. James Russell Lowell to Phillips Brooks, May 1, 1891 and Brooks' pocket notebooks for sermons in 1874 quoted in Alexander V. G. Allen, *Life and Letters of Phillips Brooks*, III, 415, and II, 236. See also *ibid.*, II, 216. For discussion of Brooks' attitude toward Norton, see William Lawrence, *Memories of a Happy Life* (Boston, 1926), p. 83. Brooks' speech, July 4, 1880, and Brooks to Robert Monachie, July 6, 1888, quoted in Allen, *Life and Letters of Brooks*, II, 396, and III, 273.

22. Lodge, *Address Before the Citizens of Nahant, Memorial Day, 1882* (Cambridge, 1882), p. 15; John T. Morse, "Henry Cabot Lodge," *Harvard Graduates' Magazine*, XXXIII (1925), 454. Worthington C. Ford, *The American Citizens' Manual* (New York, 1883), Part II, 124–125.

23. "The Effects of Immigration," *Boston Daily Advertiser*, August 11, 1882.

24. Fiske, *American Political Ideals*, pp. 105, 143; Clark, *Life and Letters of Fiske*, II, 249–250.

25. Charles F. Dunbar, "Economic Science in America," *North American Review*, CXXII (1876), 126–127. See also Alfred Bornemann, *J. Laurence Laughlin, Chapters in the Career of an Economist* (Washington, D. C., 1940), pp. 13–14.

26. Walker and Adams had collaborated in "The Legal-Tender Act," *North American Review*, CX (1870), 299 ff. Henry Adams to Walker, February 29, 1876 and Walker to Richmond Mayo Smith, January 20, 1888, quoted in Munroe, *Francis Amasa Walker*, pp. 159–160, 323–324; for reference to Fiske's friendship, see Fiske to W. L. Garrison, February 1, 1898, *Letters of Fiske*, p. 666.

27. Walker, "The Wage Fund Theory," *North American Review*, CXX (1875), 111.

28. Walker, "Our Population in 1900," *Atlantic Monthly*, XXXII (1873), 492–495. Edward Jarvis, "Immigration," *Atlantic Monthly*, XXIX (1872), 454–468; Jarvis, "Autobiography," MS, Houghton Library, pp. 205–206, 237.

29. Walker, "Occupations and Mortality of Our Foreign Population, 1870," *Discussions in Economics and Statistics* (edited by Davis R. Dewey, New York, 1899), II, 216–217.

30. Walker, "Our Domestic Service," *ibid.*, II, 234. Walker, "American Irish and American Germans," *Scribner's Monthly*, VI (1873), 179.

31. Walker, "The Growth of the United States," *Century*, XXIV (1882), 920–926.

32. Walker, "American Manufacturers," *Discussions in Economics and Statistics*, II, 182.

33. Walker, *A Plea for Industrial Education in the Public Schools, Addressed to the Conference of Associated Charities of the City of Boston, February 10, 1887* (Boston, 1887), pp. 12–13, 15–17.

34. R. T. Ely, *Ground Under Our Feet* (New York, 1938), p. 163; see Ely, "Report of the Organization of the American Economic Association," The American Economic Association, *Publications*, I (1886), 5–8. Walker, "Speech December 27, 1888 at the Annual Meeting of the American Economic Association," and "The Manual Laboring Class," The American Economic Association, *Publications*, IV (1889), 27, and III (1888), 11.

35. Walker, "The Manual Laboring Class," The American Economic Association, *Publications*, III (1888), 14, 19–20, 22–23; Walker "The Knights of Labor," *Discussions in Economics and Statistics*, II, 325–326, 334–335. Walker, "What Shall We Tell the Working Classes," *ibid.*, II, 311. See Davis R. Dewey statement, *ibid.*, II, 300, for evidence of Walker's views in 1887.

36. Walker, "Henry George's Social Fallacies," *North American Review*, CXXXVII (1883), 147–157; Walker, "Mr. Bellamy and the New Nationalist Party," *Atlantic Monthly*, LXV (1890), 248–262. Walker, "The Knights of Labor," *Discussions in Economics and Statistics*, II, 325. J. H. Nicholson's recollections of Walker's views on the extent of anarchists' influence in the United States quoted in Munroe, *Life of Walker*, p. 274.

37. Walker, "The Growth of the Nation," *Discussions in Economics and Statistics*, II, 202, 206–207.

38. Walker, "The Great Count of 1890," *Forum*, XI (1891), 418. Walker, "The Tide of Economic Thought," The American Economic Association, *Publications*, VI (1891), 32–38.

39. Walker, "Immigration and Degradation," *Forum*, XI (1891), 640.

40. In this connection, there is relevant material in Norman E. Himes, *The Medical History of Contraception* (Baltimore, 1936), pp. 224–229, 261 ff., 282, 385.

41. Walker, "Our Population in 1900," *Atlantic Monthly*, XXXII (1873), 494–495, and "Immigration," *Yale Review*, I (1892), 127.

42. *Handbook of the American Economic Association for the Year 1890–*

1891 (Baltimore, 1890), p. 8, announced the prize awarded by the American Economic Association of one hundred and fifty dollars presented by the journal *America* for the best essay on "The Evils of Unrestricted Immigration." See also "Secretary's Report of Third Annual Meeting," The American Economic Association, *Publications,* IV (1889), 92.

43. Munroe, *Life of Walker,* pp. 294, 299, 321–324, 327, 340, 400. Richmond Mayo Smith, "Memorandum on the Immigration of Foreigners into the United States, and "Control of Immigration I," *Political Science Quarterly,* II (1887), 521, and III (1888), 48–49, 56–60.

44. R. M. Smith, "Control of Immigration II," *Political Science Quarterly,* III (1888), 197, 223. Smith's reference to Walker's speech at Lehigh University revealing "The danger to American labor from the immigration of labor with a lower standard of living." *ibid.,* p. 417. See Walker's revised edition of *Political Economy* (New York, 1888), pp. 307–310. *Boston Daily Advertiser,* July 13 and 17, 1888.

45. Edward Bemis, "Restriction of Immigration," and "The Distribution of Immigrants," *Andover Review,* IX (1888), 251–263, 592, 596. Again the editor of the *Boston Daily Advertiser,* March 12, 1888, expressed interest in the new restrictionist sentiment.

46. Walker, "Immigration," *Yale Review,* I (1892), 131–132.

47. *Ibid.,* I, 134–135. Four years later he recapitulated these views, see Walker, "Restriction of Immigration," *Atlantic Monthly,* LXVII (1896), 822–829 which became a classic for later restrictionists.

48. R. M. Smith, *Emigration and Immigration* (New York, 1890), pp. 5, 41.

49. *Ibid.,* pp. 14–15, 64–67.

50. *Ibid.,* pp. 5, 63, 84, 86–88.

51. *Ibid.,* pp. 288–293.

V. FOUNDING THE IMMIGRATION RESTRICTION LEAGUE

1. Thomas Bailey Aldrich, "The Unguarded Gates," *Atlantic Monthly,* LXX (1892), 57.

2. *Boston Daily Advertiser,* May 6, 1886. *Boston Evening Transcript,* May 6, and May 11, 1886; see also Edward L. Pierce, "Address," New England Society of Brooklyn, *Proceedings,* Seventh Annual Report (1887), p. 38. Rev. Cyrus Bartol quoted in *Boston Daily Advertiser,* May 10, 1886. Frances C. Sparhawk, "The Query Club," *Education,* VII (1887), 350–353, 501–503, 506–509.

3. *Boston Daily Advertiser,* May 25, 1886, March 22, 1886.

4. Anna L. Dawes, *How We Are Governed* (Boston, 1885), p. 353. *Boston Daily Advertiser,* September 13, 1882, November 14, 1884.

5. Moses Coit Tyler quoted in Herbert Baxter Adams, "New Methods of History," *J. H. U. Studies,* II (1884), 32. H. B. Adams, "History at Amherst and Columbia Colleges," *Education,* VII (1886), 177–180; Katherine Coman, "Preparation for Citizenship at Wellesley College," *Education,* X (1890), 341–

347; Anson Morse, "Preparation for Citizenship at Amherst College," *Education*, IX (1888), 242; Arthur L. Perry, "Preparation for Citizenship at Williams College," *Education*, IX (1889), 513; Albert Bushnell Hart, "Preparation for Citizenship at Harvard," *Education*, VIII (1888), 630–638.

6. *Boston Daily Advertiser*, July 3, 1882, November 29, 1884; *Annual Reports of the Executive Committee of the Citizens Association of Boston* (1889–1892). Dr. C. F. Crehore to Elizabeth P. Gould, October 22, 1889, The Massachusetts Society for Promoting Good Citizenship, Scrapbook, Boston, Massachusetts; *Brochure of Massachusetts Society for Promoting Good Citizenship* (Boston, 1889). See also, E. P. Gould, "The Massachusetts Society for Promoting Good Citizenship," *Education*, IX (1889), 552–554; Edwin D. Mead, "Editor's Table," *New England Magazine*, new ser., X (1894), 387. Mellen Chamberlain, *Josiah Quincy the Great Mayor* (Boston, 1889), p. 23. See also J. R. Lowell, "A Great Public Character," *My Study Windows*, pp. 94–98.

7. John Fiske, *Civil Government in the United States* (Boston, 1890), p. 134.

8. "Committee on Readings in American History," *Brochure of the Massachusetts Society for Promoting Good Citizenship*.

9. William A. Mowry, "Courses of Study in Civics for Schools and Higher Institutions of Learning," *Education*, VIII (1887), 93. Dawes, *How We Are Governed*, pp. 6–7.

10. E. D. Mead, "The Old South Historical Work," *Education*, VII (1886), 259–260, 262.

11. Chauncey J. Hawkins, *Samuel Billings Capen His Life and Work* (Boston, 1889), p. 75, and Capen, "The Teaching of Morals in the Public Schools," *Education*, IX, (1889), 525. C. F. Crehore was the practical administrator of the Massachusetts Society for Promoting Good Citizenship. See Crehore, "The Influence of Race Upon Educational Methods," *Education*, VII (1887), 402–403.

12. Capen from an article entitled "The Young Man in Politics," quoted in *Boston Daily Advertiser*, September 11, 1888. See also, Hart, "The Exercise of the Suffrage," *Political Science Quarterly*, VII (1892), 307–327. See inside cover, The Massachusetts Society for Promoting Good Citizenship, Scrapbook.

13. Inside cover, The Massachusetts Society for Promoting Good Citizenship, Scrapbook; Horace G. Wadlin quoted in *Boston Daily Advertiser*, December 15, 1891. Henry Cabot Lodge, *The Question of Immigration A Lecture before the Massachusetts Society for Promoting Good Citizenship*, reprinted from *The Boston Commonwealth*, Boston, 1892, p. 7. When Lodge originally delivered this speech, he had said "We are not going to shut the door on the oppressed of any clime." See the *Boston Herald*, April 26, 1892. Significantly, in the printed version he omitted this statement, apparently a rhetorical gesture to the old immigration tradition.

14. Editorial, *Boston Traveler*, January 28, 1892. Phillips Brooks to his brother Arthur, August 15, 1891, *The Life and Letters of Phillips Brooks*, III, 443–444. Winslow Warren from a speech at the triennial meeting of the General Society of Cincinnati, quoted in *Boston Transcript*, May 14, 1896. Fiske

was state promoter of the National Society of Children of the American Revolution. See Winslow Warren Clippings at the Massachusetts Historical Society. George Perry at the Boston Festival in honor of Queen Victoria quoted in the *Boston Herald,* June 22, 1897.

15. Aldrich to George Woodberry, March 17 and May 14, 1892, May 28, 1894, Woodberry Collection.

16. Hawkins, *Samuel Billings Capen,* p. 104.

17. Barrett Wendell, "Recollections of Harvard 1872–1917," MS (1918), Harvard Archives, p. 43.

18. Samuel Eliot Morison, *Three Centuries of Harvard* (Cambridge, 1942), p. 420. Wendell, "Recollections of Harvard 1872–1917," p. 71.

19. Statement by Ralph Barton Perry, personal interview. Wendell to E. K. Rand, April 19, 1920, *Barrett Wendell and His Letters,* p. 327, where Wendell explained his functions as an educator. "My real duty, as I saw it, was not scholarly but humane."

20. Wendell, "Mr. Lowell as a Teacher," *Scribner's Magazine,* X (1891), 645–649; Wendell, "Charles Eliot Norton," *Atlantic Monthly,* CIII (1909), 82–88. Wendell to Woodberry, September 3, 1885 and September 22, 1904, Woodberry Collection. Wendell, *Rankell's Remains* (New York, 1886), p. 10. Wendell to Col. Robert Thomson, December 17, 1893, *Wendell and His Letters,* pp. 108–109. Wendell, *Stelligeri and Other Essays* (Boston, 1893), pp. 12–13, 15–16. Wendell to Norton, October 20, 1888, and in a similar vein November 20, 1896, Norton Papers. Wendell to Edward J. Lowell, January 7, 1888, *Wendell and His Letters,* p. 75.

21. Wendell to Col. Thomson, December 17, 1893, *Wendell and His Letters,* pp. 108–109. Wendell, *Stelligeri and Essays,* pp. 32–33, 109–111, 143–144. In this period Wendell reflected the prevailing Teutonist mode of thought. See Wendell to H. B. Adams, November 12, 1891, W. Stull Holt, "Historical Scholarship in the United States 1876–1901," *J.H.U. Studies,* LVI (1938), 172. Later he explained that the Dutch and French strains of the Yankee American had been absorbed before 1750. See Wendell to Horace M. Kallen, October 11, 1919, *Wendell and His Letters,* p. 318.

22. Nathaniel S. Shaler, *Autobiography* (Boston and New York, 1909), pp. 3, 109–110, 193–195, 199–200, 202–203, 378.

23. Shaler, *Autobiography,* pp. 27, 200; Shaler, "An Ex-Southerner in South Carolina," *Atlantic Monthly,* XXVI (1870), 60–61; "Mixed Populations of North Carolina," *North American Review,* CXVI (1873), 161–166; "The Negro Problem," *Atlantic Monthly,* LIV (1884), 699, 702–704; "Science and the African Problem," *Atlantic Monthly,* LXVI (1890), 37.

24. Shaler, *Autobiography,* pp. 259–260, 238, 303–306, 308; and "The Uses of Numbers in Society," *Atlantic Monthly,* XLIV (1879), 331.

25. Shaler to Norton, July 14, 1879, Norton Papers. Shaler, "The Summer's Journey of a Naturalist," *Atlantic Monthly,* XXXI (1873), 709–710, 712–713.

26. Shaler, "Journey of a Naturalist," p. 713.

27. Shaler to T. W. Higginson, November 7, 188—, Higginson Papers. Shaler, "The Use and Limits of Academic Culture," *Atlantic Monthly,* LXVI

(1890), 164. Shaler, "Race Prejudices," *Atlantic Monthly*, LVIII (1886), 512. See also his *Autobiography*, pp. 166, 363, 382.

28. See the inside of the cover page of *America*, I (1888). Shaler, "The Immigration Problem Historically Considered," *America*, I (1888), Nos. 30–31, 1–2. Ironically, in these articles Shaler declared that "the nineteenth century" would "be known, in times to come, as the age in which race prejudice began to disappear." *Ibid.*, p. 1.

29. Shaler, "European Peasants as Immigrants," *Atlantic Monthly*, LXXI (1893), 649, 651, 653–655. See *The United States of America* (edited by N. S. Shaler, New York, 1894), II, 613–614. *The Daily Crimson*, November 20, 1888, June 2, 1889.

30. H. B. Adams, *The Study of History in American Colleges and Universities* (Washington, 1887), p. 41. Morison, *The Development of Harvard University* (Cambridge, 1930), pp. 159–161. Morison, "Albert Bushnell Hart 1889–1939," The Massachusetts Historical Society, *Proceedings*, 3d ser., LXVI (1936–1941), 435. See also, Robert Lincoln O'Brien (then editor of the *Boston Herald*) to A. B. Hart, March 20, 1924, on the impact of Hart as a teacher in History 13 and English 6, Hart Papers.

31. Hart, Biographical Notes, Hart Papers. Hart to Norton, March 2, 1898, May 28, 1896, Norton Papers. Hart, *National Ideals Historically Traced* (New York, 1907), p. 265.

32. A. B. Hart, "Preparation for Citizenship," *Education*, VIII (1888), 631. *Topical Outline of the Courses in Constitutional History of the United States for the Year 1886–1887* (Cambridge, 1886), p. 8; *The Work of Students, History 13, 17 and 20 (d)* (Cambridge, 1887); Charles Warren, "History 13 Notes" (1889), all in the Harvard Archives. Richard Frothingham, *The Rise of the Republic* (Boston, 1872), pp. 30–32, 403–406; Hart, "The Rise of American Cities," *Quarterly Journal of Economics*, IV (1890), 151–152. Hart, "Town Government on Cape Cod," *Nation*, LVI (1893), 343–345.

33. Hart, "The Rise of American Cities," pp. 151–157; *Prospectus of the American History Leaflets Colonial and Constitutional* (edited by Albert Bushnell Hart and Edward Channing, New York, 1893).

34. Carroll Wright, "Statistics in Colleges," The American Economic Association, *Publications*, III (1889), 15. Hart, "Preparation for Citizenship at Harvard," p. 632.

35. Hart and George Pierce Baker, *Harvard Debating* (Cambridge, 1890), pp. 3, 18. Hart's "Outline of Arguments for Immigration Debate in English 6," published in *The Daily Crimson*, October 12, 1887. Hart, *Subjects and Methods in Political and Economic Debates* (Cambridge, 1892), pp. 3–4, lists all the sources for both sides. See Lodge's speech, February 19, 1891, *Congressional Record*, Fifty-First Congress, Second Session, XII, Part III, 2955–2958 where Lodge presented his article from *North American Review* (1891) in full.

36. Morison, *The Development of Harvard University*, pp. 223–224. Francis G. Peabody to Hart, January 25, 1890, Hart Papers. *The Daily Crimson*, December 19, 1888.

37. See Peabody, "The Soil and The Seed," and "Coming to One's Self," *Harvard Vespers Addresses to Harvard Students by the Preachers of the University 1886–1888* (Boston, 1888), pp. 25–31, 192–202. See student lecture notes on "The Social Question," Philosophy 5 (1892–1893) compiled by Ralph Clinton Larrabee, Harvard Archives.

38. Moorfield Storey, "Class Day Oration" (1866), James Holden Strong, "Class Day Oration" (1866), see also John F. Simmons (1873), Lester Williams Clark (1875), and Theodore Chickering Williams (1876), *Baccalaureate Sermons, Class-Day Orations and Poems* (Cambridge, 1866–1878). Curtis Guild, "Class Day Oration" (1881), and Arthur Richmond Marsh, "Class Day Oration" (1883), *Baccalaureate Sermons, Class-Day Orations and Poems* (Cambridge, 1879–1890).

39. Phillips Brooks, "Baccalaureate" (1884), *Baccalaureate Sermons, Class-Day Orations and Poems.*

40. Guild, "Class Day Oration" (1881), and Frank Elmer Ellsworth Hamilton, "Class Day Oration" (1887), *Baccalaureate Sermons, Class-Day Orations and Poems.* W. F. Atwood, "English 12 theme" (1885), Harvard Archives.

41. Wendell, "Notes on Fortnightly Themes for Second Half Year," English 12, 1889, pp. 50–51, Harvard Archives. *The Daily Crimson,* March 29, 1889. The whole tone of the debate was stronger for restriction than that of earlier debates. *Class of 1889, Harvard College 1889–1914* (Boston, 1914), pp. 378, 622, 625.

42. *Boston Transcript,* August 14, 1894; *Boston Herald,* August 15, 1895, March 13, 1911, April 10, 1915; *Boston Daily Advertiser,* March 7, 1893; *New York Times,* August 8, 1919; Leslie G. Ainley, *Boston Mahatma,* pp. 81–99; *Boston Globe,* November 8, 1900, March 13, 1911.

43. Charles Warren, "Lecture Notes, Fine Arts 4" (1887–1888), and "Lecture Notes, History 13" (1887–1888), Harvard Archives. *The Daily Crimson,* October 29, 1887. Charles Warren, "Plato's Republic Considered with References especially to the Functions of the State Therein and its Relation with some Modern Questions" (1889), MS, Harvard Archives.

44. C. Warren, "The Failure of the Democratic Idea in City Government" (1889), MS, Harvard Archives.

45. Robert DeC. Ward to the editor of the *Boston Traveler,* October 21, 1891. Ward to the editor of the *Boston Daily Advertiser,* November 19, 1891.

46. *Immigration and Other Interests of Prescott F. Hall* (edited by Mrs. Prescott F. Hall, New York, 1922), pp. xiv, 119–123; statements by John Farwell Moors and Henry DeCourcy Ward, personal interviews.

47. Lodge, "True Americanism," *Harvard Graduates' Magazine,* III (1894), 9–23. Winthrop T. Hodges to Henry DeC. Ward, April 18, 1940, Ward Papers.

VI. EARLY YEARS OF THE LEAGUE

1. Phillips Brooks quoted in The Immigration Restriction League, *Publications,* No. 37 (1903), frequently paraphrased by League writers. See Alexander V. G. Allen to Hall, April 21, 1903, IRL Papers.

2. John Murray Forbes to C. Warren, July 16, 1894, IRL Papers. The executive committee did not take Forbes literally enough and in a succeeding letter, Forbes to C. Warren, July 23, 1894, *ibid.,* Forbes withdrew his offer of generous assistance and sent only the regular membership dues of one dollar.

3. Elijah A. Morse to Robert DeC. Ward, July 14, 1894, Ward Newspaper Clippings. Henry Lee to Charles Warren, July 3, 1894, IRL Papers. On Lee's attitude toward Boston and her immigrants see *Boston Daily Advertiser,* March 8, 1888. Records of the Executive Committee of the Immigration Restriction League and of the Meetings of the League, June 20, July 11, August 24, 1894.

4. John Fiske to C. Warren, July 2, 1894 and August 25, 1894, IRL Papers; C. Warren to Fiske, November 15, 1894 and Fiske to James Brooks, November 20, 1894, *Letters of John Fiske,* p. 635; Fiske to R. DeC. Ward, November 20, 1894, Ward Papers. Chauncey J. Hawkins, *Samuel Billings Capen His Life and Work,* p. 84. G. F. Edmunds to R. DeC. Ward, December 1, 1894 and December 13, 1894, Ward Papers. See early letterheads, IRL Papers.

5. IRL, Records of the Executive Committee, May 31 to January 1, 1895, December 28, 1896, May 1, 1896, December 23, 1896. See *Class of 1889, Harvard College,* pp. 378–379, 626.

6. See IRL Form Letters to potential members, September 13 and December 22, 1894 and to United States Congressmen, November 13, 1895 in IRL Scrapbook 1894–1917; see also IRL, *Publications,* Nos. 11 and 16 (1896). R. DeC. Ward, "Should Immigration Be Restricted?" *Donahoe's Magazine,* XXXV (1896), 125; Lord *et al., History of the Archdiocese,* III, 384–385. *Boston Transcript,* October 27, 1894. Hall, "Immigration and the Educational Test," *North American Review,* CLXV (1897), 395; *Boston Evening Record,* October 27, 1894. See also John F. Moors to the editor of the *Boston Herald,* August 10, 1894.

7. The Immigration Restriction League, *Constitution* (Boston, 1894).

8. *Boston Daily Advertiser* and *Boston Herald,* November 21, 1894. IRL, Records of Executive Committee, February 26, 1895.

9. *Boston Transcript,* November 2, 1894; IRL, Records of Executive Committee, November 15 and 22, 1894, November 1, 1894.

10. *Milwaukee Journal,* March 5, 1895; Fiske to Abby, March 7, 1895, *Letters of Fiske,* p. 638; James K. Hosmer, "Response," December 21, 1889, The New England Society of St. Louis, *Proceedings,* First to Twelfth Annual Celebrations (1885–1896), pp. 33–38; *St. Louis Chronicle,* February 22, 1895; *New York Press,* May 26, 1895.

11. Quoted in *Public Opinion,* XVII (1894). See "Twenty Reasons Why Immigration Should Be Further Restricted Now," IRL, *Publications,* No. 4 (1894).

12. Walker, "Restriction of Immigration," *Atlantic Monthly,* LXXVII (1896), 827–828; Hall, "Selection of Immigration," *Publications of the American Academy of Political and Social Sciences,* No. 431 (1904), 173. Ward, "Steamship Influence and Ellis Island," *Harper's Weekly,* LV (1911), 6. This argument became firmly ingrained and the son of Robert DeC. Ward recalled

its importance to his father, statement by H. DeC. Ward, personal interview.

13. "Twenty Reasons Why Immigration Should Be Further Restricted Now," IRL, *Publications*, No. 4 (1894). Hall, "Some Industrial Aspects of Immigration," *Boston Commonwealth*, XXXV (1895), 3. *Annual Report of the Executive Committee of the Immigration Restriction League for 1895* (Boston, 1895).

14. Ward, "The Present Aspect of the Immigration Problem," IRL, *Publications*, No. 1 (1894), No. 4 (1894), No. 5 (1895), No. 8 (1895), and IRL, *Annual Report* (1895).

15. R. M. Smith, "Control of Immigration II and III," *Political Science Quarterly*, III (1888), 217, 417–418; Lodge, "The Day We Celebrate," *Speeches* (Boston, 1892), p. 47. Walker, "Immigration," *Yale Review*, I (1892), 130. R. M. Smith, "Control of Immigration," pp. 68, 413. Walker, "Restriction of Immigration," p. 826.

16. Hall, "Some Industrial Aspects of Immigration," p. 3; and "Immigration and the Educational Test," *North American Review*, CLXV (1897), 393.

17. Hall to the editor, *Boston Journal*, June 30, 1894.

18. Lodge, "Lynch Law and Unrestricted Immigration," *North American Review*, CLII (1891), 604; *Boston Post*, March 18, and April 6, 1891. Phillips Brooks to Robert Treat Paine, Jr., March 26, 1891, *Life and Letters of Phillips Brooks*, II, 822. Hall to W. L. Garrison in the *Boston Record*, July 27, 1894.

19. Lodge, "Lynch Law and Unrestricted Immigration," p. 605. *Boston Daily Advertiser*, July 20 and 27, 1894; *Boston Herald*, July 26, 1894. Hall, "Immigration and the Educational Test," pp. 400–401; and, similarly, John F. Moors to the editor, *Boston Herald*, August 10, 1894. *American Review of Reviews*, III (1891), 331.

20. IRL, *Publications*, No. 2 (1894), No. 11 (1896), No. 16 (1896). Horace G. Wadlin, *Illiteracy in Massachusetts* (Boston, 1889), pp. 11–15. See also Hall to the editor, *New York Tribune*, May 14, 1895.

21. IRL, *Annual Report* (1895). See also IRL, *Publications*, No. 11 (1896). United States Bureau of the Census, *Historical Statistics of the United States: 1789–1945* (Washington, 1949), p. 32.

22. Ward, "The Present Aspect of the Immigration Problem," pp. 4–5. Hall, "Some Industrial Aspects of Immigration," p. 3, and "Immigration and the Educational Test," p. 395.

23. Statement by R. T. Paine, personal telephone interview.

24. Lodge, *Early Memories*, pp. 8, 16, 265–266, 339, 346–347.

25. Lodge, "Colonialism in the United States," *Atlantic Monthly*, LI (1883), 624–625; see also *Early Memories*, p. 205.

26. Lodge, "The Anglo-Saxon Land Law," *Essays in Anglo-Saxon Law*, p. 56; *A Short History of the English Colonies in America* (New York, 1881), p. 414; *A Frontier Town and Other Essays* (New York, 1906), pp. 28–29, 47, 226, 233–234.

27. Lodge, *The Life and Letters of George Cabot* (Boston, 1887). For the "partisan" caliber of the work see Henry Adams, "Lodge's Cabot," *Nation*, XXV (1877), 12–13. Samuel Eliot Morison, "Edward Channing A Memoir,"

The Massachusetts Historical Society, *Proceedings*, 3d ser., LXIV (1931), 260. H. Adams to Charles W. Eliot, March 2, 1877, *H. Adams and Friends*, p. 81.

28. Claude M. Fuess, "Carl Schurz, Henry Cabot Lodge and the Campaign of 1884," *New England Quarterly*, V (1932), 453–482.

29. Lodge, "The Tariff," *Speeches and Addresses 1884–1909* (Boston, 1909), pp. 89–110; *Boston Journal*, November 3, 1898. IRL, *Publications*, No. 12 (1896). Lodge, "The Census and Immigration," *Century*, XLVI (1893), 738.

30. Lodge, "Speech Before the Republican State Convention of Massachusetts, March 27, 1896," *Speeches and Addresses 1884–1909*, pp. 273–274; *Early Memories*, pp. 209, 211–212, 216–217; *A Frontier Town*, p. 27.

31. Lodge, "The Day We Celebrate, December 21, 1880," *Speeches and Addresses 1884–1909*, pp. 45–46.

32. Lodge, "Senator Hoar," *A Frontier Town and Other Essays*, pp. 200–201.

33. Lodge, *Address Delivered Before the Citizens of Nahant* (Cambridge, 1882), pp. 14–15. Lodge was still a free trader here; "The Day We Celebrate," *Speeches and Addresses 1884–1909*, p. 47; *Congressional Record*, Fifty-First Congress, Second Session, XXII, Part I, 12; *Congressional Record*, Fifty-Second Congress, First Session, XXIII, Part I, 204; Fifty-Second Congress, *Senate Reports*, II, 143–148; "The Restriction of Immigration," *North American Review*, CLII (1891), 32; see also Lodge, "The Political Issues of 1892," *Forum*, XII (1891), 104–105; "The Distribution of Ability in the United States," *Historical and Political Essays* (Boston, 1892), pp. 142–166.

34. Lodge, *The Restriction of Immigration* (Washington, 1896), pp. 7–8, 12, 14.

35. Lodge, *Boston* (Cambridge, 1891), pp. 204–205.

36. *Ibid.*, pp. 198–199. Lodge, *A Short History of the English Colonies*, p. 228; contrast his discretion in *Immigration*, Speech in The House of Representatives, February 19, 1891 (Washington, 1891), p. 8. Lodge, *The Restriction of Immigration*, p. 11.

37. Joseph Lee quoted in a statement by John F. Moors, personal interview.

38. IRL, *Annual Report* (1895). The idea of a literacy test was not original, see Edward Bemis, "Restriction of Immigration," *Andover Review*, IX (1888), 262–263. Ward, "The Present Aspect of the Immigration Problem," p. 13; IRL *Publications*, Nos. 14, 16 (1896).

39. *Congressional Record*, Fifty-Fourth Congress, Second Session, XXIX, Part I, 235–239. Lodge was willing to make an exception of Cubans for a limited time during their fight for independence.

40. Three telegrams from Lodge to Ward, February 17–24, 1894, and nine letters from Lodge to Hall, December 22, 1896 to December 24, 1897. Of these, the final letter shows how close the bill was to Lodge's heart. "If I can place it [the Bill] on the statute book, I shall feel more gratified than I can say, for I consider it one of the most vitally important measures which has been before the Congress in my time." See also Samuel McCall to Ward, May 21 and May 25, 1896, Ward Papers. *Boston Transcript*, January 26 and

27, 1896; *Boston Herald,* January 24, 1896. Fiske to Ward, December 30, 1895 quoted in part, *Boston Transcript,* January 27, 1896.

41. Quoted in the *Boston Herald,* March 3, 1897.

42. IRL, Records of Executive Committee, January 10 and 17, 1898, November 9, 1898. IRL, *Annual Report* (1898, 1899, and 1900).

43. *Nation,* LXIX (1899), 293–296; Hall, "Present Status of Immigration Restriction," *Gunton's Magazine,* XVIII (1900), 305–307.

44. IRL, Records of the Executive Committee, November 4 and 11, 1899. IRL, *Annual Report* (1898, 1899, and 1900). Hall, "Present Status of Immigration Restriction," pp. 305–307.

45. Norton, "Records of the Hour War Time" (1898), Norton Scrapbook. Fred Harrington, "The Anti-Imperialistic Movement in the United States, 1898–1900," *Mississippi Valley Historical Review,* XXII (1935), 211–230; Anti-Imperialist League, *Pamphlets* (1898–1911), and Imperialism News Cuttings, Widener Library; see also Edward Waldo Emerson, "John Murray Forbes," *Atlantic Monthly,* LXXXIV (1899), 396.

46. *Boston Transcript,* December 22, 1898 and March 24, 1899. Lodge, *The Retention of the Philippines, Speech in the Senate of the United States* (Washington, 1900) pp. 16–17. See the Resolutions of the Faneuil Hall Meeting and Speech of George McNeil at the Faneuil Hall Meeting, June 12, 1898, Anti-Imperialist League, *Pamphlet.* Lodge's discussion at Lawrence, Massachuetts, quoted in the *Boston Journal,* November 3, 1898.

47. William Graham Sumner, *The Conquest of the United States by Spain* (Boston, 1899), pp. 11–12.

48. Harrington, "Literary Aspects of American Anti-Imperialism," *New England Quarterly,* X (1937), 666.

VII. THE LEAGUE AT HIGH TIDE

1. Frederick Bushée, "The Declining Birth Rate and Its Cause," *Popular Science Monthly,* LXIII (1903), 360.

2. Prescott F. Hall, "Present Status of Immigration Restriction," *Gunton's Magazine,* XVIII (1900), 309. IRL, *Annual Report* (1903). John Fiske to W. L. Garrison, February 1, 1898, *The Letters of John Fiske,* pp. 666–671.

3. IRL, Records of Executive Committee, April 1, 1899, November 20, and December 5, 1901, February 28, 1903; see Henry Holt, *Garrulities of an Octogenarian Editor* (Boston, 1923); when in 1907 Franklin MacVeagh became the head of the Immigration Department of the National Civic Federation, he resigned his vice-presidency in the League despite his continued belief in its aims, IRL, Records of the Executive Committee, October 24, 1906.

4. Letterheads of the IRL, 1913.

5. IRL, Records of the Executive Committee, January 11 and October 18, 1902, April 25 and May 13, 1905. James H. Patten was still working for the Boston League, IRL, Records of the Executive Committee (1921–1931), November 2, 1931, belonging to Henry DeC. Ward.

6. IRL, *Publicatons,* No. 37 (1903), 2–3; see also, IRL, *Annual Reports*

(1904–1907). Hall, *Immigration* (New York, 1906), pp. 206–207, 276, 310. Henry Cabot Lodge quoted in IRL, Records of the Executive Committee, October 9, 1905; for Gardner's continuous surveillance of restrictive legislation see Gardner to his wife, April 14, 1910, Constance Gardner, *Some Letters of Augustus P. Gardner* (Boston, 1920) and see also the "Introduction," pp. 63–64; xi–xiii. A conversation between Gardner and the Managing Director of the National Liberal Immigration League quoted in B. A. Sekely, *Immigrant Labor and the Restriction of Immigration* (New York, 1917), p. 6. See also IRL, Records of the Executive Committee, October 20, 1906, April 13, 1907, October 3, 17, and 31, 1913.

7. Robert Lord *et al., History of the Archdiocese of Boston,* III, 582–583. IRL, Records of the Executive Committee, January 18, 1902, July 3, 1905, July 13, 1905, May 19, 1909, December 1, 1909, January 5, 1910. Hall veiled his anti-Catholic sentiments rather thinly in the handwritten comments in his own copy of *Immigration,* especially pp. 144–145, Houghton Library. See also H. F. Bowers, the founder of the American Protective Association to Hall, April 21, 1910, IRL Papers.

8. IRL, Records of the Executive Committee, June 8 and 21, 1905.

9. Ward to *Manufacturer's Record,* Baltimore, Maryland, May 6, 1909; Ward, "Immigration and the South," *Atlantic Monthly,* XCVI (1905), 611–617. Patten, *The Immigration Problem and the South* (Raleigh, North Carolina, 1906), p. 16, reported in a Norfolk, Virginia newspaper, November 12, 1907, Hall Newspaper Clippings.

10. IRL, Records of the Executive Committee, November 7, 1903, September 2 and 30, 1904, April 25, 1905, and January 4, 1906. See also the vote of thanks to Peter C. Brooks for contributing $500, *ibid.,* October 9, 1905. See Prescott F. Hall's Notebook of Contributors (1910–1919), Houghton Library, confirmed by Mrs. Margaret Southard, daughter of Joseph Lee, that her father had always paid Patten's salary, personal interview. Madison Grant to Ward, May 27, 1924, Ward Papers.

11. Hall, "New Problems of Immigration," *Forum,* XXX (1901), 557–558; J. Lee, "Immigration," The National Conference of Charities and Correction, *Proceedings,* XXXIII (1906), 584.

12. Jeremiah Jenks, "The Racial Problem in Immigration," The National Conference of Charities and Correction, *Proceedings,* XXXVI (1909), 217.

13. Edward A. Ross, *Social Control* (New York, 1901), pp. 17, 439–440 and *Seventy Years of It* (New York, 1936), pp. 245–246. Richmond Mayo Smith, "Theories of Mixture of Races and Nationalities," *Yale Review,* III (1894), 177. Ross, "The Causes of Race Superiority," *Annals of the American Academy of Political and Social Sciences,* XVIII (1901), 67–68.

14. Smith, "Theories of Mixture of Races and Nationalities," *Yale Review,* III (1894), 177.

15. William Z. Ripley, *The Races of Europe* (New York, 1899), pp. 96, 477, 484–485, 511, 516.

16. *Ibid.,* pp. 25, 516, 559.

17. On the influence of *Races of Europe,* see Lawrence Martin to Ripley,

January 18, 1937; William Ridgeway to Ripley, January 2, 1909; Charles Seymour to Ripley, December 23, 1936, Ripley Papers. Ripley, *The Races of Europe,* pp. 52–53, 111–112, 516.

18. Poultney Bigelow to Ripley, undated letter, included in the Ripley Papers. Poultney Bigelow's complaint upon driving through Connecticut, finding the children of the foreign-born everywhere, their homes ruining the state, quoted in Ross, *Changing America* (New York, 1912), p. 142. Ripley to Hall, February 16, 1909, IRL Papers.

19. Ripley to Hall, February 16, 1909, IRL Papers, Houghton Library, Ripley, "The Census Revelations of Our Peril from Uncontrolled Immigration," *Boston Transcript,* June 21, 1913.

20. Barrett Wendell to F. J. Stimson, December 28, 1904, *Barrett Wendell and His Letters,* p. 162. Ripley, *The European Population of the United States* (London, 1908), p. 225. Ross, "The Causes of Race Superiority," pp. 74, 88. Later Ross enjoyed the fact that he launched the phrase "race suicide" two years before Theodore Roosevelt made it famous.

21. Ripley, *The European Population of the United States,* p. 240; Franklin Giddings, "The American People," *International Quarterly,* VII (1903), 298–299. Albert Bushnell Hart, "A Hopeful View of Democracy," *Outlook,* LXV (1900), 504–507; see also Carroll Wright, *Outlines of Practical Sociology* (New York, 1899), pp. 106, 109–110. Giddings, "Comments on the Foregoing," *Century,* LXV (1903), 690–692. J. Lee, "Assimilation and Nationality," *Charities,* XIX (1908), 1453–1455.

22. R. M. Smith, "Theories of Mixture of Races and Nationalities," pp. 182, 186.

23. John R. Commons, *Myself* (New York, 1934), pp. 7–11, 16, 21, 33, 39, 43, 68–69. It was voted to "retain" Commons to appear at the hearings of the currently pending literacy bill, IRL, Records of the Executive Committee, January 11, 1902. See also IRL, Records of the Executive Committee, October 17 and 22, 1901, January 18, 1902, October 17, 1903, June 29, 1905, January 11, 1909, April 29, 1911 and March 13, 1913.

24. Commons, *Races and Immigrants in America* (New York, 1920), pp. 1–5.

25. *Ibid.,* pp. 13–16, 22–38, 63–106, 198–200, 208, 211–213.

26. *Ibid.,* pp. 3–4, 10–12, 39–62, 175, 214, 220–221; Commons, *Myself* illuminates his approach to industrial America. Commons, "Review of Prescott Hall's *Immigration,*" *Charities,* XVII (1906), 504. In contrast, see W. F. Willcox, "Review of Hall's *Immigration* and its Effect upon the United States," *American Historical Review,* XI (1906), 921–922.

27. IRL, Records of the Executive Committee, April 4, 1912, March 3, 1913, September 19, 1913; Ross, *Seventy Years of It,* pp. 1–105, 223.

28. Ross, *Social Control;* see also "The Cause of Race Superiority," p. 89. Commons struck the same note in *Races and Immigrants in America,* p. 214. Ross, *Changing America,* pp. 143, 147, and *Seventy Years of It,* pp. 93, 126, 223–224, 276–277. Ross, *The Old World in the New* (New York, 1914).

29. Commons, *Races and Immigrants in America,* p. 76; Ross, *Seventy Years*

of It, pp. 223–229, 231–232, and *Changing America,* pp. 32–46; Thomas Nixon Carver, *Recollections of an Unplanned Life* (Los Angeles, 1949), pp. 261–263, and *Essays in Social Justice* (Cambridge, 1915), pp. 261, 372.

30. Carver, *Recollections of an Unplanned Life,* pp. 5–9, 92–112, 131 ff. and Carver's Economics 3, Notes of James Ford and of Albert G. Waite (1904–1905), Harvard Archives.

31. Carver, "Immigration and the Labor Problem," *American Journal of Politics,* III (1893), 78–81, especially 80–81, documented with references from Walker and Mayo Smith; "Life in the Corn Belt," *The World's Work,* VII (1903), 4238. *Working with Immigrants* (Boston, 1910), a Prospectus published by the State Executive Committee to the Young Men's Christian Associations of Massachusetts and Rhode Island. IRL, Records of the Executive Committee, November 7, 1903, March 11, 1910, June 11, 1911. Carver, *Recollections of an Unplanned Life,* pp. 141–142, 261–267, and *Essays in Social Justice,* pp. 8, 11.

32. A. B. Hart, *National Ideals Historically Traced,* pp. 83–84. A. L. Lowell, "The Colonial Expansion of the United States," *Atlantic Monthly,* LXXXIII (1899), 150.

33. Robert A. Woods, *English Social Movements* (London, 1892), pp. 182–226; Joseph Lee, *Constructive and Preventive Philanthropy* (New York, 1906), pp. 2, 7, 10–20; Jeffrey R. Brackett, "The Duty of the Church to the Needy," *Charities,* VIII (1902), 315–321. Richard C. Cabot, *Social Service and the Art of Healing* (New York, 1909), pp. 46–47. Robert A. Woods quoted in Eleanor H. Woods, *Robert A. Woods,* p. 58; Jane Addams, "The Subtle Problems of Charity," *Atlantic Monthly,* LXXXIII (1899), 177.

34. J. Lee, *Constructive and Preventive Philanthropy,* pp. 8, 10–20. Mrs. Fields quoted in E. H. Woods, *Robert A. Woods,* p. 60. (This same lady used to instruct her maid to put out a glass of cold milk for her postman, just before he arrived on a hot day. Statement by Eva Whiting White, personal interview.) Robert Treat Paine, "The Importance of Stopping Outdoor Relief to Chronic or Hereditary Paupers," *Charities,* X (1903), 134–137. Mary Richmond, *Friendly Visiting Among the Poor* (New York, 1899), pp. vii–viii, 40.

35. John F. Moors, "Joseph Lee," *Recreation,* XXXI (1937), 535–537. J. Lee, *Expensive Living—The Blight on America* (Boston, 1900), pp. 6–7, and *Play in Education* (New York, 1915), p. 376.

36. "The Play Life of Joseph Lee," *Recreation,* XXXI (1937), 516–518; Mary Lee, "Joseph Lee Loved to Play," *ibid.,* p. 519; Theodate Geoffrey, "Joseph Lee, Philosopher," *ibid.,* p. 232. R. A. Woods, *The Neighborhood in National-Building* (Boston, 1923), p. 232.

37. J. Lee, *Play in Education,* p. 433, and "The Need to Dream," *Journal of Proceedings and Addresses of the Fifty-First Annual Meeting of the National Education Association of the United States,* LI (1913), 159–169.

38. J. Lee, *Play in Education,* pp. 13, 464, 474–475; *Expensive Living,* pp. 5, 19.

39. *Class of 1883 Harvard College* (Boston, 1913), p. 110. *Class of 1883*

Harvard College (Boston, 1933), p. 189. Eva Whiting White, "Joseph Lee—His Contribution to Social Work," *Recreation*, XXXI (1937), 543–544.

40. J. Lee, *Constructive and Preventive Philanthropy*, p. 233.

41. J. Lee to the editor, *Charities*, XVIII (1907), 632; "Assimilation and Nationality," *ibid.*, XIX (1908), 1453–1455. J. Lee, *Expensive Living*, pp. 7–8.

42. J. Lee, *Expensive Living*, p. 19.

43. Lee quoted in T. Geoffrey, "Joseph Lee, Philosopher," p. 571. Edward Hartman, "Joseph Lee, Creative Philanthropist," *Recreation*, XXXI (1937), 546–547. J. Lee, *Constructive Philanthropy*, p. 235, and *Expensive Living*, p. 8.

44. IRL, Records of the Executive Committee, December 21, 1901; The League listed other charity organizations which adopted resolutions favoring restriction within the decade, IRL Papers. Amos G. Warner, *American Charities, A Study in Philanthropy and Economics* (New York, 1894); Brackett, "The Duty of the Church to the Needy," *Charities*, VIII (1902), 315–321. *Boston Transcript*, April 13, 1904; E. H. Woods, *Robert A. Woods*, p. 149. IRL, Records of the Executive Committee, June 1, 1905, June 8, 1908, June 16, 1911, and May 31, 1912. Similarly John F. Moors and Prescott Hall spoke to the Monday Evening Club of paid charity workers in Boston, IRL, Records of the Executive Committee, April 30, 1904.

45. Statement by Mrs. Robert A. Woods, personal interview.

46. E. H. Woods, *Robert A. Woods*, pp. 1–3, 13–14, 17–23.

47. R. A. Woods, *English Social Movements* (London, 1892), pp. 261–265.

48. *Ibid.*, pp. vi, 151, 264. Woods to Anna L. Dawes, December 20, 1892, letter in possession of Mrs. Robert A. Woods.

49. R. A. Woods, *The Neighborhood in Nation-Building*, pp. 3, 34, 138.

50. *Americans in Process* (edited by R. A. Woods, Boston, 1902), pp. 364, 372–373; Woods, *The Neighborhood in Nation-Building*, pp. 30–31.

51. R. A. Woods to A. L. Dawes, December 20, 1892, belonging to Mrs. R. A. Woods; E. H. Woods, *Robert A. Woods*, p. 82; Woods, *The Neighborhood in Nation-Building*, pp. 13, 57–62, 66. By contrast, South End represented "the zone of emergence" for many slum dwellers. Statement by Eva Whiting White, personal interview.

52. South End House, *Annual Report* (1906), p. 33, and (1912), pp. 22–23. Woods, *The Neighborhood in Nation-Building*, pp. 13, 59, 94.

53. South End House, *Annual Report* (1912), pp. 22–23, and (1922), p. 13. Woods, *The Neighborhood in Nation-Building*, pp. 13, 56. Statement by Mrs. R. A. Woods, personal interview. IRL, Records of the Executive Committee, October 19, 1911.

54. Hodges' Journal, January 9, February 5, February 10, October 17, 1894, January 15, February 4, November 20, 1897, February 2, 1898, June 17, 1899, April 12, 1900. Hodges Papers. Hodges, Notes on "A Quiet Day for Social Workers," April 9, 1897, Hodges' Journal. Hodges' Notes for a speech at Denison House, November 19, 1894, Hodges' Journal. Hodges, "Christian

Socialism and the Social Union," Church Social Union, *Publications*, No. 30 (1896), 10–11. Notes, April 4, 1895, Hodges' Journals.

55. Vida D. Scudder, *A Listener in Babel* (Boston, 1903), pp. 74, 76, 85, 233, 251, and *On Journey* (New York, 1937), pp. 15–16, 57–69, 72, 77–85, 110–112.

56. Richard Cabot, *Social Service and the Art of Healing*, pp. 4–7.

57. James A. Field, *The Progress of Eugenics* (Cambridge, 1911), pp. 4–38. Henry Holland, "Heredity," *Atlantic Monthly*, LII (1883), 447–451 related eugenics and the political state. Francis Galton, "Eugenics: Its Definition, Scope and Aims," *American Journal of Sociology*, X (1904), 1–25.

58. Louis Agassiz, "Evolution and Permanence of Type," *Atlantic Monthly*, XXXIII (1874), 98; Nathan Allen, "Changes in New England Population," *Popular Science Monthly*, XXIII (1883), 443–444; Field, *The Progress of Eugenics*, pp. 39–40.

59. Edward Bellamy, *Looking Backward 2000–1887* (Boston and New York, 1929), pp. 223, 267–268. J. R. Commons, "Natural Selection, Social Selection and Heredity," *Arena*, XVIII (1897), 94, and Amos G. Warner, *American Charities*, pp. 119, 122, 135.

60. David Starr Jordan, *The Days of a Man* (New York, 1922), I, 1–100, 153, 673, II, 490 and *The Human Harvest* (Boston, 1907), p. 50; Jordan, *Foot-Notes to Evolution* (New York, 1907), pp. 121, 309–310. IRL, Records of the Executive Committee, March 30, 1908, April 4, May 31, June 4, 1912; Edward McNall Burns, *David Starr Jordan Prophet of Freedom* (Stanford, California, 1953), pp. 72–77.

61. Alexander Graham Bell, "A Few Thoughts Concerning Eugenics," *National Geographic Magazine*, XIX (1908), 119–123. Bell to P. F. Hall, May 31, 1911; see also IRL, Records of the Executive Committee, February 29, 1912 on Bell's refusal to accept election as a vice-president of the League.

62. Charles B. Davenport, *Heredity in Relation to Eugenics* (New York, 1911), pp. 199–211, 221–224. Davenport was a member of the New England Society of Brooklyn, see the New England Society of Brooklyn, *Proceedings*, 14th Annual Meeting (1894), p. 87.

63. Ward to Davenport, February 5, 1912, Ward Papers.

64. Ward to Davenport, November 22, 1911, Ward Papers. See also Hall's list of doctors who were interested in more stringent immigration legislation, IRL Papers.

65. Ward, *The Crisis in Our Immigration Policy*, pp. 7, 21. P. F. Hall, "'The Future of American Ideals," *North American Review*, XCCV (1912), 101. Ward to Davenport, March 21, 1910, Ward Papers.

66. Dr. Alexander Forbes to P. F. Hall, June 8, 1911. In contrast, there were many distinguished Boston physicians who responded to Hall's line of reasoning in this context. For example, Dr. James Lincoln Huntington to Hall, October 1, 1911, IRL Papers.

67. Thomas W. Salmon, "Insanity and the Immigration Law," reprinted from *New York Hospital Bulletin* (1911), Hall Collection. Salmon, "Immigration and the Preventing of Insanity," *The Boston Medical and Surgical Journal*, CLXIX (1913), 297–301.

68. IRL, Records of the Executive Committee, June 4, October 30, 1912, October 13 and 31, 1913 and May 8, 1914. *Congressional Record,* Sixty-Third Congress, Third Session, Part I, pp. 203–224, which includes letters written by Dr. Salmon on the subject. *New York Times,* March 3, 1914.

69. IRL, Records of Executive Committee, December 14, 1911; Ward, "The Restriction of Immigration," *North American Review,* CLXXIX (1904), 236. F. A. Bushée, "The Declining Birth Rate and Its Cause," pp. 355–361; Ward, "The Immigration Problem," *Charities,* XII (1904), 149; Hall, "Immigration Restriction and World Eugenics," IRL, *Publications,* No. 71 (1919). Hall, "The Future of American Ideals," pp. 94–102; Hall, "Eugenics, Ethics and Immigration," IRL, *Publications,* No. 51 (1909).

70. Hall, "The Future of American Ideals," pp. 94–102, and "Eugenics, Ethics and Immigration," pp. 2, 8.

VIII. *TESTING THE RACES: STEREOTYPES OF THE FOREIGN-BORN*

1. Jeremiah W. Jenks, "The Racial Problem in Immigration," The National Conference of Charities and Correction, *Proceedings,* XXXVI (1909), 216–217.

2. Oscar Handlin, "American Views of the Jew at the Opening of the Twentieth Century," American Jewish Historical Society, *Publications,* XL, Part 4 (1951), 328–329.

3. Herman Jackson Warner to H., December 29, 1882, *New Letters of an Idle Man* (edited by George E. Woodberry, London, 1913), p. 9. "Politics," *Atlantic Monthly,* XXXI (1873), 125. Nathaniel S. Shaler, "The Scotch Element in the American People," *Atlantic Monthly,* LXXVII (1896), 516.

4. Barrett Wendell to Prescott F. Hall, March 22, 1910, IRL Papers. Henry Cabot Lodge, *The Restriction of Immigration,* p. 11; *Report of the Industrial Commission* (Washington, 1901), XV, 268–275, 958–962, and Hall's repetition of these statements, *Immigration,* p. 37. Robert A. Woods, the preface of *Americans in Process,* pp. iv–v. Bushée, "The Invading Host," *Americans in Process,* p. 56.

5. Henry Childs Merwin, "The Irish in American Life," *Atlantic Monthly,* LXXVII (1896), 289; Sara Orne Jewett, *Strangers and Wayfarers* (Boston, 1890), pp. 87–88 and *Tales of New England* (Boston, 1895), p. 259. Joseph Lee, *Constructive and Preventive Philanthropy,* pp. 198–199. John R. Commons, *Races and Immigrants in America,* p. 182, repeated by Hall, *Immigration,* p. 188. Henry Pratt Fairchild, *Immigration* (New York, 1913), pp. 310, 368; Edward A. Ross, *The Old World in the New,* p. 39. William Z. Ripley, "Race Factors in Labor Unions," *Atlantic Monthly,* XCIII (1904), 305.

6. Ripley, *The European Population of the United States,* p. 230.

7. Bushée and Rufus F. Miles, "Nationalities in the West End," *Americans in Process,* p. 69. J. Lee, *Play in Education,* p. 193; William I. Cole, "Criminal Tendencies," *The City Wilderness* (Boston, 1898), p. 174. E. A. Ross, *The Old World in the New,* p. 34.

8. Bushée, "Population," *The City Wilderness,* pp. 39–40; E. A. Ross, *The*

Old World in the New, p. 44. Bushée, *Ethnic Factors in the Population of Boston* (New York, 1903), pp. 150–152.

9. Louisa May Alcott, *Little Women* (Boston, 1896), pp. 536–537, 541, 559, 568, 581–582.

10. Hall, *Immigration,* p. 47.

11. Charles Follen Adams, *Yawcob Strauss and Other Poems* (London, 1910), pp. 82, 166–172, 269. These poems became widely known through Adams' public readings and also appeared as syndicated newspaper items and in *Harper's Monthly. DAB,* I, 40.

12. Hugo Münsterberg, *American Traits* (Boston, 1901), pp. 1–6, 21–22; H. J. Warner to H., December 19, 1885, *New Letters of an Idle Man,* p. 43. Freeman, *Some Impressions of the United States* (London, 1883), p. 34.

13. Josiah Flint, "The German and the German-American," *Atlantic Monthly,* LXXVIII (1896), 657–658; Ross, *The Old World in the New,* pp. 47–53.

14. Sara Orne Jewett to Mrs. Henry Parkman, undated in 1902, *Letters of Sara Orne Jewett* (edited by Annie Fields, Boston, 1902), p. 190, corroborates Münsterberg, *American Traits,* pp. 7–8, 15–22. In the resurgence of anti-German feelings in 1917, Anglophiles drew again upon negative elements of the stereotype to demarcate the German from the true American. See Walter Hines Page to Arthur Page, July 8, 1917, Burton J. Hendrick, *The Life and Letters of Walter H. Page* (New York, 1922), II, 287, on "kinship in blood and ideals of the two great English-speaking nations. We were actually coming to believe ourselves that we were part German and Slovene and Pole and What-not, instead of essentially being Scotch and English."

15. Hall, *Immigration,* pp. 46–48 based on the assessment of the German group in the *Report of the Industrial Commission,* XV (1901), 326–461. Similarly, see Commons, *Races and Immigrants in America,* p. 132. Ross, *The Old World in the New,* pp. 50–53, 59–60, 62, 64. Bushée, *Ethnic Factors in the Population of Boston,* p. 154. *The Reports of the U. S. Immigration Commission* (Washington, 1911), II, 232, 246, 249, and V, 66.

16. Lodge, *The Restriction of Immigration,* pp. 10–11; Hall, *Immigration,* pp. 47–48; E. A. Ross, *Changing America,* pp. 164–165.

17. Oscar J. Falnes, "New England Interest in Scandinavian Culture and the Norsemen," *New England Quarterly,* X (1937), 211–242. R. M. Smith, *Emigration and Immigration,* p. 146.

18. Kendric Charles Babcock, "The Scandinavian Contingent," *Atlantic Monthly,* LXXVII (1896), 666–670; Hall, *Immigration,* p. 62; *Report of the Immigration Commission,* V, 120.

19. Hall, *Immigration,* p. 62; Carver, "Life in the Corn Belt," *The World's Work,* VII (1903), 4238. Ross, *The Old World in the New,* pp. 70, 81–85, 89, 91–92.

20. Henry W. Longfellow, "Evangeline" (1847–1857), *American Poetry and Prose* (edited by Norman Foerster, Boston, 1934), pp. 645–670. For Parkman's views, see Edward Saveth, *American Historians and European Immigrants* (New York, 1948), pp. 100–111.

21. *Connecticut Report of the Bureau of Labor* (1885), quoted in R. M. Smith, *Emigration and Immigration*, pp. 135, 145. Carroll Wright, *Massachusetts Report of the Bureau of Statistics of Labor* (Boston, 1881), p. 469. Marcus L. Hansen, "The Second Colonization of New England," *New England Quarterly*, II (1929), 557.

22. William Dean Howells, *Suburban Sketches* (Boston, 1884), p. 62. Shaler, "The Summer Journey of a Naturalist," *Atlantic Monthly*, XXI (1873), 713.

23. Hall, *Immigration*, p. 43; Commons, *Races and Immigrants in America*, p. 151; Ripley, "Race Factors in Labor Unions," p. 302. Lodge, "A Million Immigrants A Year," *Century*, LXVII (1904), 467. Carroll Wright, *Outline of Practical Sociology* (New York, 1899), p. 109. Henry Loomis Nelson, "French-Canadians in New England," *Harper's New Monthly Magazine*, LXXXVII (1893), 180 ff; William MacDonald, "French-Canadians in New England," *Quarterly Journal of Economics*, XII (1898), 260; John Davidson, "The Growth of the French-Canadian Races," *Annals of the American Academy of Political and Social Sciences*, VIII (1896), 213–235.

24. E. P. Clark, "The Immigration Problem," *Nation*, LIV (1892), 4–5; Nelson, "French-Canadians in New England," pp. 180–187. Max B. Thrasher, "One of the Strangers at Our Gates," *New England Magazine*, XVI (1897), 29–31. Edward Everett Hale, "New England and Emigration," *Chautauquan*, XII (1891), 634. MacDonald, "French-Canadians in New England," p. 268. Commons, *Races and Immigrants in America*, pp. 97–98. Dr. William Henry Drummond, *The Habitant and Other French Canadian Poems* (New York and London, 1912), p. 27.

25. Howells, *Suburban Sketches*, pp. 37–39.

26. Eliot Norton, *Fourth Report of the Society for the Protection of Italian Immigrants* (New York, 1904–1906); E. Norton, "Diffusion of Immigration," *Annals of the American Academy of Political and Social Science*, XXIV (1904), 161–165; Vida D. Scudder, quoted in *Denison House Annual Report* (1909), pp. 14–17; Mary G. Smith, quoted in *Denison House Annual Report* (1913), p. 29.

27. Henry James, *The American Scene* (New York, 1946), pp. 118–119, 126–128, 231, 265, 270. Poultney Bigelow quoted in Ross, *Changing America*, p. 142.

28. Howells, *Suburban Sketches*, pp. 38, 50. Lodge, "Lynch Law and Unrestricted Immigration," *North American Review*, CLII (1891), 604–605; "A Million Immigrants A Year," *Century*, LXVII (1904), 467. Commons, *Races and Immigrants in America*, p. 78; Ross, *The Old World in the New*, pp. 97–101; *Reports of the United States Immigration Commission*, V, 81–82.

29. Vida D. Scudder, "Experiments in Fellowship Work with Italians in Boston," *Survey*, XXII (1909), 47–51.

30. Owen Wister, *Philosophy 4 A Story of Harvard University* (New York, 1903), pp. 14, 23, 26, 35–38, 52, 93–95. Wister had been identified with the Boston Restrictionists since 1899. See above, p. 123.

31. Lodge, "Lynch Law and Unrestricted Immigration," pp. 608–609; Dr.

Joseph Senner, U. S. Commissioner of Immigration, denied Lodge's contentions. He showed how the enactments of 1893 had practically eliminated "birds of passage," Dr. Joseph H. Senner, "Immigration from Italy," *North American Review*, CLXII (1896), 654. Shaler, "European Peasants as Immigrants," p. 653.

32. Robert A. Woods, "Notes on the Italians in Boston," *Charities*, XII (1904), 451–452; Frederick A. Bushée, *Ethnic Factors in the Population of Boston*, p. 158. William I. Cole, "Law and Order," *Americans in Process*, pp. 207–209. Bushée, "Italian Immigrants in Boston," *South End House Bulletin No. 10* (1897), p. 15. Philip Edmund Sherman, "Immigration from Abroad in Massachusetts," *New England Magazine*, XXIX (1904), 676.

33. John Foster Carr, "The Coming of the Italian," *Outlook*, LXXXII (1906), 419–431. Alice Bennett, "The Italian As a Farmer," *Charities*, XXI (1908), 57–60; Ross, *The Old World in the New*, pp. 97–101.

34. Hall, "The Future of American Ideals," pp. 94–102. Ross, *The Old World in the New*, pp. 95, 113, 119–140. Broughton Brandenburg, "Racial Traits in American Beauty," *Cosmopolitan*, XLI (1906), 57–64, for Anglo-Saxon, Celtic, Scandinavian, and Teutonic portraits of feminine beauty.

35. See C. E. Norton to Edward Lee-Childe, September 24, 1876, *The Letters of Charles Eliot Norton*, II, 64. Charles Dawson Shauly, "Germany in New York," *Atlantic Monthly*, XIX (1867), 555. John Fiske to Abby, February 25, 1877, *The Letters of John Fiske*, p. 361.

36. On Carlyle's attitude, see C. E. Norton to Miss E. C. Cleveland, June 7, 1869, *Letters of Norton*, I, 334–336. Anna L. Dawes, *The Modern Jew His Present and Future* (Boston, 1886), pp. 23–24.

37. Bushée, *Ethnic Factors in the Population in Boston*, p. 9; Hall, *Immigration*, pp. 20–21. Arnold White, *The Problems of a Great City* (London, 1886), p. 142, and "Immigration of Aliens," *Charities*, III (1893), 70, 77. Ward to editor, *Boston Daily Advertiser*, February 19, 1892. Broughton Brandenburg, "Underground Immigration," IRL, *Publications*, No. 43 (1905). *New York Sun*, June 17, 1895. Henry Cabot Lodge quoted in the *Boston Herald*, August 5, 1895. W. Z. Ripley, *Races of Europe*, p. 372–373.

38. Ripley, *Races of Europe*, pp. 373, 382–384, 395, 398, 400.

39. J. Lee, *Play in Education*, p. 358 and *Constructive and Preventive Philanthropy*, pp. 198–199; Bushée, "The Invading Host," *Americans in Process*, p. 62. Ross, *The Old World in the New*, pp. 157 ff.

40. Bushée, "Population," *The City Wilderness*, p. 43, and *Ethnic Factors in the Population of Boston*, p. 157.

41. Hall, *Immigration*, pp. 51, 165. See also Roger Mitchell, "Recent Jewish Immigration to the United States," *Popular Science Monthly*, LXII (1903), 341–342. Ward underlined passages in this article dealing with the moral degradation of the Jewish immigrant, Ward Newspaper Clippings. Ross, *The Old World in the New*, pp. 147–148, 155–157. Bushée, "Population," *The City Wilderness*, pp. 39–40; Cole, "Two Ancient Faiths," *Americans in Process*, pp. 284–285. Bushée, *Ethnic Factors in the Population of Boston*, pp. 156–157, and

"The Invading Host," *Americans in Process*, pp. 49–50. Woods, "Work and Wages," *The City Wilderness*, p. 91.

42. Commons, *Races and Immigrants in America*, p. 153; repeated in Ripley, "Race Factors in Labor Unions," *Atlantic Monthly*, XCIII (1904), 302. In retrospect, Commons felt he had judged wrongly for he had not distinguished between "race psychology and industrial psychology," Commons, *Myself*, pp. 68–70. Ross, *The Old World in the New*, pp. 289–298; Hall, *Immigration*, pp. 50, 303. J. Lee to the editor, *Charities*, XIX (1907), 1107.

43. Edward Everett Hale, *A Summer Vacation* (Boston, 1874), pp. 63–69. Charles W. Eliot, Introduction to *The Immigrant Jew in America* (edited by Edmund J. James, Oscar R. Flynn, Dr. J. R. Paulding, Mrs. Simon N. Patton, Walter Scott Andrews, New York, 1906), p. 4.

44. Edward Atkinson to John S. Williams, June 30, 1902, MS, Atkinson Papers, Hale, "How to Deal with Our Emigrants," *Social Economist*, IV (1893), 82. Hutchins Hapgood, "The Earnestness That Wins Wealth," *The World's Work*, VI (1903), 3458–3459. Esther G. Barrows, *Neighbors All* (Boston, 1929), p. 73. Evelyn Foster Peck, "The Russian Jew in Southern New England," *New England Magazine*, XXXI (1904), 26–27.

45. Shaler, *Autobiography*, pp. 376, 384. Shaler, "The Scotch Element in the American People," *Atlantic Monthly*, LXXVII (1896), 515–516, and *The Neighbor* (Boston, 1904), pp. 72–103.

46. Shaler, *The Neighbor*, pp. 108, 112, 121–124, 319–320.

47. *Ibid.*, pp. 286, 325, 328.

48. In addition statement by Horace M. Kallen, personal interview. Another student of Wendell's affirmed this preference for Hebraic as opposed to Jewish culture, Mark DeWolfe Howe, "Settlers in the City Wilderness," *Atlantic Monthly*, LXXVII (1896), 119–123. Edith Wendell Osborne, *Recollections of My Father* (Boston, 1921), p. 17. Wendell to Horace V. Kallen, June 5, 1912, Wendell to Sir Robert White-Thompson, March 31, 1917, *Barrett Wendell and His Letters*, pp. 249, 281–282. Samuel McCall, *The Patriotism of the American Jew* (New York, 1922).

49. C. B. Davenport, *Heredity in Relation to Eugenics*, p. 216.

50. Hall, *Immigration*, pp. 51–53. H. C. Lodge to Theodore Roosevelt, July 26, 1908, *Selections from the Correspondence of Theodore Roosevelt and Henry Cabot Lodge* (edited by Henry Cabot Lodge, New York, 1925), II, 306–307. Hall, "The Immigration Situation in Congress," *Outlook*, LXXXIV (1906), 611–615; Cyrus L. Sulzberger, "Immigration Restriction: Its Fallacies," *Charities*, XV (1906), 924–929. Hall, handwritten comment, Hall Newspaper Clippings, X, 77. *Boston Herald*, February 8, 1913, *Boston Morning Globe*, January 4, 1913, *Lawrence Massachusetts Telegram*, January 9, 1913.

51. Hall to Miss Helen E. Freeman, December 9, 1912, IRL Papers. Hall to Louis Brandeis, April 7, 1915, IRL Papers; Hall, "The Future of American Ideals," *North American Review*, XCCV (1912), 94–102.

52. Ross, *The Old World in the New*, pp. 164–165.

53. H. G. Wells, *The Future in America* (New York, 1906), p. 135.

54. Esther Barrows, *Neighbors All*, p. 4, referred to Miss Mary Coe's view of

the Syrians. C., "Syrians in Boston," *Survey*, XXVII (1911), 1088. This letter may have been written by Miss Coe. Her view was shared by Bushée, "Population," *The City Wilderness*, pp. 46–47. Sara O. Jewett to Miss Louisa Dresel, June 14, 1898, *Letters of Sara Orne Jewett*, pp. 153–154.

IX. THE MINORITY WITH FAITH

1. Charles W. Eliot to Grace Norton, April 10, 1920, John Graham Brooks Papers.

2. Edward Atkinson, "Incalculable Room for Immigrants," *Forum*, XIII (1892), 364–367.

3. *Ibid.*, p. 368.

4. Atkinson, "Incalculable Room for Immigrants," p. 370. See also Godfrey L. Cabot of Harvard Class of 1889, later a successful entrepeneur in aeronautics, who opposed restriction despite "friends and kindred." Cabot to the editor of the *Boston Transcript*, February 13, 1897.

5. *Boston Daily Advertiser*, April 15, 1889. Edward Everett Hale, *Letters on Irish Emigration* (Boston, 1852), pp. 52–53, 56, and Hale, "How to Deal With Our Immigrants," *Social Economist*, IV (1893), 76–77. Thomas Wentworth Higginson, *Book and Heart, Essay on Literature and Life* (New York, 1897), pp. 156, 163.

6. *John Graham Brooks-Helen Lawrence Brooks 1846–1938, A Memorial* (Boston, 1940). John Graham Brooks, "The Human Side of Immigration," *Century*, LXXIII (1907), 635. Brooks, *The Social Unrest* (New York, 1903), p. 344, and *As Others See Us* (New York, 1908), pp. 314–315.

7. Hale, *A New England Boyhood and Other Bits of Autobiography*, pp. 241 ff; Hale, *Letters on Irish Emigration*, p. 53. *Boston Daily Advertiser*, July 27, 1894; *Boston Post*, February 10, 1897; *Boston Morning Herald*, May 23, 1904; *Boston Traveler*, January 10, 1906; *Boston Daily Advertiser*, January 10, 1906; *Springfield Weekly Republican*, April 12, 1906. Hall kept notes on Eliot's speech of December 16, 1905 to the Economic Club and wrote "The Ethics of Immigration" as a direct answer. MSS, IRL Papers.

8. Brooks, "The Human Side of Immigration," p. 635; Hale, *Letters of Irish Emigration*, pp. 52–53; Hale, *The Duty of the Church in the Cities*, p. 7. Eliot, "One Remedy for Municipal Misgovernment," *Forum*, XII (1891), 154. Atkinson, "Incalculable Room for Immigrants," pp. 364–365, 370; Brooks, "The Human Side of Immigration," p. 636

9. Hale, "The Quarantine Bill," *Lend A. Hand*, X (1893), 4. Higginson, *Book and Heart*, pp. 160–164. W. L. Garrison, the son of the abolitionist in *Boston Daily Advertiser*, July 27, 1894.

10. Hale to his wife, February 21, 1891, Edward E. Hale, Jr., *The Life and Letters of Edward Everett Hale* (Boston, 1917), II, 343. Charles W. Eliot, "Address," Cambridge Historical Society, *Publications*, I (1905), 42.

11. Higginson, *Book and Heart*, p. 158. Eliot to ———, November 21, 1892, quoted in Henry James, *Charles W. Eliot*, II, 53. William James to

Henry Rutgers Marshall, February 8, 1899, *The Letters of William James* (edited by Henry James, Boston, 1920), II, 88.

12. Josiah Royce, *California* (Boston, 1886), especially pp. 225–227, 229, 360–363, 500–501. Royce, *Race Questions and Other American Problems* (New York, 1908), pp. 8–9, 35.

13. Eliot, "Family Stocks in a Democracy," *American Contributions to Civilization and Other Essays and Addresses* (New York, 1898), pp. 138, 157; Eliot, "Five American Contributions to Civilization," *ibid.*, p. 22.

14. Eliot to Frederick G. Bromberg, December 6, 1901, Letters, Miscellaneous Notes Relating to President Charles W. Eliot, collected by Ralph Barton Perry, Harvard Archives. Eliot, "Liberty in Education," *Educational Reform* (New York, 1898), p. 134.

15. Samuel A. Eliot (President Eliot's son) to Albert Bushnell Hart, December 27, 1929, Hart Papers. Eliot, "The Function of Education in Democratic Society," *Educational Reform,* pp. 415–416.

16. James, *Charles W. Eliot*, I, 34. Eliot, *The Contemporary American Conception of Equality among Men as a Social and Political Ideal* (University of Missouri, Columbia, Missouri, 1909), p. 18, IRL Papers. Eliot, "The Aims of Higher Education," and "The Function of Education in Democratic Society," *Educational Reform,* pp. 236–238, 414.

17. Eliot to ———, November 21, 1892, James, *Charles W. Eliot*, II, 52–54. Eliot, *The Contemporary American Conception of Equality among Men as a Social and Political Ideal,* pp. 21–23; Eliot to Edward Lauterbach, January 10, 1911, sent to Congress with Eliot's permission by the Liberal Immigration League, *Congressional Record,* Sixty-First Congress, Third Session, XLVI, Part I (Washington, 1911), p. 918. Eliot, "What Is an American?" *A Late Harvest* (Boston, 1924), pp. 251–252.

18. James, "On a Certain Blindness in Human Beings," *Talks to Teachers on Psychology: and to Students on Some of Life's Ideals,* pp. 232–234. James, "What Makes a Life Significant?" *ibid.,* pp. 265–266, 275–277; James, *Memories and Studies* (New York, 1911), p. 322.

19. J. G. Brooks, "The Human Side of Immigration," p. 636.

20. Higginson, *Book and Heart,* pp. 230–237; Higginson, "On the Outskirts of Public Life," *Atlantic Monthly,* LXXXI (1898), 192–194. Higginson, "George Frisbie Hoar," *American Academy of Arts and Sciences,* XL (1905), 761–769.

21. Eliot to his Mother, undated (approximately April 1865), James, *Charles W. Eliot*, I, 141. Eliot, "The Aims of the Higher Education," *Educational Reform,* p. 238. Eliot to John O'Brien (editor of the *Sacred Heart Review*), February 12, 1900 and James Higgins to Eliot, January 12 and 15, 1900, Eliot Papers. James to Mrs. Henry Whitman, July 24, 1896, *Letters of William James,* I, 296–297.

22. Eliot to Lauterbach, January 10, 1911.

23. Atkinson to John S. Williams, June 30, 1902 at the Massachusetts Historical Society. James to William M. Salter, September 11, 1899, *Letters of James,* II, 100–101. James to Thomas I. Davidson, 1899, quoted in R. B.

Perry, *The Thought and Character of William James* (Boston, 1935), II, 691–692. Statement by R. B. Perry, personal interview. See also James to Mrs. Henry Whitman, June 20, 1891, *Letters of James,* I, 309. James to Professor Bowditch, January 21, 1884, quoted in A. A. Roback, *William James His Marginalia, Personality and Contribution* (Cambridge, 1942), p. 146. This was originally written in German and translated by Roback.

24. J. G. Brooks, handwritten note, undated, in Brooks' Notebook. Brooks showed an enduring interest in the Jews from 1870 to 1930, Brooks Papers. Eliot, *The Contemporary American Conceptions of Equality Among Men as a Social and Political Ideal,* pp. 21–23. Eliot, Introduction to *The Immigrant Jew in America,* p. 4, and Foreword to McCall, *The Patriotism of the American Jew,* pp. 12–13. Eliot, "Jacob H. Schiff," *Menorah Journal,* VII (1921), 16–21. As an old man, Eliot attributed the growth of anti-Semitism to the undesirable traits which the Jew had developed over centuries of persecution. Eliot looked to the establishment of a Jewish homeland in Palestine to eliminate these unattractive qualities. See "Zionism," *A Late Harvest,* pp. 253, 259–260.

25. Eliot to Ward, December 30, 1913, Ward Papers. Eliot, Marginal Comments on Ward's *The Crisis in Our Immigration Policy,* Ward had sent Eliot a reprint of Ward's article which presented the eugenics argument for restriction. Eliot sent back the article with his own comments in the margin. This annotated copy is now in the Ward Papers.

26. *Ibid.,* pp. 7, 11, 15–19, 24–25. Eliot to Lauterbach, January 16, 1911, Eliot Papers.

27. Eliot, marginal comment on Ward's *The Crisis in Our Immigration Policy,* p. 24.

28. Eliot to Ernesto G. Fabri, January 15, 1907; Eliot to Ralph W. Easley, December 23, 1905, May 4, 1906, April 25, 1906, Eliot's secretary to Samuel B. Donnelly, March 5, 1906, Frank J. Warne to Eliot, September 6, 1906; Eliot to N. Behar, April 23, 1910, Eliot Papers.

29. Eliot to Behar, February 24, 1914, typewritten copy, Eliot Papers. Eliot, "Inaugural Address as President of Harvard College," *Educational Reform,* p. 21, on the value of "the poverty of scholars." See also Eliot to James H. Patten, July 29, 1905, IRL Papers. Eliot, "Closed Shop or Open," *Harvard Alumni Bulletin,* XXVI (1923), 303–308.

30. Emily Balch quoted in the *Boston Daily Globe,* March 6, 1947. Statements by Emily G. Balch, personal interview.

31. *Ibid.*

32. Emily Balch, *Our Slavic Fellow Citizens* (New York, 1910), pp. 34–37, 50–55, 80.

33. *Ibid.,* p. 136.

34. Balch, Notes "Immigration Policies" (Brooklyn, Connecticut, 1913) for lectures at Wellesley College, MS belonging to Miss Balch. Eliot to W. S. Richards, December 29, 1905, "Ignorance and dirtiness can be cured at least in the second generation." Letters, Miscellaneous Notes Relating to President Eliot, Harvard Archives.

35. Balch, Notes on "Immigration Policies," and *Our Slavic Fellow Citizens,* pp. 6, 20.

36. Balch, Notes on "Immigration Policies," and *Our Slavic Fellow Citizens,* p. 419.

37. See Paul Kellogg, "An Immigrant Labor Tariff," *Survey,* XXV (1911), 529–531. Significantly, although concerned with the standard of living, Miss Balch specifically rejected Walker's contention that immigration had caused the decline of the native birth rate.

38. Balch, Notes on "Immigration Policies." See also Higginson, *Book and Heart,* p. 156. "But as there can proverbially be no omelet without the breaking of eggs, so there can be no fusing of all nations except by bringing the nations here to be fused."

39. Eliot, "What Is an American," *A Late Harvest,* pp. 251–252. Hale, *The Five Great Duties of the Twentieth Century* (n.p., 1901), pp. 8–9.

40. Royce, *The Philosophy of Loyalty* (New York, 1908), pp. 214, 245, and *Race Questions,* p. 76. Royce, "Reflections after a Wandering Life in Australasia," *Atlantic Monthly,* LXIII (1889), 825–826. See *The Social Philosophy of Josiah Royce* (edited by Stuart Gerry Brown, Syracuse, N. Y., 1950), especially pp. 27–28, 174, where Brown quotes from Royce, *The Hopes of the Great Community.*

41. Royce, *The Philosophy of Loyalty,* pp. 211–212.

42. Royce, *Race Questions,* p. 61. Royce himself insisted that his concept of loyalty did "not foster class hatreds" nor rationalize "race prejudices," *The Philosophy of Loyalty,* p. 214.

43. Balch, Notes on "Immigration Policies."

44. Higginson, *Book and Heart,* p. 164.

X. THE CONSEQUENCES

1. Edward Grant Conklin, "Some Biological Aspects of Immigration," *Scribner's Magazine,* LXIX (1921), 358.

2. A. Lawrence Lowell to Ward, December 12, 1913, Ward Papers. Prescott F. Hall, "The Recent History of Immigration and Immigration Restriction," *Journal of Political Economy,* XXI (1913), 743.

3. Theodore Roosevelt to Henry Cabot Lodge, March 23, 1896, *Selections from the Correspondence of Theodore Roosevelt and Henry Cabot Lodge,* I, 216. Roosevelt to Hall, March 26 and December 28, 1896, IRL Papers.

4. Lodge to Ward, February 20, 1904, Ward Papers; IRL, Records of the Executive Committee, February 27, 1904. Ward's article, "The Immigration Problem," *Charities,* XII (1904), 138 ff., stressed the race suicide of the native stock as the most important consequence of immigration. Ward to T. Roosevelt, September 30, 1905, in which Ward made specific suggestions for the President's message, Theodore Roosevelt Collection, Library of Congress. Compare Theodore Roosevelt in *Message of the President of the United States Communicated to the Two Houses of Congress at the Beginning of the First Session of the Fifty-Ninth Congress* (Washington, 1905), pp.

38–42. See also Ward to Roosevelt, March 15, 1905; Lodge to Ward, March 17, 1905; and William Loely (Roosevelt's secretary) to Ward, November 6, 1905, Ward Papers. IRL, Records of the Executive Committee, September 28 and November 9, 1905. Roosevelt to Ward, June 14, 1906, January 29, 1907, and September 15, 1908, Ward Papers.

5. IRL, Records of the Executive Committee, October 6, 1906, January 26, 1907, December 14, 1907, January 15, 1908, February 10 and 16, 1908, January 11, 1909, January 26, 1909. Lodge to Roosevelt, July 26, 1908, *Selections from Correspondence of Roosevelt and Lodge*, II, 306–307; Roosevelt to Hall, June 24, 1908, *The Letters of Theodore Roosevelt* (edited by Elting E. Morison, Cambridge, Mass., 1952), VI, 1096–1097.

6. Jeremiah W. Jenks and W. Jett Lauck, *The Immigration Problem* (New York and London, 1912), pp. 2–4; Roosevelt to Joseph Gurney Cannon, June 27, 1906 and January 12, 1907, to Charles Patrick Neil, June 28, 1906, and to Ralph M. Easley, Jeremiah W. Jenks, and James B. Reynolds, February 24, 1906, *Letters of Theodore Roosevelt*, V, 165, 322–323, 550.

7. IRL, Records of the Executive Committee, January 15, February 24, and March 16, 1908, March 8, and July 13, 1909.

8. *Ibid.*, December 1, 1909, January 5, January 19, March 25, July 14, November 2, November 16, November 28, and December 15, 1910; see also Statement of the IRL, *Reports of the Immigration Commission*, XL, 101–138.

9. This phrase, quoted from the original Report in Jenks and Lauck, condensed popular version, *The Immigration Problem*, p. 364, was welcomed by Hall; see his "Review," *American Economic Review*, II[2] (1912), 675–667. Significantly, Lothrop Stoddard later cited the same phrase as a tribute to the Immigration Commission's part in ending "the purely 'economic' attitude toward immigration." Stoddard, *Re-Forging America* (New York, 1927), p. 200. Contrast the Immigration Commission's request to Harvard College to register students according to "the race of father and mother" whether or not it agreed with the nationality of the parents. Theodore Hinckels to Charles W. Eliot, September 1, 1908 and to Joseph Warren, September 25, 1908, Eliot Papers.

10. E. A. Spears to Jenks, February 19, 1915, Scrapbook of the Far Eastern Bureau, Widener Library; Carver, *Recollections of an Unplanned Life*, pp. 109–111; Jenks, *Syllabus of Political Questions, New York University* (New York, 1900), pp. 16–17; Jenks, *Principles of Politics* (New York, 1909), pp. 3–4; Jenks, "The Racial Problem in Immigration," The National Conference of Charities and Correction, *Proceedings*, XXXVI (1909), 217. Jenks, "Restriction of Immigration—Discussion," *American Economic Review*, II[1] (1912), 78. *Reports of the U. S. Immigration Commission*, V, 48.

11. Hall, "Review of Jeremiah W. Jenks' and W. Jett Lauck's, *The Immigration Problem*," pp. 675–676; Jenks and Lauck, The Immigration Problem, pp. 10–11.

12. Paul V. Kellogg, "An Immigrant Labor Tariff," *Survey*, XXV (1911), 529–531; Emily F. Balch, "Discussion," following Henry P. Fairchild, "The Restriction of Immigration," *American Economic Review*, II (1912), 63.

Percy Stickney Grant, "American Ideals and Race Mixture," *North American Review*, CXCV (1912), 513–525.

13. Charles W. Eliot to Edward Lauterbach, January 17, 1913, Eliot Papers. John Graham Brooks, *American Syndicalism* (New York, 1913), pp. 2–3.

14. Brooks, *American Syndicalism*, pp. 2–3, 76, 120. Robert A. Woods, "The Breadth and Depth of the Lawrence Outcome," *Survey*, XXVIII (1912), 67–68. Florence Kelley to J. G. Brooks, August 15, 1913, Brooks Papers.

15. J. G. Brooks, "The Shadow of Anarchy," *Survey*, XXVIII (1912), 81–82. Woods, "The Clod Stirs," *ibid.*, XXVII (1912), 1929. Lauck, "The Significance of the Situation at Lawrence," *ibid.*, XXVII (1912), 1772–1774. Jenks, Form Letter to United States Senators and Congressmen, February 2, 1915, Scrapbook of the Far Eastern Bureau.

16. William Z. Ripley, "The Job at Babels," *Survey Graphic*, I (1922), 447–452, 484. Florence Kelley to J. G. Brooks, August 13, 1913, Brooks Papers.

17. IRL, Records of the Executive Committee, December 1, 1909. On Grant's efforts to influence Woodrow Wilson, see Frank Knox to Prescott Hall, June 24, 1914, IRL Papers.

18. Madison Grant, *The Passing of the Great Race* (New York, 1916), pp. 7, 64–65, 74, 79–81, 198. Concerning the influence of this book, see Lothrop Stoddard, *Re-Forging America*, p. 339. For Grant's anti-Catholicism and anti-Semitism, Grant to John Jay Chapman, March 27, 1925, Papers of John Jay Chapman.

19. Ross, *The Old World in the New*, p. 304. Hall, "Review of Henry P. Fairchild's *Immigration*," MS, IRL Papers. Grant, *The Passing of the Great Race*, p. 193.

20. Hall, Form Letter to Members of the Immigration Restriction League, February 22, 1917, Hall Newspaper Clippings.

21. Grant, *Restriction of Immigration: Racial Aspects*, reprint from *Journal of National Institute of Social Sciences* (New York, 1921), p. 9. Lothrop Stoddard, *Re-Forging America*, p. 181. Henry P. Fairchild to the editor, *Nation*, XCIII (1911), 626–627. Wayne MacVeagh, "The Impassable Chasm," *North American Review*, CCII (1915), 26–34.

22. Fairchild, "After-War Immigration Crisis," *New York Times*, October 12, 1919; Grant, "The Racial Transformation of America," *North American Review*, CCXIX (1924), 344.

23. Stoddard, *The Rising Tide of Color Against White World Supremacy* (New York, 1920), pp. 116–120, 165; Stoddard, *The Revolt Against Civilization: The Menace of the Under Men* (New York, 1922), pp. 84–113.

24. Stoddard, *The Rising Tide of Color*, pp. 253–260; Stoddard, *Re-Forging America*, pp. 170 ff., 199–200.

25. Cornelia James Cannon, "American Misgivings," *Atlantic Monthly*, CXXIX (1922), 150–151. Ward, *Our Immigration Problem To-Day, An Address given at Hartford, Connecticut, February 19, 1923* (Boston, 1923), pp. 4–5, referred to the testimony of Dr. H. H. Laughlin, Lt. Col. Robert M.

Yerkes, Dr. Arthur Sweeney, Prof. Carl C. Brigham, and Mrs. Cannon. E. G. Conklin, "Some Biological Aspects of Immigration," p. 358. Dr. Arthur M. Sweeney, "Mental Tests for Immigrants," *North American Review,* CCXV (1922), 609, 611. H. H. Laughlin, *Eugenical Sterilization in the United States* (Chicago, 1922), p. 349.

26. IRL, Records of the Executive Committee, March 14, 1912. A. L. Lowell, *Public Opinion and Popular Government* (London, 1913), pp. 31–36. Albert Bushnell Hart to A. L. Lowell, May 11, 1922; and Hart to Lowell, May 27, 1922, Hart Papers. Henry Starr, "The Affair at Harvard," *Menorah Journal,* VIII (1922), 263–276. A New England educator recalled that Lowell at a conference acted as if "lying and cheating were exclusively Jewish traits." ——— to Sara Norton, August 24, 192–, Brooks Papers.

27. Stoddard, *Re-Forging America,* p. 202; Ward, "The New Immigration Law and Its Operation," *Scientific Monthly,* XXI (1925), 53.

28. IRL, Records of the Executive Committee, June 3, 1929. Richards M. Bradley, typewritten copy of a statement of protest in 1934 (apparently intended as a petition to congressmen) against potential liberalization of the national immigration policy. Joseph Lee quoted in *Class of 1883, Harvard College* (Cambridge, 1933), pp. 189–190.

29. Herbert B. Ehrmann, *The Untried Case* (New York, 1933), p. 182. Statement by Herbert B. Ehrmann, personal interview. G. Louis Joughin and Edmund Morgan, *The Legacy of Sacco and Vanzetti* (with an Introduction by Arthur M. Schlesinger, New York, 1948), pp. 96–97, 156, 203, 220, 267–268, 333, 368–370, 437–438, 510–511. *Walled in This Tomb; Questions Left Unanswered by the Lowell Committee in the Sacco-Vanzetti Case . . . Including the Report of the Lowell Committee* (Boston, 1936), especially pp. 18–20, 27.

Index